LOGOS

Also by Raymond Tallis and published by Agenda

Of Time and Lamentation: Reflections on Transience

Logos

THE MYSTERY OF HOW WE MAKE SENSE OF THE WORLD

Raymond Tallis

agenda
publishing

First edition published in 2018 by Agenda Publishing

Agenda Publishing Limited
The Core
Science Central
Bath Lane
Newcastle upon Tyne
NE4 5TF
www.agendapub.com

ISBN 978-1-78821-087-4

British Library Cataloguing-in-Publication Data
A catalogue record for this book is available from the British Library

Typeset by JS Typesetting Ltd, Porthcawl, Mid Glamorgan

Printed and bound in the UK by Clays Ltd, St Ives plc

For dearest Danilo and Jay – who are just setting out on their journey of making sense of the world. And for their loving guides on the journey Adela and Jules, Ben and Lawrence

Contents

Acknowledgements

Yet again, I am deeply indebted to my publisher, Steven Gerrard. I am enormously grateful for his tremendous support for my writing and his scrupulous labours during the journey to the press.

Two referees – Professor Sebastian Gardner of University College London and Dr Tom McClelland of University of Warwick – reviewed the manuscript and made many helpful suggestions which have greatly improved the book. I am very grateful to them for their generosity. It goes without saying that any errors are my own.

Preface

> [A] philosopher worthy of the name has never said more than
> a single thing: and even then, it is something he has tried to say,
> rather than actually said.
>
> > Henri Bergson, Address to the Fourth International
> > Congress of Philosophy, Bologna, 1911

The inquiry that follows is a philosophical homecoming. At any rate, it is an attempt to return to the place whence I set out in my teens, dozens of published books, and many more dozens of unpublished manuscripts, ago.

My philosophical awakening was shaped by fears. Some were well-founded, such as that sooner or later I, and everyone I cared for, would die in pain and terror. Other fears were equally commonplace but less well-founded: that my freedom was illusory; and that the world as I experienced it might be a dream. These philosophical concerns were, a few years later, offset by something quite different: an overwhelming astonishment *that* I existed, *that* I could think that I existed; *that* I could make everyday sense of myself and my world; in short, *that* there is "that". It was accompanied by an unexpected joy that I still cannot fully explain although I am grateful for it.

One moment I have recalled so frequently that not one detail will have survived undistorted. As I remember it now, I am standing in a little attic room, fragrant with cabbage soup and the fishy smell of a malfunctioning anglepoise lamp. These were my student digs: 60 Park Town Crescent, Oxford, where I was lodged with Mrs Pasternak-Slater, the exiled sister of Boris. I am talking to my friend Chris Verity, then a medical student and now a retired consultant. I can't remember what we were talking about. Suddenly I heard my own voice and, beyond my voice, the "that" implicit in it – located somewhere between "that I am", "that x is the case", "that the world exists" and "that I am making sense of something". Thus, my encounter with "thatter". "Mystery" is, perhaps, too narrow a word; rather a revelation tinged with surprise, feeling itself to be on the threshold of a further revelation that in the subsequent fifty or more years has not revealed itself.

My career as a doctor kept me rather too much in touch with mortality, and the many limitations of freedom arising out of illness and the confusions that threatened to invade us all, as cooperation between the "it is" of the body and the "I am" of the self starts to breakdown. In my philosophical thinking, therefore, I have often focused on the joyful astonishment of realizing and accounting for the "that" which had filled me with such inexplicable delight, that seemed to bring me to the verge of an alternative sense of reality.[1] It has been a presence – to varying degrees on- and off-stage – in many of my books. It was most obvious in *The Explicit Animal* (1991) and in the discussion of propositional awareness in *The Knowing Animal: A Philosophical Inquiry into Knowledge and Truth* (2004). But it was also a motivating force in *Not Saussure: A Critique of Post-Saussurean Literary Theory* (1988, 1995) and *Enemies of Hope: A Critique of Contemporary Pessimism* (1997, 1999) and even in my monographs on Heidegger and Parmenides.

I could trace the itinerary of this motif through the "Collected Works of Raymond Tallis" at great length but even authorial vanity can bore itself. The point is the centrality of the theme of "That" or "That!" to my thinking. I have been tenacious in loitering in its vicinity; and it has motivated my critique of many anti-humanist intellectual trends ranging from scientism to post-Saussurean thought. It has toyed with me for decades and has come to sit at the heart of my humanist belief in the uniqueness of human consciousness and our status as true agents, who are points of origin in the world rather than merely dissolved into external – physical and cultural – forces. Of a humanism, in short, that while denying our supernatural status, does not conclude, as I did in the more despairing moments of my early teens, that we must be entirely part of the natural, the material, world, helplessly subordinated to its laws.

Logos is an attempt, more direct than any of my previous books, to be true to, or to prolong, this astonishment that has, at increasingly long intervals, lit up within me. It is an endeavour to wake out of, or to, ordinary wakefulness: to discover the strangeness in the blindingly obvious.

There is something necessarily artificial, flawed, about this endeavour, not just because the pace and rhythm of writing and reading does not match that of thinking and contemplation (which anyway cannot be requisitioned to order) but also because, *pace* Kant, our reason is only rarely driven by an inward need to pose metaphysical questions.[2] The seriousness of our lives often seems to point elsewhere and even "the examined life" passes for the most part free of examination. On the contrary, it is life that tends to examine us, or at least to set the questions. We are too busy being our localized selves to ascend to the uncompromised awareness of a consciousness that belongs to no-one, nowhere, and nowhen, in particular. This can make the elective astonishment of philosophy seem frivolous or artificial.

Philosophy is necessarily dialogic. While there are many interlocutors named during the course of this inquiry, there is one whose presence is more ubiquitous than is explicitly acknowledged. As I began the second attempt at this book I re-read Thomas Nagel's *The View from Nowhere.*[3] Notwithstanding the copious underlinings and marginal instructions to "NB" this and "NB" that in my dog-eared copy, I do not recall my first reading of the book, although I was aware of the impact it had made on me. Re-reading Nagel brought home the significance of his subtle, complex, and self-questioning arguments. In the thirty or more years since its publication, its stature has grown. To borrow a metaphor from George Santayana applied to Spinoza, "like a mountain obscured at first by its foothills he rises as he recedes".[4] It is exasperating how many contemporary intellectual trends – reductionist and computational theories of the mind and evolutionary epistemology to name only the most dispiriting examples – have continued to flourish since Nagel demonstrated their inadequacy. That is another story. I mention Nagel here only to highlight how the passage from my open-mouthed awe to specific lines of inquiry has been influenced by *The View from Nowhere*.

In *Logos*, therefore, I have tried to return to something that feels like a fundamental or "ur-thought" I have been on verge of having. And if some of what follows is quite technical, the audience I have in mind is the fabled "general reader". That reader is someone like myself who passes most of his conscious hours in a sub-philosophical frame of mind, even when he is philosophizing. Many philosophical thoughts, after all, are easier to discuss than to think.

The remark from Bergson at the head of this Preface – which is applicable to anyone who truly struggles to philosophize – is an advance warning that a thought I have never quite managed to think is still incompletely thought by the end of this inquiry. In short, *Logos: The Mystery of How We Make Sense of the World* is a failure, although not I hope a pointless one. There is a purpose, even nobility, in aiming "to fail better".[5] Meanwhile understanding or doing justice to that intuition of half a century ago, whose admittedly intermittent light is undimmed, remains as a regulative idea. Who knows, I may have succeeded better than I fear. But for that I depend on you, the reader, the writer's always underestimated invisible partner.

Overture

The greatest mysteries are those we are most likely to overlook, because they are the ground on which we stand when we puzzle over things that surprise us. Chief among these is the very fact – though "fact" is hopelessly inadequate – that the world makes sense to us. As Einstein observed, "the eternal mystery of the world is its comprehensibility".[1]

A couple of decades earlier Einstein believed he had come close to fulfilling the Pythagorean dream of discovering the mathematical structure of the natural world – of space, time, and the entities occupying or taking place in them – and rendered the material universe transparent to thought. His euphoria was short-lived. Quantum mechanics – a seemingly unintelligible but immensely powerful way of describing the physical world and an incompatible complement of general relativity – came to occupy more and more explanatory space. Nevertheless, Einstein's surprise, and delight, his wonder, remain valid: even the partial intelligibility of the world is mystery enough. The conflict between these two spectacularly successful theories did not make their theoretical and practical potency any less astonishing.

That the world makes sense and we make sense of the world and of ourselves in the world whose givens impose a kind of sense on us is a many-layered miracle. Even those who do notice it – artists, theologians, philosophers, scientists – do so only intermittently. Typically, it is the (local) *failure* of sense that provokes us into thought. Otherwise we are too complicit in the necessary assumptions of common sense, paying sufficient attention to get by but not enough to see the extraordinary stuff out of which its fabric is made. We rarely wake to the miracle of our wakefulness and the possibility of waking out of it to some more illuminated state.

Of course, if we did not make moment-to-moment sense of what was going on around us, there would be no "us". Inhabiting an entirely unintelligible world in which nothing could be understood, anticipated, or acted upon with reliable consequences, would be incompatible with inhabiting.

But there is no "of course" even about this. That human existence *requires* a more or less intelligible world simply moves the mystery on. After all, the vast majority of organisms flourish – and act, or at least react – without making sense of the world in the way that we humans do. That A is explained by B is not the kind of thing that bacteria (by certain criteria the most successful organisms) entertain; and at a higher level, the laws of nature as we understand them are beyond the cognitive reach of all but a small subset of *H. sapiens.* Human flourishing has not for most of the history and prehistory of humanity depended on the kind of gaze that could discern laws connecting the fall of a cup off a table with the clockwork of the solar system, or a theory that folds the gravitational field into the structure of space-time. Man-the-sense-making-animal therefore remains deeply mysterious and Man-the-Explainer or would-be Explainer of the universe – *H. scientificus* – doubly so.

Let us unpack this a little. We live in a world in which happenings seem to be explained by other happenings: "this happened because of that". We not only observe causes but actively seek them out. We also note patterns, connect and quantify those patterns, and arrive at the natural laws which have proved so empowering, enabling us to predict and manipulate events, to work with and around them, in pursuit of our ends. All of this takes place in a boundless public cognitive space, draws on a vast collective past, and reaches into an ever-lengthening and widening future.

Observed patterns may be exploited as rules to guide or permit effective action. Sense-making makes what happens into a nexus of norms and norms seem to prescribe what *should* happen: they are quasi-normative. There is surprise, even outrage, at the unexpected, as if the material world *ought* to observe its own regularities, notwithstanding that there is no ought in nature.

The extraordinary character of man, the sense-making animal may be highlighted by contrasting the direct and limited "epistemic foraging"[2] of a beast looking for the origin of a threatening signal with a team of scientists listening into outer space to test a hypothesis about the Big Bang, having secured a large grant to do so.

The reference to astronomy suggests another way of coming upon the miracle of our sense-making capacity: our ability to discern the laws informing a universe that far outsizes us. You don't have to identify the human mind with the human brain to be legitimately astonished at the disparity of size between the knower and the known, between what we physically are and what we know. Consider the relative volumes of our heads (4 litres) and of the universe (4×10^{23} cubic light years). In these less-than-pinprick bonces, closer to the size of the atom than to the size of the universe, the universe comes to know itself as "The Universe" and some of its most general properties are understood.[3] The mystery is beautifully expressed by the American philosopher, W. V. O. Quine when he describes his attempt to explain: "how we, physical denizens of the physical world, can have projected our scientific theory of that whole world from our meagre contacts with it: from the mere impacts of rays and particles on our surfaces and a few odds and ends such as the strain of walking uphill".[4]

That our knowledge and understanding are incomplete does not diminish the achievement. It hardly matters how precise are the figures we arrive at regarding the size or the longevity of the universe. The question "what kind of being must we be to be mistaken over *this*?" is as compelling as the question "what kinds of beings could arrive at this kind of knowledge?". What knower could house gigantic ideas such as "the universe" or (come to that) "life"? These items do not deliver themselves prepackaged as mind-sized miniatures. The cognitive depth these ideas require of us is the same irrespective of whether we have religious or secular outlooks; whether we believe the universe was made or just happened; whether its unfolding is postulated to be driven by a deity or by an intrinsic momentum of change; whether its necessity is represented by mindful Fates or by mindless laws and causes. "God" does not make the order of the universe and our capacity to grasp it any more probable. It is simply another name for that improbability, as we shall investigate in Chapter 2.

Indeed, the intuition that our knowledge is bounded by ignorance, that things (causes, laws, mechanisms, other galaxies) may be concealed from us, that there are hidden truths, realities, modes of being, has been the powerful motor of our shared cognitive advance. We are creatures who cultivate doubt. We have the extraordinary capacity to infer from a mistake in one instance the possibility of being mistaken in a whole class of cases. This, at least as much as our habit of (provisional) generalization and our uniqueness as "the measuring animal", should astonish us. So, too, the fact we can tolerate the extraordinary state of affair that as our knowledge grows, we ourselves, as the objects of our collective knowledge, shrink: our tiny bonces, in galaxies light-years in diameter.

The headline achievements of the human mind, however, are built on lower-level sense-making capabilities that are no less remarkable. Scientific inquiry and religious or philosophical speculation are the upper storeys of a mode of consciousness that is awake to a world other than itself. Perception discerns objects that it senses as being incompletely revealed, that it intuits as having intrinsic properties such as density or microscopic structure, operating in the absence of consciousness. Our everyday consciousness inhabits a realm of knowledge and reasons and words that transcend the material circumstances of the human organism. We are aware of *truths* singular, particular, general, universal, and of the perpetual possibility of getting things wrong.

There is a spectrum of sense-making, ranging from wondering what caused that noise over there, to what shapes the order of things, leading up to the ultimate question of why there is anything rather than nothing. The speculative and spectacular sense-making of the scientist is rooted in a many-layered soil of everyday making sense of ourselves, expressed in the coherence of the succession of moments, the narrative of our lives, our plans, supported by the "artefactscape" in which we pass so much of our lives. There are important differences, however, as we shall discuss.

Sense-making is not the product of the individual mind, although this is where it has ultimately to be registered or indeed realized. It is fashioned in the boundless community of minds, woven out of the explicitly joined attention we pay to the world, shared through a trillion cognitive handshakes, overwhelmingly mediated by the languages – words, non-verbal signs, and artefacts – that constitute the fabric of intelligible, known reality.

The present volume is not an exercise in Cartesian "systematic doubt" or in Cartesian certainty, but in surprise; in cultivated, organized, even systematic surprise. It does not provide many answers: it is closer to "Oh!" than to "QED". The exploration will in many places merely be reminders of what we all know about our knowledge. While it will be structured, the structure will be imposed on something that is intrinsically unstructured. What is on offer is not an explanation but merely a description one of whose chief aims is to reinforce resistance to an unsurprised reductionism. The inquiry into how it is we make sense of things seems always to lead on to higher-order sense-making that requires explanation.

Chapter 1 "Seeing the Sense-Making Animal" attempts to scope the territory. I will trace some of the paths between sense-experience and the higher sense-making Einstein felt to be mysterious. The chapter shall not follow the conventional curriculum of theories of explanation and philosophies of science. I shall not separate and adjudicate between teleological ("to what end"), functional ("serving what function"), reductive ("A boils down to B"), and psychological explanations of phenomena. Nor shall I examine the relations

between the invocation of causes, laws and entities such as elementary particles and forces, as instruments of sense-making. Nor, again, shall I discuss the
relationship between the explanatory power and truth of explanations, or the
contrast between anti-realist and realist accounts of explanation. This is not
only because I have nothing original to say about these matters but also (and
more importantly) because the purpose of this chapter is to dig into the many
layers of cognitive soil out of which particular and general explanations arise.[5]

In the next chapter, "*Logos*: A Brief Backward Glance", I will glance at a few
of the most influential prescientific stories humans have told themselves in
their endeavour to make sense of the fact that the world is to an astonishing
degree intelligible to us. My potted, potholed, history will be anchored to a
term that seems to gather up much that is central to our inquiry in its volumi-
nous denotative and connotative folds: *Logos*.

The next two chapters look at two ways of accounting for our ability to make
sense of the world. In Chapter 3 "Deflating the Mystery 1: Putting the World
Inside the Mind", I examine the idea, most closely associated with Immanuel
Kant, that we understand the natural world because the laws of nature that
structure our experience originate *within* our understanding. In Chapter 4
"Deflating the Mystery 2: *Logos* as Bio-*Logos*" I offer a critical examination of
the contrary view: that the world is amenable to our understanding because
understanding has been shaped by the material world in such a way as to
ensure our survival.

Having set aside these attempts at demystification I return to the task of
clarifying the challenge of making sense of the fact that the world makes
sense. Chapter 5, "The Escape from Subjectivity", highlights the perspectival
and parochial nature of the awareness from which understanding necessarily takes its rise, given that we are embodied, and the miracle of our transcendence of those limits. This sets the scene for the examination in Chapter
6, "Thatter: Knowledge", of the essential nature of knowledge and the realm
of "thatter", in which we are immersed and in relation to which we conduct
much of our lives. The very nature of knowledge presupposes, at least on a
realistic account, that it is about something other than, and independent of,
itself. Consequently, there has to be an irreducible gap between our minds
and the universe of which we are mindful. The gap is between two relata: the
knower and the known. Chapter 7 "Senselessness at the Heart of Sense" exam-
ines the necessary residual opacity in the two protagonists. The final chapter "Towards a Complete Understanding of the World?" gathers up several
threads of the inquiry. It problematizes the idea of progress in understanding
and addresses the inescapable limits to the intelligibility of the world. The

question of whether humanity cognitively advances by some absolute criterion remains vexed.

There are addenda to some chapters. Whether they are necessary elaborations, clarifications, or simply digressions will be for the reader to judge. The truth is that the topic does not have natural boundaries. As with other philosophical inquiries, its limits are imposed rather than intrinsic.

Two things will be apparent. The first is that it is not a work of scholarship, although it enters areas in which the primary, secondary and tertiary literature is enormous. Secondly, its aim is the relatively modest one of removing some of the barriers to seeing the mystery of our capacity to make sense of things and the mysterious fact that we pass our individual lives steeped in knowledge and understanding that, albeit incomplete, nevertheless far exceeds what we are or even experience; and, that collectively, we seem to have grounds for believing that we understand more of the world than those who came before us and who lived, as we still do, in a patchwork of ignorance and knowledge, confusion and clarity, nonsense and sense.

CHAPTER 1

Seeing the sense-making animal

In what follows, I will trace a path from everyday observations which may generate or solve local puzzles, transitions from events that are clues to other events, against the background of already-made sense, to scientific sense, in a naive way that would make philosophers of science and historians of human cognition reach for the smelling salts. My primary aim is to make the richness, the complexity, and the multi-dimensionality of human sense-making more visible. There is no intention to retrace the actual path that humanity and individual human beings have taken in progressing from pre-scientific gawping (and reacting) to a scientific world-picture whose success may be measured in part by the extent to which it has marginalized the natural world in favour of a landscape of technologies. Nor will I give an adequate account of the collective cognitive journey from seeing patterns to seeking them by means of reliable methodologies. My aim is merely the more modest one of highlighting the scale of the long and winding intellectual journey to our present mode of comprehending the world in which we live, that Einstein celebrated. We shall be dipping our toes in deep and muddy waters.

When we try to take the measure of the extraordinary fact that we make (partial) sense of the world, we run into a thicket of connected and overlapping terms: "understanding", "explaining", "figuring out", "grasping and solving", "recognizing", "interpreting", "classifying", "generalizing", "detecting patterns", "seeing order", "observing structures"; various modes of a "because" that invokes causes, reasons, and other ways of registering intuitions of necessity; noting connections, observing law-like behaviour, uncovering fundamental reality (or realities) or general truths. This is just some of the foliage in the lexical shrubbery. Any exploration of the "sense-making" animal seems obliged, however, to begin with sense experience.

There are many reasons for thinking of the deliverances of our senses as "the ground floor" of our awareness, the platform of all cognitive ascent, the basic stuff out of which sense must be made. Admittedly, almost from the beginning, there is a shaping of experience into a structured world, a nexus of significance. World-building, and learning how to be in the world, are products of an iteration between sense experience and sense-making. Even so, it is reasonable to think of sense experience as basic. If, to modify Kant, experiences without ideas are blind, ideas without experiences are empty,[1] without sense experience, there would be nothing to make sense of. They are traditional starting points of philosophical theories of knowledge, particularly those influenced by the empirical tradition associated in anglophone philosophy with John Locke and David Hume. And Kant started with the assumption that all knowledge begins with experience.[2]

There has been an equally strong tradition – beginning in European philosophy with Parmenides and Plato – according to which sense experience was a barrier to apprehending truth and reality. The latter would be seen only when intelligence burned away the sensory mist. This was not, however, the path to the kind of sense-making that so justifiably astonished Einstein.

Our senses, after all, are our fundamental connection with that which is "out there". Arguably, they are that in virtue of which there is an "out there": the material world does not, of itself, have either inside or outside, here or there. Sense experience is our exposure to what we might call a "proto-epistemosphere". They offer a revelation of a reality manifested as handy or distant, populated with the presences or absences of elements basic to our health, well-being and survival: food and predators, threats and promises, friends and adversaries, or more globally daylight or weather. The "out there", felt on our body, experienced inside our body, revealed to seeming immediate awareness, straddles *what* we are and *where* we find ourselves.

Even this basic "outsideness" of (the) "out there" – the given into which we are pitched, our primary situation, the locus of our starting points and our destinations – is more complex and mysterious than might at first appear (and we shall return to it in Chapter 3). There is the far from simple truth that whatever we are aware of as "out there" has somehow to be inside or part of us and yet at the same time be posited as distinct from us, in-itself as well as for-us.

Contemporary theories of this basic aspect of sense-making try (vainly) to resolve the tension between our sense experiences as items that are within us and as items that are "of" something outside of us. A currently popular approach among philosophers attempts to do so by postulating that sense experiences are material effects within us (specifically our brains) of the objects we are aware of as being outside of us. The passage from Quine, quoted in the Overture, which speaks of "our meagre contacts with the physical world" and "the mere impacts of rays and particles on our surfaces and a few odds and ends such as the strain of walking uphill"[3] beautifully encapsulates the idea that our knowledge begins with experience and that the latter is due to a causal interaction between our own bodies and those that are outside of it. The gap between the sensor and the sensed that holds open the "outside" is thus apparently bridged at the same time as it is maintained.

The reasons why this causal approach does not work are more interesting than might initially appear and will figure in the chapters to come, particularly Chapter 4. If I mention it at the outset, it is to pre-empt any suggestion that the mystery of making sense begins only at a higher level than sense experience, and that the latter is straightforward. On the contrary, that mystery pervades all our consciousness.

Moreover, sense experience is not a pure substrate upon which sense-making operates, in innocence of what happens at higher levels. As already noted, except perhaps in the very early days of life, our sensory awareness of the world is pervaded by something that goes beyond it. That characteristic is what makes awareness "of" – x, y, or z. In short, there isn't a basic state of consciousness in which we are bathed in a sea of pure sensation. Our experiences are organized and ascribed to things in a world. The experienced world is structured; otherwise what is "out there" would be slop and the mind would be delirium. The world is not first served up as a blizzard of unprocessed sensory experiences arising from inside or without the body which is then gathered up into sense-making categories.

This is one of the fundamental truths that prompted Kant's focus on the synthetic power of the mind.[4] We do not piece together the objects of perception, the things we locate "out there" and engage with, out of showers of discrete sense experience, then classify them, and then see what we might do with them, and finally explain them with reference to other items similarly built up. As many philosophers have pointed out, our experiences are not atomic, sequins of uncategorized bits of sound, luminosity, tingles, and the like. They belong to a field, to a continuum of what we might call "disclosure", and this field is not merely a network of physical spatiotemporal relations but a nexus of significations – of meaningful "whats" laid out before us connected with one another by means of visible and invisible "whys". A blizzard of flashes and tingles, etc., would not add up to "surroundings" – to an outside. A huge literature testifies to the effort that has gone into observing how, and in what ways, sense experience relates to a world.

Our consciousness of what is "out there" – even imagined as an instantaneous time-slice – is not (just) of a sphere of material elements belonging to a succession of present moments. It is also an unfolding realm of possibility, and consequently a theatre of ongoing, past, future, or potential action. We are not, after all, merely, or even primarily, spectators. Our spectatorial self is a luxury self and, even then, is caught up in ongoing agency. Even *flâneurs* must continue doing all those things that are necessary to keep them alive and safe – in order to be able to be intrigued, or bored, caring or careless as they turn their supposedly disinterested gaze on the world.

A "ground floor outside", constructed out of pure sensory experience of what is out there (or of our own bodies as the most proximate layer of out there), is therefore a myth. Sentience is impregnated from the outset with higher-order sense-making. The obverse is, however, also true: higher-order sense-making is tethered to more basic experience.

Take a paradigm case of higher-order sense-making: the scientist making a measurement. She must handle the apparatus, having seen that it is in front of her and, indeed, near to her. And she is not protected from the world accessed directly by her senses. Preoccupied by the light from distant stars, she trips over a loose cable.

Consider another case. The reader following a novel harvests light off the pages on which the story is written, pages that have other physical properties, shared by the material objects of the room in which the book is being read, and carrying many characteristics – such as creases – that are irrelevant to the sense being extracted from the written word. While we may lose ourselves in a book, in a space of abstract meanings, we never leave behind the realm of basic sense experience. The weight of the book in the hand is mingled with the sensations associated with our anxiety as to what might happen next to the character for whom we are concerned. I may be following the hero down a street in Moscow but I can still be made to jump by the cleaner suddenly appearing at the window with his cloth. We are always available for, or exposed to, the connectedness of the material world that physically surrounds us. We never entirely vacate the spaces of nature and sense experience for those of discourse and reason.

All of this can be accepted but, nevertheless, the endeavour to distinguish and unpack the many layers of sense-making can fruitfully begin with sense experience, and the no-longer and not-yet, the undisclosed and the manifestly hidden, with which our sensory fields are dappled. It is here we enact the basic modes of "sussing out". We look to see what is around the corner, under the stone, behind a wall, beyond the visible beyond. We immediately identify or slowly realize the nature of an object we encounter, recognizing it as an instance of a type. We see, or look to see, why something happened, identifying a cause.

What discrete acts of (explicit) understanding have in common is that they are triggered by an *interruption* in sense or discontinuity of an encircling horizon. The interruption is typically registered by surprise, by puzzlement, by the overturning of an expectation that might only then become explicit. Sense-making takes the form of a search for local answers to "What?" that gives the clue to "Why?". There is a dawning in a local darkness.

While, sniffing, palpating, tasting may yield answers to "What?" or even "Why?", it is the distance senses – vision and hearing – that are most associated with the primordial search for sense prompted by an interruption in the continuum of sense. We walk round an enigmatic item to see what it is or what we might do with it, what makes it tick, or how it came to be here. We listen actively: "What is/what caused that sound?". Active sense-making is even more apparent in the case of sight, where heightened and even trained awareness turns seeing into scrutinizing or peering or some other mode of active, disciplined, attention. Even in these rather homely instances, the resultant understanding draws on prior sense-making that itself goes beyond sense perception: the classification of items; and a sense of how items of a certain sort hang together. Elementary and advanced sense-making are mingled in moment-to-moment awareness of what is happening, of what is out there.

Making unfolding sense of the unfolding experienced world is not always active; it is sometimes just a matter of waiting – to see what happens next, what is disclosed. Or not even waiting: "this" is followed by "that" in some meaningful succession, even if the connection is naked conjunction, with "and" dominating over "therefore" and "because", the staccato of disconnected events or the legato of process, as simultaneous happenings compete for our attention. The ringing in my ears, the tap of the keyboard, the steady chugging of the washing machine below, and the occasional cough from the next room, fill my unawaiting ears, unsurprised by the downpour of happening. Even (seemingly passive) waiting, however, can be active and attuned, shaped by expectations that may be evident only in retrospect when the unexpected surprises us. The temporal relation between waiting and sense-making may be complex or even back to front, as when I look out for another flash of lightning to confirm that the rumble I have just heard was that of thunder.

Frequently, of course, sense-making is more than just a matter of waiting. It is the product of active investigation: parting the bushes to identify what is making the rustling noise; turning an object over to see what it is; climbing to the top of a tree to find the source of an illumination. The investigations seeking the answers to local "whats" and "whys" are often solitary rather than systematic. Under such (customary) circumstances, they may be so much part of a seamless flow of individual experience that the notion of (distinct) "explanation" hardly gets a toe-hold. There are simply local realizations – "recognitions" – that are inseparable from seeing, hearing, or otherwise sensing.

Ultimately, we come to more complex, purposive sense-making journeys, explorations, where we seek in order to find, where we look out for signs, or make measurements and, having made measurements, compare our findings with others, see patterns, and make calculations on the basis of them, ascending from a series of individual measurements to a perceived pattern and, descending from the pattern, anticipate, or count on, an individual outcome. The purposive search for sense, for explanation, may be driven by puzzlement (coloured by a range of feelings ranging from idle curiosity to fear) that demands relief. In saying this, I am highlighting something that is insufficiently noticed: the widening distance between informal, continuous sense experience – where solutions to puzzles are as it were in a solvent – and formal planned observations leading eventually to precise measurements in the context of scientific questions, to the production of theories, and the putting of those theories to practical use; between the continuity of fulfilled expectations that are visible only when they are unexpectedly defeated, and – via basic and less basic "sussing out" and crossword-level puzzling and proofs that seem satisfactory – the "Eureka!" moments that have echoed down the years. Such moments may still be driven by sense experience. After all, the original Eureka moment, was made possible by Archimedes going back to sensory basics and seeing the water rise as he stepped into his bath, thus enabling him to reach the solution to a problem he had failed to solve by abstract thought.[5]

Thus, aspects of the ascent from the basic connectedness of successive moments, the recognition that "what is going on now" as part of something that is ongoing, to the sense that what is going on here can be relied upon to be happening elsewhere, indeed everywhere, to ever-growing powers of prediction, ceaselessly strengthened by reflected-upon correction.

Sense-making above a very elementary level is often a shared activity, even though the cooperating partners may not be physically co-present. It begins with manifestly joined attention which in turn presupposes a complex awareness of another person, or groups of one's fellows, as we draw on a common pool of sense and sense-making. From our earliest months, we are surrounded by explainers, classifiers and connectors – foremost among them our parents, and others responsible for our upbringing. This development of *shared* sense-making is an essential step in the cognitive growth of humanity away from the animal *umwelt*. At any rate, the joint pursuit, or confirmation, of the sense we have made ranges from puzzling together over the nature of something jointly visible, "that thing over there", to the mighty collective enterprises of science in the research laboratory; from the child's "Wazzat?" to CERN, where sustained, formalized, funded, regulated curiosity is directed towards an agreed set of questions.

Sense-making is simplifying. The infinitely complex reality that surrounds us is treated largely as foreground signal to background noise. Our senses are filters and that which is not filtered out is itself subject to further filtration, as the non-salient is exiled to a penumbra of relative inattention. This is evident at a very basic level: active looking (as opposed to mere gawping) involves *over*looking: seeing that thing over there, my gaze overflies everything that intervenes between me and it. The most powerful and effective mode of simplification is something deeply mysterious: the generalizing ability of our consciousness – more broadly of our mind (as some classification may be unconscious or liminal). We see an individual as an instance of a type and, conversely, see types as instantiated in individuals. Very little of the observed item is registered in the process of whatever is necessary to diagnose its general nature, to allocate it to a class. To describe something as a "tree" is to overlook the millions of individual leaves, its height and location, the patterns in its bark, and so on.

It scarcely needs saying that the generalizing capacity of human consciousness is vastly extended, and its products stabilized so that they can be further built upon, by speech and writing. Language gives generality a realm of its own and relocates a world of items set out in physical space to a different kind of space that we may call "hermeneutic", "semantic", "discursive", "rational" or "truth value" space. Its inhabitants are set out in a manner entirely different from the side-by-side of material objects. The boundless multi-dimensional trellis of articulated meaning does not fit into the physical world. Its elements do not map onto points in the space and time occupied by things we walk between, as moving bodies between other bodies. It is this that lies behind the truth, articulated by the cognitive psychologist Jerry Fodor that "the semantic (and/or the intentional) will prove permanently recalcitrant to integration in the natural order."[6]

As has been observed since ancient Greek philosophy, the relationship between particulars and the general classes to which they are allocated is teasingly chicken-and-egg. The class of "stones" is built up out of individual stones but stones can be allocated to that class only if we have the idea of the latter beforehand. Without the idea of a class of stones, I could not know that this item is a stone, or that this item and that item are both to be allocated to the class of stone; and without stones the class would be empty. Given, however, that we enter a world populated by classifiers (our fellow humans), we are presented with the chickens and the eggs side by side.

Even so, the transformation of "what is in front of us" into membership of classes has provoked much, and much profound, discussion. The menagerie of classes makes explicit the mystery of generality in a physical world constituted of particular items. The problem of "universals" has been a major strand in the history of thought, and rightly so. To look at a cup, occupying a location in space, and enduring over a definite stretch of time, and to connect it by membership of a class with a realm that is not so located, is to exercise a fundamental power of our own consciousness and of ourselves as sense-making animals.

It is hardly surprising that the classes to which items are allocated – stabilized in words – were elevated into the Forms and Ideas of Plato and construed as inhabitants of a divine realm. The Platonic story respects the miracle of our own understanding, evident even in this, its seemingly most elementary, form. The Platonic divine realm is a *projection* – from our sense of our own transcendence of the material world in which we are bodily located. Ideas of the eternal, disembodied mind, spirit, or soul of human beings are nourished by the Platonization of the seemingly humble notion of distinct classes that find a home in them. To reject these items as the "mere" result of reification of the referents of general terms, is to miss something important. Universals are a striking reflection of the mystery of the explicit generality that lies at the heart of sense-making. This remains true irrespective of whether universals are understood realistically, as (say) properties that exist in themselves, or in a nominalist fashion in which they are identical with certain linguistic predicates.

The extreme realism of the Platonist tendency to manufacture supernatural entities out of the classes to which we allocate objects – and consequently to envisage a world parallel to (and even superior to) that which is accessed by our senses – has complex roots. It may be in part due to the two-faced nature of words as on the one hand verbal tokens that can be seen and heard and, on the other, the invisible and inaudible verbal types (such as the names of classes) they instantiate and that to which they refer. In virtue of being written down or spoken on an individual occasion, they are separate from the items they can be used to mean, even when those meanings constitute reference to particular entities. The classes can be tokenized in a locality – as in the case of the words on this page you are reading – but they are not themselves confined to any place where a token occurs. They seem to have a reality other than (and, for Platonists, superior to) the transient material of the tokens that express them. Classes, unlike classified individuals, do not *occur*.

The Platonic vision inadvertently highlights something else that reaches to the heart of the (uniquely human) relationship to the world. A classified object is not merely a stimulus whose sense is tied to a mandated response. Take something simple such as a cup. It is out there; I recognize it for what it is; I may use it to drink from; or simply note it; or I classify it in another way – as, for example, an item to measure out a quantity of flour, or as a collectible, or as a way of impressing someone else, or as a missile. The class "cup" is thus doubly dissociated from the material objects that instantiate it: the word "cup" can be applied to an indefinite number, and a wide range, of objects; and a given object may fall under a wide range of general terms ("cup", "souvenir", "ladle"). Most importantly, the item is held in readiness, as something that may be mobilized at any time to serve some purpose. It has a sense that is, as it were, frozen, or at least paused, rather than being gathered up into the flow of consciousness and action. The classification that allocates items before us to a "what" shapes our anticipations of what to expect of it, and guides us how to interact with it, but also opens it up to other possible uses. More importantly, verbal classification elevates the classified object above the space and time in which it is encountered. The connection of an entity with its class is a path that does not belong to the natural world, as the quotation from Fodor highlights.

Classified stuff – ready to be elevated to ingredients, aids, and other items that may help us meet our desires (however remote from immediate or any biological needs) or embody anticipated threats (again often remote from, or only very indirectly connected with, threats to our organic existence) – forms the background of the taken-for-granted, of the good-enough sense, that we navigate our busy way through as we pass our lives. It is, of course, supplemented by the closely woven fabric of higher-order sense that forms the specifically *human* contribution to our world: the intelligible behaviour of others informed by our personal expectations of, and relations with, them; by the law and institutions with their regulations that may run to thousands of pages; and by all the formal and informal unreciprocated and mutual obligations that attach to our many roles in private and public life.

I have sketched some of the elements that go into making the background against which we make ordinary, continuing, sense of the, or of a, world or indeed of the multiplicity of worlds we enter and leave in the incessant, often involuntary, tourism that constitutes our lives, the natural and human public realm that endures from moment to moment, day to day, year to year. It is out of this humus there flowers the sense-making that has prompted this book: the kind that leads to the miracle of the highest level of (partial) comprehensibility of the universe.

For each of us, that background is a private take on a collective reality sustained not only by the habits of the material and natural world, but also by language and other sign systems (and anything may become a sign if someone uses or sees it as such), by practices, artefacts, institutes and obligations. Such background intelligibility has a coherence and unity – at least from one moment to the next. It is not episodic or focal but a sustained, connected, distributed field of mattering or of that which might matter. It is a *landscape* of familiarity, a *continuum* of meaning. The explicit sense-making we associate with "working things out", puzzling over things, typically arises in response to an interruption in sense: it is sense-making that dawns only after a delay, a surprise, a trip in an otherwise seamless flow of sense-making consciousness, an affront to our expectations. Our cognitive advance has been driven to a very great extent by making the most of such interruptions, resisting immediate understanding; by breaking with familiarity, "untaking" the "for granted". Let us look at this a little more.

Disciplined inquiry is frequently in rebellion against automatic (common) sense-making. The sciences (and sometimes the humanities) actively cultivate uncertainty and "problematize" the seemingly unproblematic.[7] The kind of sense-making, the comprehensibility that astonished Einstein sufficiently for him to speak of it as "an eternal mystery", is different in this important respect from the sense that I make of what is around me as I walk in the park of an afternoon, although much of that sense will have been the result of previous effortful sense-making going back to my infancy. Science is the product of sustained and deliberate bafflement, a cultivated and cooperative puzzlement shared over centuries across vast numbers of individuals who are often aware of each other only as fellow contributors to the great game of understanding the natural world. If we think of one of the drivers to the general theory of relativity – the observation of the anomalous path of the planet Mercury that puzzled Einstein for nearly a decade before he completed his theory – we get a startling example of how science advances through individuals capable of being astonished by phenomena that are simply not observed by others, and who are willing to stick with their astonishment until it is resolved at an appropriate level.

16

The example illustrates something else: sense-making that is neither produced or consumed on the spot or indeed indexed to a particular spot but is permanently available to be invoked or mobilized to repair a hole in understanding, to address uncertainty. A theory is stored sense, pickled or frozen interpretation, available to be used when required. The other aspect of this is the way scientific inquiry requires a willingness to pass through, and even dwell in, a desert of senselessness – evident in contingent laws, naked numbers standing for constants – en route to technologies that can enhance agency.

The long delay often seen before scientific sense-making delivers practical application (or even confirmation) is perhaps its most striking and impressive feature. Not only do we see something far removed from the response of an organism to a stimulus but an unequivocal expression of something disinterested at the heart of scientific inquiry – a feature to which we shall return in Chapter 4. The equation or law discovered by investigators working at a particular place and a particular time will have drawn on the cooperative sense-making of a largely invisible congregation of predecessors. And it will find its subsequent use in the work of any number of individuals at any place and any time. This patience in exploiting understanding – a willingness to cultivate understanding that does not deliver immediate benefits – is perhaps more readily tolerated because, after the agricultural revolution, humans became accustomed to actions whose purpose was fulfilled in the remote future. Sowing seed in the spring made sense only in relation to the expected harvest in the autumn.

To emphasize the distance between sense-making and application in solving problems of daily life, is not to be starry-eyed about science.[8] Scientists are as venal, vain, competitive and ambitious as their fellows. But for the most part they will advance their reputation only by separating their immediate interests from the sense they make of the cells, atoms, or volcanoes they are researching. The great French physiologist Claude Bernard famously (perhaps apocryphally) advised his colleagues to "Put off their imagination as they put off their overcoat as they enter the laboratory, and put it on again, as you put on your overcoat, as you leave". Ditto ambition.

The reward for this self-denying ordinance is technologies that have put the biblical miracles in the shade. Our capacity to talk to someone 10,000 miles away who has been picked out by a satellite makes Moses' striking of the rock unimpressive and Jesus' conversion of water into wine small beer. And science – its methods and fruits – pervade every aspect of our lives. As Ernest Geller has put it: "[W]hile once upon a time there was science within the world, now it is as if the world were within science; science became the container, the world the content".[9]

It is difficult to exaggerate the importance of the "de-localization" of sense-making, and the decoupling of sense-making from the time and circumstance of encounter with that which has to be made sense of. We make better sense of the world through this delay. So, while much science may be motivated by a desire to control the natural world rather than purely to understand it, these motives are often better served by a pursuit of what appears to be pure, disinterested understanding. Blue skies research may ultimately deliver more practical benefits than more narrowly instrumental inquiry. A willingness to scratch our individual and collective heads over a conundrum that may be seen to be illustrative of more general problems has served us well in our endeavours to free ourselves from nature. It marks a distance between on the one hand solving problems by trial-and-error, seen in many species, and on the other, approaching them with reason and insight scarcely developed outside of humanity. Likewise, the habit of setting ourselves problems for the pleasure of solving them, irrespective of whether such recreational sense-making has practical benefits. The delay between encounter and sense-making draws on and expands a temporal order, a temporal depth, that is not known in the natural world. This, and a comparable liberation from space as we make shared sense of things, is key to our capacity to act upon the natural world from a virtual outside.

Delay is an important feature of human inquiry in another sense. It takes the form of rising above the flow of experience to formal observation. This is most striking when we make a measurement. We take measurement for granted and do not see how strange it is. It is special not merely because it is quantitative and objective but because it seems to stand outside of experience: it is as it were "an experience by appointment"; one that is requisitioned and designed for a purpose. Measurement is the key to the journey that leads from the flow of everyday consciousness to the discovery of hidden causes, laws, or general principles.

While it is important to highlight the delay between human sense-making and the need for action, it is important not to exaggerate it. Even where we are spectators of the world in which we are immersed, we are necessarily engaged spectators. The objects revealed to us are "affordances" – to use a term introduced by the psychologist J. J. Gibson: "The affordances of the environment are what it offers the [human] animal, what it provides or furnishes for good or ill".[10] Affordances are occasions for action: objects as *manipulanda* that are understood as having to be negotiated in the context of an ongoing or envisaged action. Our relationship to the natural and human world that surrounds us is influenced by our needs and our sense of possible or meaningful transactions. Our actions may act on, and to some degree "cash out", much of the sense we make of things. *Aesthesis* and *kinesis* are inseparable.

This may have two consequences: our sense-making may be lived out in goal-related behaviour; and the latter may deepen and extend that sense that is made. We may see a mutual ratcheting of sense-directed behaviour and of behaviour-driven realization, elaboration, of sense. One mode of sense-making that straddles action and understanding – making things that "work", that do things that we cannot do unaided or wish to outsource according to principles we understand – entrains and develops many modes of discovery and realization and may in turn become a platform for further sense-making. The paths to sense-making are many and various.

The delay between sense-making and action, and between the emergence of a hiatus in sense and its being filled, is an extension of what is seen in everyday, pre- or extra-scientific engagement with the world – namely an uncoupling of behaviour that makes agency different from mere reaction to stimuli. "Figuring out" is often general rather than tethered to a particular obstacle to the flow of action or understanding. The contrast with animals that may seem to solve a particular problem but do not generalize the solution to neighbouring problems could not be more striking.[11] This uncoupling is a feature of a creature – a human being – who *faces* the world rather than being immersed in it, albeit as a distinct part. Our face is often a collective face, equipped with a gaze that is informed by the cumulative understanding of contemporaries and ancestors. We are creatures who operate through things *that* are the case. We shall examine this in Chapter 6.

While the sense-making of the higher, more general kind may be remote from meaning-led immediacies of everyday activity, the divorce is not complete. And certainly not in the first instance. We have already mentioned how seeing an item as "a cup" stabilizes its sense and gives the latter a reality that is out there and available, even if not being consumed in actions or subsumed into a continuum of familiarity. Even so, the classification of distinct items and events and situations and states of affairs together is the basis for seeing patterns in the world. A pattern connects, even unifies, items that are at the same time experienced as distinct; similarity is highlighted at the expense of difference. The patterns can be tested for the scope of their generality, and as they are modified, so they may have greater scope. Patterns justify expectations, enabling us to anticipate what is going to happen and the outcome of those happenings we are responsible for.

Of course, patterns are not always, or even generally, self-declaring. As I look around me now, I see states of affairs unfolding. They do not exemplify patterns without assistance from me: something has to be picked out as an instance, connected with other instances, and these connected instances have to be linked with past connections through personal or shared memory or available reports.

In the case of natural science, the patterns may be suggested in the first instance by direct perceptions. In post-Galilean science, they more typically emerge from measurements made under controlled conditions carried out in conformity with agreed standards, with postulated patterns being upheld by confirmed predictions. At the highest level, measurements may be crucial tests of theories and a huge burden of proof rest on a single observation. The iconic example is the observation of the bending of light during a total eclipse, made by members of an expedition that had crossed half the world, in support of a theory that encompassed all of physical space, time and matter – the general theory of relativity.

This illustrates two further important aspects of the cognitive development presupposed in science. Firstly, much of what is hypothesized is beyond the scope of sense experience. The "universe" of science is largely a construct of the mind that can be experienced only indirectly or piecemeal. Secondly, our scientific inquiries are often driven by new kinds of surprise generated by assumptions that our pre-scientific ancestors would not have entertained. The anomalous perihelion of Mercury, already referred to, would not have troubled Neolithic man, though the puzzle it presented provided a crucial test of general relativity. Advancing technology generates new items that demand explanation. This may have begun some while back in the history of *Homo faber*. Before the agricultural revolution, the failure of certain plants to flourish would not have seemed like a puzzle to be addressed any more than it was an urgent problem to be solved. After the agricultural revolution, it was an important source of surprise; indeed, of shock.

Sense-making does not of course follow a straight path, as if experiences were premises and laws were conclusions, and there were a direct and inevitable route from scattered inquiries to a coherent system of understanding. There are false starts, digressions into the *Wunderkammer* of collections and whimsies, with classifications and lexicons and cabinets full of imaginary beings. There are striking examples, such as phlogiston and caloric: long journeys into sidings, broken toys in what will prove to have been incubators of future, more powerful theories. There are equally false endings, the most spectacular of which was the completeness of physics at the end of the nineteenth century.

And there is the motive force of metaphors, images, analogies, isomorphisms, and echoes that may be fruitful or pave a road to a wilderness of confusion.

At the heart of sophisticated sense-making are the *facts*. We may think of facts as frozen fragments of made sense. Unlike experiences, they do not have visual appearances, and are not audible or tangible, and cannot be tasted or smelt. Connected with this is that they belong to no individual. They are part of the cognitive commons that each of us has access to and they feed into and prompt shared, collaborative inquiry. As the number of collaborators, the informal and formal teams, separate and intersecting, increases so the rate of acquisition of stored or frozen sense accelerates. Instruments, institutions, dogmas, vested interests, take understanding even further from the sense experience of individuals.

Because observations increasingly generate facts that are pure quantities, science at the highest (or the most abstract) level, finds a world that is a "system of magnitudes" and the answers to its questions are numerical. What is "out there" is reduced to the values of variables that are in themselves lacking in everyday meaning ("2 cms/sec" has no stand-alone significance) or qualitative content ("2 cms" and "1 sec" are colourless, silent, tasteless, weightless, etc.). The laws connecting variables in turn express the connections between inputs and outputs of defined systems, or states of affairs (highly defined to make sure they are identical in salient ways) at time t with the same states of affairs at time t + 1.[12]

The patterns evident even in elementary scientific laws – such as Charles's law which states that when the pressure of a dry gas is held constant, its volume will be proportional to its temperature – go far beyond those directly available even to the most intelligent gaze observing how gases expand when they are warmed up. The laws themselves do not capture the stuff of stuff: no gas merely has, or is separable from, its temperature or volume; and volume and temperature are not stand-alone properties, such that the gas could have the one without the other, or indeed without many others.

In being used to calculate expectations or to design artefacts that link visible means with visible ends, patterns captured in physical laws connect with, but stand out from, the background of the general taken-for-granted. In virtue of their very generality – a law of motion may apply equally to a person tripping over a stone and a rotating planet, to what is happening this morning and what happened 1 billion years ago – they are viewless. No-one can directly sense $F = ma$; and $E = mc^2$ or the Schrödinger wave equation are even more remote from the experiences that ultimately triggered the sense-making that led up to them.

The widening gap between everyday sense-making and a mode of understanding that applies to the whole of physical reality highlights something that bears reiteration. It is that the kind of sense-making evident in disciplinary inquiry is not made to be consumed on the spot. That is why $F = ma$ – unlike "This creature looks like it is going to bite" – can be of equal use at any spot. The former may be banked until a time when it is needed. Making sense of an object next to my hand, or of a sound from a hidden source, or of a predator coming towards me, is rooted to the circumstances of an occurrence. It does not travel. If, when we want to understand why a crash occurred, we invoke one or other of the laws of motion, or when we are trying to design a gadget we think of Ohm's law, there is a clear separation between the sense-making and that which is made sense of. This is one of the glories of the generality of conscious experience extended further to an indefinite range of instances, some of which may not be envisaged when the law was first promulgated by the scientist who discovered it or was taken up by the community of scientists and technicians who use it.

Although (as we shall discuss in Chapter 7) the laws of nature are intrinsically senseless, they carry an aura of sense because they lie behind (or seem to lie behind) the predictability of the world. Our knowledge of them enables general trends to be connected with our ends, transforming the character of our surroundings into a realm of ingredients, handles and machinery. The laws extend our ability to suborn the material world to our ends, making it a partner of ever more complex aims. By a process of projection, the natural world may seem increasingly to be tinctured with *telos* – to have an order for which, since we can exploit it, we might be grateful. At the same time, however, as the laws become increasingly general and extricated from the particular settings where we make everyday, moment-to-moment, sense of the world, so they seem drained of sense. "This is like that" or "This is essentially the same as that" effaces difference and singularity. Laws and equations and fundamental elements such as atoms are faceless – one of the reasons why the more comprehensive our theories of the universe, the less meaningful the latter seems. The journey to fundamental reality becomes a journey away from meaning. And away from change: very general laws such as the conservation of mass, of energy, or of mass-energy, imply that nothing in the end truly changes.

Laws are one expression of patterns and of order – they are the patterns of the unfolding of patterns. An ordered world, regulated by the shaping force of necessity as defined by natural laws, is more mind portable.[13] A succession of instances that is entirely random is difficult to hold in one's mind but an ordered series is susceptible to algorithmic compression, to be capturable in a simple formula, and lies within our mind's capacity to contain. Such items are more easily collected because they appear to be packaged in their own principles of collection – so they can be (to speak etymologically) *"con-ligo"*, bound and read together.

Thus, dots arranged in a circle or in a square can be recalled more easily than the same number of dots randomly scattered on a surface. It is for this reason, spatially ordered items can seem to make more sense – or to be more sense-complete – than items that lack such spatial order. And the same applies to temporal order: repeated successions of events appeared more imbued with sense than patternless ones. Fulfilled expectations carry their charge of rightness. Eventually, as David Hume pointed out, regular associations between classes of event – such that As are always followed by Bs – will give a sense of inevitability to the point where the connection between As and Bs is taken to be necessary and we imagine that As *ordain* Bs. The patterns in space and time give a sense of *coherence*: in virtue of holding together, they are more mind-friendly. Hence, they "make sense".

At the heart of sense-making at the scientific and the immediately pre-scientific level is the notion of material necessity: "this happened *because* of that". "Becausation" is a very busy junction at which many modes of understanding intersect. There is the (much contested)[14] notion of cause, most typically understood as a preceding event that brings about its successor, having itself been brought about by its predecessor. The putative link between causes and effects is the motor that connects one event with another such that the former may even be seen as *sufficient reason* for the latter, in virtue of the former's power. This is the guarantor of the coherence of the world.

At its very basic level, the causal relationship is the transmission of energy preserved through time, as when one object bumps into another and donates some of its inertial energy to it. This kind of causation is part of fundamental common sense and it is experienced directly in agency, when we initiate one event to bring about another, either directly or indirectly, in the push-pull realm of mechanics.

Singular "becausation" straddles the border between explanation and mere description. For the invocation of a cause to count as an adequate explanation, something has to be postulated to account for its causal efficacy. I have already referred to "powers" and "energy". These are very general terms that connect singular causes with general principles. Individual causes instantiate general causal laws, if their circumstances of operation are such as to provide no hindrance. The effect becomes a quasi-rational consequence: such "becausation" sidles up to "because" understood as a reason. It does not quite qualify as a full-blown reason such as the goal-directed motivation associated with a voluntary action or the logic-based passage of a conclusion proceeding inescapably from premises. A material cause is remote from anything like "reasonableness". We shall return to this in a moment.

The ascent to generality – from observed singular causes to inferred causal laws to the grand laws painstakingly uncovered, tested and revised by science – is fraught with risks. These hazards are evident long before we reach the Humean limits to induction, according to which even the assumption that the sun will rise tomorrow may turn out to be just that. If A caused B is based on the observation that A is "constantly conjoined" with B (to use Hume's term) then we need something more than observation to underpin the conclusion that A will inevitably be followed by B, and to justify the move from the correlation between A and B to the notion that A will mandate B. The inference has had a difficult time since it was challenged by Hume. The causal laws that are intuited as underwriting individual causal connections will seem to become more robust as they are linked with other laws of increasing generality. Ultimately, explanations of particular events are connected with general explanations of all events. A pattern seen to link As with Bs seems to be less of a human imposition if it is discovered to be a (relatively) local expression of more general patterns.

The reliability of a pattern is not, of course, a measure of the extent to which it makes sense, as will have been evident from our discussion of natural laws such as those of mechanics. Untutored intuition might anticipate that, for example, the inverse square law of gravitational attraction should be an inverse cube law, given that the space through which it operates is three-dimensional. So the inverse square law seems more a raw fact of physical reality rather than something that makes satisfying sense. While a higher-order law may seem to offer an explanation of a lower-order one, the higher-order law is in truth simply a wider statement as to how things are. Eventually, ascent to higher generality reaches an explanatory ceiling – studded with contingent physical constants – marking a terminus to sense-making. The dynamic of explanation – "becausation", "this because of that" – halts at the stasis of description.

The ultimate blankness of "this is how things are" is concealed because of the profusion of quasi-explanatory connections between lower and higher levels en route to the highest-level laws. The law-like behaviour we see in everyday life based on direct, untutored observations, seem to have what we might call a self-explanatory force. This is different from the Humean translation of constant conjunction into necessary connection. Essentially, it is the feeling that as things generally are, so they ought to be: the principle of precedence expressed in the most general and intransigent habits of nature, seems to be sense enough, at least to occasion no surprise. If the sun rises in the morning, there is no explanatory work to be done. There is nothing surprising, no "What the heck is going on?". Only if it does *not* rise in the morning is there something to explain. "This is how things are" consequently seems like explanation enough most of the time: this is the order of things; this is how things are when nature is not out of joint.

The cognitive glory of humanity lies not only in seeing patterns in the order of things but also in refusing to take the surface order of things, the utterly ordinary, as not requiring explanation; seeing the sunrise as a cognitive challenge as acute as an eclipse, and as a prompt for general, and generalizing, inquiry. Treating common sense, the sense of "of course", with disrespect is the start of the long journey culminating in contemporary science. In their latest iteration, the laws of nature, empty of human meaning, on the one hand, and of phenomenal qualities on the other, are ultimately non-explanations, as is betrayed by the seemingly arbitrary physical constants that lie at their heart. In the ascent to a comprehensible universe, the very taste of sense seems to be lost. The other side of this is breaking down the barrier between nature and the laws of nature. Matter in the general theory of relativity melts into the structure of space-time; and the universe of quantum mechanics is a wave-function defined mathematically.

Admittedly some lower-level laws may correspond directly with the deliverances of daily life. $F = ma$ fits with the experience that the harder and longer you push something the faster it goes – as Quine noted in his reference, in the passage quoted earlier, to "a few odds and ends such as the strain of walking uphill". And one aspect of the law of gravity is captured in the observation that the longer something falls, the faster it falls. But there is much that does not fit with this: the fact that a feather typically falls more slowly than a pebble concealed the nature of the gravitational force for thousands of years. And the truth that "down" is not an absolute direction or that there is no fundamental difference between moving at a constant speed in a straight line and being at rest is equally repugnant to common sense. It took the genius of individuals like Galileo and Newton to wake us out of the folk mechanics of daily life and intuit principles that hold sway in places where common sense does not care to tread; for example, the distant galaxies or the microscopic spaces between atoms.

We accept as explanations laws that are either remote from common-sense experience, or reach beyond the scope of common sense; that involve *constants* identifying proportionalities – numbers without qualitative content or other sources of meaning; and – something that I have not mentioned hitherto – involve entities (atoms, subatomic particles), stuffs (phlogiston, fields), forces (intra-nuclear) and energies (ultraviolet light) that are not part of everyday sense-making and are remote from sense experience. In short, we are willing to take as an explanation – or accept as explanation – something that does not offer the usual satisfactions of either a solved puzzle (What is that noise? Why did that happen?) or conform to the visible habits of a world that seems to be behaving as usual and so not requiring explanation.

Unlike the anthropomorphic explanations mobilized in magic thinking and religious discourse, the appeal to laws of nature ultimately lacks the usual satisfactions of answers to "Why?". Prior to science, religion, too, had addressed questions about things that could seem to be taken for granted – the usual order of things such as the sun rising in the morning – but the answers still belonged to a transcendental projection of common sense, invoking an agency that was projected from human agency. In the case of the Abrahamic religions, that agent was sufficiently close to human beings to share the latter's emotions and even some of their historical preoccupations. The natural world of scientific explanations, rooted in measurement drained of meaning and phenomenal quality, is mindless, equally remote from human free will and divine plan. Its material causes are insentient agents of change; mere happenings that made other happenings happen. Its laws are not decrees, its forces are not the expression of a will. Law-governed nature is the unmandated tendency of what-is to repeat itself, an empty necessity exercising power without consciousness.

It is time to summarize – or at least to bundle together – the gleanings from this tour through aspects of human sense-making. We have seen how the idea of sense-making and intelligibility is distributed through a tangle of loosely associated mental states, casual observations, individual challenges, and deliberate inquiries. Its aspects include recognizing familiar objects and patterns of behaviour of the material world (including that of our fellows), summarizing them in descriptions, noting order, identifying causes and seeing physical and narrative connections. There are many layers of sense-making: realizing that such-and-such is the case; sorting out something that is puzzling; seeing a pattern in events (either through casual noticing or formal observation) that makes a kind of sense out of fulfilled expectation; and then, via formal experimentation and measurement, advancing to laws that go beyond what is available to the senses, encompassing galaxies beyond our own, the interstices of living cells, and energies imperceptible to senses. There is no well-defined ladder leading from a ground floor composed of sense-experiences continuous with those shared with, for example, our nearest primate kin to higher reaches of natural science. There is much to-ing and fro-ing between levels at which we individually and collectively "suss out" what is going on around us. This makes it more, not less, of a miracle that we have the capacity to speak of things that are billions of times larger than our mouths, to think of and be right about spaces that are orders of magnitude larger than any that could be visited or occupied by any of us. For this has its origin in our willingness to seek explanation outside of our usual sources of sense-making: to make a kind of sense that lacks the taste of everyday understanding, and consequently has little intuitive appeal.

We have implicitly indicated ways in which human sense-making is different from that even of our nearest primate kin. The parting of the cognitive ways between ourselves and the non-human animals begins at a basic level. The difference between the hunting animal and human epistemic foraging, on a quest driven by an idea, is profound. As we have noted, our cognitive reach owes much to our tolerance of delay in sense-making, separating answers from the situations that provoke question, and a willingness to provoke and address puzzlement that does not deliver immediate benefits. These virtues are connected with the uniquely human sense of that which is "out there", that which is utterly other than myself. The hidden is sensed as an explicit possibility and as such is necessarily general. This may be rooted in our unique status as embodied subjects (as opposed to mere sentient organisms) that confer on the objects that surround us the status of items that are not consumed by our experience of them.

The extraordinary cognitive ascent of humanity from a sensory field to a *Weltbild*, from sensing immediate surroundings to mapping the world, and ultimately to locating all spaces and times in relationship to one another, is also in part a consequence of our capacity to share our consciousness in a community of minds. The sharing goes beyond explicit teaching to the absorption of assumptions, categories, and ways of speaking and thinking, of modes of proposing, conjecturing, imagining, and supposing, as well as common practices drawing on shared facilities located in a multiplicity of common spaces. As Thomas Suddendorf has put it: "Although our individual understanding is often flawed and our foresight misguided, by linking our minds to those of others we have enormously increased our predictive capacities and powers of control. With theory of mind and language we are able to wire our scenario-building into much larger networks."[15]

Working within that community we have been willing and able:

- to see what is normal as an appropriate subject for inquiry: to be as astonished at the fact that the sun rises as at the eclipse that hides it;
- to cultivate uncertainty and surprise, to welcome interruptions in sense, to problematize the world in a manner that goes beyond worrying about answers to local questions – "What is that noise?", "Is that safe to eat?", "What will happen if I do this?", "What do those footprints mean?";
- to wake out of background assumptions that define what demands explanation and what counts as a satisfactory, or at least adequate, explanation;
- to accept answers that offer very little intuitive or emotional sustenance – no gods, no minds – following the possibility of generalization beyond the point where thoughts lose contact with the visible, the audible, or the ordinarily meaningful;
- to de-localize the sources of sense, or at least of explanation;
- to await patiently the rewards of sense-making – to live with unanswered questions, and with answers whose hour of use that may never come;
- to work with hidden entities, forces, energies, that act as intermediaries connecting the widest collection of possible states of affairs and processes;
- to acknowledge the boundaries of our sense-making not only by trying to extend our knowledge and understanding but also by mocking the sense we make of things, by humour, and by cultivating nonsense: man is uniquely the (deliberate) nonsense-making animal.

Thus, aspects of the sense-making animal.

It is evident that the "comprehensibility" of the world that Einstein spoke of with justifiable awe is the uppermost storey of the many-layered intelligibility we have collectively achieved, often driven by ever more abstract and egregious modes of surprise, of a sense of gaps in sense. Such active sense-making is always at risk of being interrupted by the passive, or at least involuntary, sense-making instanced in the response to pain, the unexpected, and the various pressures of biological and social life, and our propensity to distraction.

A point of overall convergence of sense-making eludes us. There is the episodic, localized sense-making expressed in working out what something is and there is the unrolling fabric of practical sense-making that corresponds to being in a room, negotiating a journey, coping with a stressful day. There are stories of sense-making – of acquiring knowledge and understanding, of becoming accustomed – that may unfold into explicit narratives with beginnings, middles, and ends, in which the completion of a local sense is suspended. Here or hereabouts we find the various ways in which we make sense of *ourselves* – our relationships, adventures and misadventures, careers, our sense of what is owing to us, duties, and destinies in the light of the kinds of creatures we are.

There is, in short, much that fills the gap between homely and grand sense-making, between working out that a heap on the floor is a pullover to developing theories about the origin and destination of the universe and any deity that may or may not have created and steers it. Between making sense of spaces – defined by buttons, doors, fences, horizons, and national boundaries with their physical, social, legal elaborations – and making sense of space as a physical category. Between on the one hand watching the time in our hurries and boredoms and anxieties, and wondering what time it is as we wait and anticipate and speculate, and on the other measuring the time of events, uncovering the clock of the universe, and making sense of time itself with and without eternity. Additionally, in the interstices of the cool hermeneutics of trying to understand the world, eluding the grasp of the purely propositional world of concepts and facts, is the intense sense-making corresponding to emotional states, those physiological storms that talk to themselves, uttering themselves into and out of existence, opening up possible worlds lit by fear, longing, excitement, joy, love, and (folded over and over) embarrassment or angry entitlement.

Thus the humus out of which the grand sense-making of theology, the arts, philosophy and, most recently, natural science arises. It now seems appropriate to take a backward glance at earlier attempts to make sense of the fact that man is the supreme sense-making animal.

CHAPTER 2

Logos: a brief backward glance

The irreducible knottiness of the present investigation will be apparent from its most succinct characterization: to make sense of the fact that we make sense of the world; or to make better sense of the fact that we progress (or seem to progress) towards better sense of the world. Thus characterized, it wears on its sleeve the impossibility it has in common with many philosophical inquiries. Trying to understand time notwithstanding that we are temporal beings, endeavouring to characterize the stuff of the universe of which we ourselves are a part, or consciously striving to get an outside view of consciousness – these seem equally self-undermining projects.

The present engagement with the enigma of the sense-making animal is a late entry into a very long conversation that has engaged innumerable thinkers approaching the matter from a variety of starting points. It may therefore be helpful to glance back at some ways in which the intelligibility of the world has been viewed. It is salutary to be aware of the struggles of those who have gone before us.

What follows is not a scholarly inquiry. I am not sufficiently deluded to imagine that I can do justice to such a vast and complex aspect of our cognitive past; even less deepen our understanding of it. It has the more modest aim of placing in a wider context the present attempt to get to grips with the fact that our minds seem to make more sense of more of the universe than one might reasonably expect. The mysterious, even miraculous, relationship between our individual and collective intelligence and the seemingly intelligible order of the world is one that has exercised some of the most luminous minds. While the focus in this book will be secular, some of the most influential and profound responses to the mystery of intelligibility have involved a third party – God – mediating between mind and world and He will dominate in the present chapter.

Logos lies at the heart of the attempt to understand human understanding. The word (term, concept, idea) has waymarked a long journey of self-reflection weaving between religious and secular attempts to understand our understanding. The story visited in this chapter will end with the extraordinary climax of Christianity. Indeed, it is difficult for one such as myself brought up in the vicinity of the Christian faith not to begin with the most famous – and fateful – *topos*: The Gospel According to St John, Chapter 1 Verse 1: "In the beginning was the Logos [The Word]".

For many theologians, Christianity *is* the religion of the *Logos*. The concept, however, goes far beyond even the wide realm of the Christian faith that has infused 2,000 years of human history with hope, joy, kindness, bloodshed, terror, and domestic and political oppression. St John's assertion was not the debut of *Logos*. Even less was this the first report on human consciousness encountering its own awe-inspiring mystery, when the inner light of understanding tried to illuminate itself with words and reach for its own source. While the Christian *Logos* was the beginning of a long journey, it was also a climactic moment in an even longer one. Before we trace some of that journey, a little etymology is in order.

There are many translations of *Logos*. This much, however, is clear: it is derived from the Greek word "*lego*" meaning "I say" – hence the cognate sense: "word", "speech", "discourse". More narrowly, it can be translated into "plea" or "opinion"; or it can open into "ground", "account", "description", "hypothesis" or "theory". Somewhere in the middle of all these senses is to be found reference to psychological states such as "expectation" and the inward intentions underlying a speech act. Most significantly, it can mean "reason" underpinned by logic, which, as we shall see, can be located either in the reasoning mind or in the world that is reasoned about. The register of its tentacular meanings would include ratio, proportion, principle, standard; reasoning power; hypothesis, grounds for belief or action. *Logos* is also the common root of all those organized, rational investigations into the world suffixed by "logy" that make up the natural and human sciences, the disciplines that aim to advance our understanding of the world in which we find ourselves and the selves we find ourselves to be. Hereabouts we find the deep connection with another root meaning of "*legein*": to gather together, to arrange, and to put in order. The Proto-Indo-European root is *leg* which means "to collect" as well as "to speak". There could be no more ambitious act of collection than that which results in a world picture.

If *Logos* seems to duck and weave between meanings, this is hardly surprising, given that (as we shall see) there is so much prior understanding involved in making sense of how we understand the world, given also that there is no stable distance between that which is being interrogated, the process of interrogation, and the interrogator. Where distances are established, they often come from extraneous sources: most notably, as in the religious use of *Logos*, the longings and needs of humanity and the power relations between human beings. In sum, *Logos* is a word, or a concept, yes; but it is more than a word or a concept. It is a semantic field of nodes here and there specified in particular translations. It speaks of a variety of responses to the astonished encounter of human understanding with itself.

And corresponding to this also, there are many characters in the story of, or the story told of, *Logos*. They include: The Universe (as the Great Other in which we find ourselves); God the guarantor of the intelligible order of things; the Community of Minds or human Reason; and those prophets, priests, thinkers, scholars, whose words interpret *Logos* for us. What follows is an elementary historiography of ideas and world-pictures.[1] As an account of this crucial aspect of the encounter of humanity with its own astonishing cognitive capacity, it is ludicrously inadequate. It will, I hope, be sufficient for the humbler purpose of making the topic of this book more visible.

It is uncertain when *Logos* or a concept equivalent to it was first articulated. Historians go back to the Pyramid Texts of Heliopolis, nearly 2,500 years before St John's fateful declaration, and the myth of the god Atum, the self-created first of the gods.[2] *Logos* makes its initial, comparatively unencumbered, appearance in the writings of early Greek philosophers, although the use they made of it was remote from the Egyptian world picture: it was less God-centred.[3] The Presocratics (sixth and fifth century BCE), those "tyrants of the spirit" as Nietzsche called them, "who wanted to reach the core of all being with one leap",[4] employed it partly to congratulate themselves on their own reason-based approach to questions about the nature of the cosmos.

In Presocratic philosophy, *Logos* is particularly associated with Heraclitus.[5] He identified the philosopher as one who activated the reason within his own mind to gain access to the reason that was inherent in, expressed by, and shaped, the unfolding world. *Logos* justified the philosophers' trust in their own arguments and explanations: it was that in virtue of which human rationality was reflected or expressed in discourse. There was *Logos*-in-the-world and *Logos*-in-the-mind. The latter, wisdom, was "one thing ... to know the thought by which all things are steered through all things".[6] As for the former, Heraclitus developed – in flashes of mental lightning – the idea that it was both the rational structure of the world – the law-governed process of change – and the source of that structure; the principle that governs everything that is or happens and the immanent reason or plan that accounts for the orderly unfolding of things. It was the hidden harmony behind the discords and antagonisms of existence, regulating the eternal war between the elements that kept Being in motion, leaving nothing immune from change.[7]

Heraclitus' views are, it is usually assumed deliberately, enigmatic in their expression. Nevertheless, it seems plausible that he believed that, while the rational order of things did not make the world rational in itself, or conscious, or capable of thought, it became rational and conscious and thoughtful in the human *Logos*. In the mind of the philosopher, the microscopic human *Logos* was united with the macroscopic *Logos* of the *Cosmos*. Specifically, *Logos*, in the sense of The Word, provided the link between rational discourse and the world's rational structure, the universal reason governing and permeating the world. This, possibly the first attempt to account for the mystery of the comprehensibility of the world, perhaps marginalized God as the underwriter of a sense-making world. At any rate, it is possible to see a tension between on the one hand a God-centred mythological cosmology and on the other a natural philosophy shaped by argument, tinged with a smidgeon of observation, in the Presocratic philosopher's endeavours to understand the fact that the world makes sense.

This is an appropriate juncture to reflect on the boundaries between *Mythos* (stories told as religious myths or in works of art) and *Logos* (in the narrow sense a reasoned account). The boundaries will of course be forever contested. After all, myths, too, are reasoned accounts of a kind: they make sense of making sense and they use words. And *Logos* must work with what is delivered to it by pre-rational means, using terms laden with historical baggage. Theo-logy and the scholarship applied to sacred texts are sprinkled with careful arguments that respect the laws of logic. In short, the conviction that there is a clear boundary between *Logos* and *Mythos* and that they are absolutely opposed may be a meta-myth, derogating myths from the standpoint of *Logos*. The meta-myth remains vulnerable so long as *Logos* is not complete and the sense we make of the world (including the fact that we make sense of the world) is not rounded off. Nevertheless, the distinction – though neither sharp nor absolute – has been and remains one of the most powerful motors of the intellectual history, indeed the collective self-awareness, of the human race.

A classic – but much-contested – study of the transition from religious *Mythos* to philosophical *Logos* – is due to the English scholar F. M. Cornford.

His central argument that "Behind philosophy lay religion; behind religion ... lies social customs – the structure and institutions of the human group"[8] reflects the overwhelming influence of the French sociologist Émile Durkheim in the early part of the twentieth century. It is a thought to which we shall return in Chapter 8.

Cornford even suggested that Heraclitus "all but divined ... what this book [Cornford's own book *From Religion to Philosophy*] is intended to prove – that *physis* or Nature is, ultimately and in origin, a representation of the social consciousness". He arrives at this surprising conclusion on the basis of Heraclitus' identifying the nature of things with "that 'common world' or 'common reason' which is accessible to all, if only their eyes are open to perceive it, and they do not turn aside, as the many do, to slumber each in his individual world of private opinion or 'seeming'".

Thus Heraclitus, the intellectual ancestor of Durkheim! Less contentiously, we may think of the philosopher as a demythologizer, insofar as the gods with personalities who figured in religion were replaced by the ultimate impersonality of a ubiquitous stuff: fire. Even when fire hurts, it does not intend it; even less does it intend any comfort it may bring.

There was, of course, much life in the old God yet. Plato's *Logos* was the rational activity of the world soul created by the "Demiurge". The Demiurge is variously understood either as a being, himself created, second to the One or Monad, or as an uncreated being who is the Creator of the world. In either case, he is importantly an *artisan* – a craftsman, a benevolent being who shapes the world and hence makes it habitable and intelligible. Access to that intelligibility is gained by the intellect, typically through engagement in the dialectic of philosophical debate, which is able to look through the veil of appearance delivered by the senses. Thus, the Platonic *Logos*.[9]

For Plato, the Heraclitean flux corresponded to the material world accessed through the deceitful senses, while the underlying reality, unveiled to the intellect, was the immobile Parmenidean Being. The *Logos* was therefore the kind of discourse or thought that accessed that which is unchanging, real and true, as opposed to sense experience which is unstable and untrue. Such discourse was possible because (as Socrates averred) there was a minute spark of cosmic fire within humans – analogous perhaps to the warmth round the ankles of flowers reflecting the sun's giant furnace.

Aristotle is archetypically presented as (an iconic) iconoclast in Raphael's "School of Athens" bringing *Logos* from Platonic heaven down to earth. In his thought, *Logos* was the inherent formula determining the nature, life and activity of the body as well as, more narrowly (and somewhat confusingly), "significant utterance". The term's most particular reference was to argument from reason – which was deemed appropriate when matters of fact and understanding were at issue. More narrowly still, *Logos* was one of the three modes of persuasion (reasoned discourse), the other two being *pathos* (or emotion) and *ethos* (the honesty and morality of the speaker that justified trust). However, the Aristotelian *Logos* as applied to discourse, was elaborated and formalized in logic that defined the valid relationships between elements picked out by asserted propositions.

Logos recovered its Presocratic majesty in Stoic thought. For the Stoics, it was the source of all the activity and rationality of an ordered world that was both intelligible and intelligent. A supreme directive and animating principle, a kind of fire – *pneuma* – it impressed its form and life on the entire world. Manifest in all the phenomena of nature, it was a "seminal reason", which could bring things into being as well as bring them into order, a force, securing the inner cohesion of bodies and the world. It thus accounted not only for their intelligible structures and their energetic movements but also for their very existence.

For the Stoics, as for Heraclitus, the world was intelligible to humans because the human soul participated in the cosmic *Logos*. Given that the one *Logos* is present in many human souls, men can be in communion with each other: we all partake of common sense – another echo of Heraclitus. Humans are truly happy only when they live in a state of harmony in which the *Logos* of their own soul resonated with the universal *Logos*, the harmony of nature.

One of the most consequential and astonishing turns in the history of *Logos* – indeed in the history of humanity's self-understanding – was the thought of Philo of Alexandria (ca. 20 BCE – 40 CE). Philo, a near contemporary of John of the gospel, was a Jewish philosopher steeped in Greek thought, who devoted his life "to expressing the essence of Judaism using the terminology of Hellenic philosophy".[10] He inadvertently laid the theological and philosophical foundations for a religion that has so far outlived him by 2,000 years and brought much sorrow to his co-religionists: Christianity.

Philo united the revelatory teachings of the prophet Moses with Platonic and Stoic thought; the historical thinking of the Old Testament, its interventionist God and directional history, with the eternal, frozen reality of Plato. Philo's *Logos* is the creative act of God and also his thinking; the Divine Mind, the Idea of Ideas, the Form of Forms, the Divine Power in the Cosmos, that orders and shapes formless matter; the Divine purpose or agent in creation and an intermediary between God and man. Crucially the single law – the *Logos* that governs the entire world and is imprinted on nature – also subsumes the more parochial Mosaic Law. Philo's synthesis of the Greek metaphysical *Logos* with the God of Moses generated a doctrine that was immensely more complicated (and compromised) than "the rational, intelligent and thus vivifying principle of the universe"[11] of Greek philosophy.

Most striking among Philo's many descriptions of the *Logos* is as the First-Born Son of the Uncreated Father.[12] The path to this extraordinary reunion of philosophy and religion, which locates humanity at the centre of the universe, is not straight: "The *Logos* has an origin, but as God's thought it also has an eternal generation. It exists as such before everything else all of which are secondary products of God's thought and therefore is called the 'first-born'."[13] As Edward Craig has put it, *Logos* – as the Word – was "a derivative divine power, at first seen as subordinate but eventually coordinated with the Father".[14]

Evidently, Philo's *Logos* was a point of convergence of many diverse strands of thought: it is both the template according to which the universe is created and the agent by which it was brought about; and it encompasses the creative principle, divine wisdom, the image of God, and man, the word of the eternal god. At the same time, it is the archetype of human reason, that through which the supreme god contacts his creation; the intermediary between God and the world, and between God and man.

Logos comes to be identified as Christ. Man, related to God through the *Logos* of his soul, is how God lets himself into his own creation. By connecting the "divine thought" with "the image" and "the first-born son of God", "the archpriest" and "the intercessor", Philo paved the way for the Christian conception of the incarnate "word become flesh". In the Old Testament (Ecclesiastes, The Song of Solomon), the Wisdom of God was personified as He who selected among the divine ideas those which were actually to be created. Philo read this as "The Idea of Ideas", the divider, who arranged the pattern of ideas for Creation. He/It was God's elder Son, the created World being the younger. The Word by which He made the world, His law, and indeed Himself, known to man was realized in Christ. *Logos* was thus both domesticated – as a man, born of woman, and meeting an excruciatingly painful death – and ascribed a boundless majesty. The Word-as-Flesh was Divine as well as Incarnated.[15]

Thus, in Philo's synthesis of Hebrew and Greek thought, in which philosophical mysteries were back-lit by religious revelations, the ground was prepared for a new kind of mediator between the intelligibility of the world and the intelligence of the sense-making humans[16] – divinity took on human form. And so we arrive back at St John's Gospel: "In the beginning was the Logos".

This *Logos* is a person who mediates between God and the world, between the Creator and the creation, that through whom God could be apprehended, however imperfectly. The *Logos* is the second person in the Godhead, distinct from, although eternally inseparable from, the Father:

> In the beginning was the Logos, and the Logos was with God, and the
> Logos was God. (1:1)
> And the Word became flesh and dwelt among us, full of grace and
> truth. (1:14)

While the Divine Flesh stands for all humanity and, beyond humanity, for the intelligibility of the world, He does so in a particular body at a particular time. The *Logos*-as-flesh spoke words and performed deeds: he walked the earth communing, during his thirty-three years of ontological slumming, with men as a man among men. When the Word became flesh, the eternal thought became a corruptible body, a transient token.

Those words were recorded and incessantly repeated. They bred interpretations that were asserted, debated, contested, and fought over. The paradox of the Word-become-flesh, of the-God-become-man, symbolized, embodied, the mysteries of a world that made (partial) sense to its human inhabitants and of the relationship between the sense that is made of the world and of the lives of those self-conscious beings that live in it and what it is that they make sense of. *Logos* became entangled with the particulars of human life: it was a mode of being that was equidistant from the mirroring of the sense-making human mind and the intrinsic order of the world.

If the Christian doctrine is a response to the challenge of connecting the small change of our daily sense-making with the intelligibility that is immanent and ubiquitous in the world, it gains existential heft at the cost of metaphysical sense. That the *Logos* should become flesh that is born, walks the earth, weeps, eats supper, suffers agony and dies, is of course profoundly absurd. More precisely, it is profound in one sense *because* it is absurd in another.

The reduction of *Logos* to "word" at the same time as it expands into divinity – such that it was "the Word" that became flesh in the person of Christ – is not simply a way of linking the advent of Christ with an Old Testament promise. It is also – notwithstanding what I have just said – a means of affirming a core meaning of *Logos* transmitted via Plato from Presocratic philosophy. *Logos* as "the Word" and Jesus as "the Word become flesh" highlights the profundity, and the tension, at the heart of the notion of "the intelligibility of the world". Jesus was both a singular and a universal: he took on the flesh not of a human being but of humanity. His flesh was a word standing for a general category: a token standing for a type; a Platonic intersection between something temporal and something eternal.

In many respects this transformation of *Logos* represents the terminus of a remarkable journey in which *Logos* metamorphoses from being the impersonal order of the universe reflected in individual (preferably philosophical) minds, to something embodied in a deity that straddles the generality of the universe and the particularity of its human inhabitants. There were, of course, further developments inside and outside the rich Christian conversation often feeding into or from structures of power and violence as well as of belief but they need not concern us here. I have indicated those aspects of the 5,000-year argument most directly relevant to our inquiry.[17]

The Christian story is true to the intellectual (or spiritual) tragedy (or comedy[18]) of our endeavours to make sense of the world. Our sense-making is inextricably mangled with our being organisms as well as persons. As we shall discuss in Chapter 5, when we strive to look beyond the horizon of the visible we do so from the marsh of our own bodies. This was a key preoccupation of the "carnophobic" philosophical tradition from Parmenides (for whom the senses were sources of delusion) that, through Plato, fed into Christianity; but it also concerns those who are at ease with the body, and whose central role as the existential underwriting of the biological authority of thought, we shall discuss. The poignant drama of Christ come down to earth also replicates the inexpressible relationship between words and that which is said or written, including the fact that it is expressible insofar as it can be stated, and what happens when a cry "That ...!" (see Chapter 6) becomes folded into utterances, books and libraries, and the many institutions of, or underpinned by, thought and language. It occupies a pivotal place in reflections on the mediated relationship between the intelligible world and the intelligent mind. Christ, the essential mediator between Divine Wisdom and Human Understanding in an incarnate *Logos*, a divinity who lived side by side with humankind, sharing its joys and sorrows, injustice, and death, and leaving His footprints on the ground on which they, too, walked, is a startling self-image of human understanding.

It is perhaps fanciful to see the mystery – or paradox, or (latterly) mere awkwardness – of eternal meanings instantiated in a transient token as a distant reflection of Plato's tragic vision of the eternal Forms barely accessible to the intellect trapped in sentient flesh. Even so, the shocking mystery of Christ remains just about recognisable in the impossibility of understanding the relationship between mind (or self) and body in contemporary Western philosophy and the place of the mind in a largely mindless Cosmos. The resistance of articulate consciousness to reduction to material events in a material object (the brain) presents a formidable barrier to the completion of the project of developing a naturalistic worldview (discussed in Chapter 4) which claims that *Logos* loses its mystery because the material world and human beings were generated by the same processes.

The First-Born *Logos* was a key moment in an unfolding story told by humanity of the twin origin of Being and Knowing, of Stuff and Sense, of a God who is both creator and architect. It is a notion that has expanded and contracted like a beating heart, as Diarmaid MacCulloch makes clear on the first page of his history of Christianity:

> *Logos* echoes with significances that give voice to the restlessness and tension embodied in the Christian message. It means not so much a single particle of speech, but the whole act of speech, or the thought behind the speech, and from there its meanings spill outwards into conversation, narrative, musing, meaning, reason, report, rumour, even presence. John goes on to name this *Logos* as a man who makes known his father God: his name is Jesus Christ.[19]

And so we retrace the boundaries of the wider conception of *Logos*: the *Logos* of Heraclitus and Plato and of Philo's First-Born; the *Logos* that is the mysterious intelligibility of an equally mysterious world, connecting self-consciousness, agency, selfhood, intelligence on the one side with, on the other, a natural world ordered mathematically, or logically subordinated to the principle of sufficient reason, regulated by discernible laws and patterns of causation, a "becausative" reality.[20]

Notwithstanding its rich meanings and its pervasive presence in the history of thought and, more widely, belief, *Logos* and the reasons for invoking it, seem to have been pushed to the margins in many areas of contemporary inquiry into the sense of the world and the fact that *we* seem capable of making that sense. Insofar as we seek to understand understanding, we often look to science, most recently neuroscience, which is thought to hold the key to the connection between the *Logos* within each of us and the *Logos* of the universe. Even those scientists who have religious beliefs, draw a line between the reason and principles that inform their work and those beliefs. *Logos* is fragmented into "logies" – disciplined inquiries into aspects of the world. Without the attachment to God, the Author of sense, in "theo-*Logos*", *Logos* loses its capital initial letter. The double helix of *mythos* and *Logos* is unwound and what remains of *Logos* goes its own way.

A few glances at the history of the jewel in the crown of natural science, mechanics, will, I hope, suffice to carry this point. This was implicit in Galileo's separation of the question of "how the heavens go" from "how to go to Heaven".[21] Newton's belief that space was the sensorium of God had no influence on the formulation of the laws of motion and of gravity. And when Einstein – who brought classical mechanics to its glorious completion – referred to God as "the Old One" who would not play dice with the world, it is difficult not to see this as an affectionate, and somewhat patronizing, nod to an idea rather than a felt reality. Subsequent allusions to reading "the mind of God" by those who sought to arrive at the equations that would, in virtue of uniting general relativity and quantum mechanics, amount to a Theory of Everything are more a deliberate provocation of the clergy than a statement of a deistic faith.[22]

The laws uncovered by natural science may be evident in the world, underpinning its intelligible order, but are not, as we noted in the previous chapter "decreed". Far from being the Mind of God, they are godless and mindless. *Logos* as Cosmic Law is simply the reliable habits of Nature – habits that can be gathered in a book or even "a mindful" because if they could not be thus gathered, they could not be conceived as a totality. The shaping power of the Creator has been reallocated to the (uncreated) Creation. The very reason why the world seems ordered may be because it can be totalized – added up to a Universe – only if seen through the lens of a few, simple, ordering principles. The intuition of idea of *The* Universe brings with it the notion of a universal, informing intelligence. This alone makes it mind-portable.

Separating the mystery of the world making sense from the idea of sense-giving (and law-giving) gods, replacing the will of God by the mechanical laws of disenchanted Nature, the principles that make the world comprehensible from (say) a man crucified upon a cross, is not entirely unwelcome.[23] However, it leaves us with a challenge that we must address in the chapters that follow: to find a basis for the intelligibility of the world without invoking an informing intelligence permeating that world and reflected in our minds; without supposing that the universe has an intelligible order because it was created by an intelligent being for intelligent beings.[24] The infinite distance between God and man crossed by *Logos* has its secular equivalent in the disproportion between the individual knowing mind and the universe that it, at least in part, knows. Consigning religious answers to the ("childish"[25]) past of the human mind does not take away the question. We should not lose the profundity of the question through rejecting the answers that have been offered it.

In the next two chapters, we shall look at two attempts to face this challenge of understanding the intelligibility of the world, without directly or indirectly appealing to God. On the surface very different, these two approaches have in common the endeavour to collapse the distance between the sense-making mind and the world of which it makes sense.

Addendum
Beginnings: bangs, flashes and commands

Creation myths requisition a variety of ingredients: Stuff, Light, Sound, Words, Commands – brought into being and united by some primordial power. Being, order, and sense-making are generated by the divine act that secures an intelligible universe. Scant attention is paid to the ordering of carts and horses – although this is a fault common to religious and secular cosmogonies. The godless creation of the universe out of a quantum vacuum – so that Nothing can magic itself into something – assumes that the laws of nature are in place before there is anything for them to operate on.[26]

When we look back from the Gospel According to St John to the Book of Genesis, we find the Word at the very beginning: it is there in the *command* "Let there be light!". At this point of origin, word and light are one in the *Logos*, the word of God that is no mere word, no mere commentary, or description, after the fact, but a generative command. In Genesis, the moment of creation is simultaneously one of illumination and articulation. The questionable ordering of carts and horses may be seen as an allegorical representation of the problematic relationship between that which is there and that which is articulated; between that which is supposed to exist in itself and that which is made explicit and articulated; of the difficulty of saying, or conceiving, or imagining Being before speech, before conception, or the illumination of an image.

The *Logos* of the world is guaranteed by the inseparability, in divine speech, of making and making intelligible; the co-creation of Stuff and Sense. "In the beginning was the *Logos*" seems to apply equally to the Old Testament story of the Creation and to the New Testament story of redemption from a Fall that began a process of an awakening to knowledge of things that only God should know. That beginning marks both the emergence of Something out of Nothing and the guarantee that that Something will make sense to the privileged human beings within it.

Both ends of St John's assertion that "In the beginning was the *Logos*" are puzzling. No *event* is in itself a beginning. It is picked out only in the light of what succeeds it, the putative endings to which it points. The opening of a story is an opening in virtue of the future closure. The cart invokes the horse: the beginning is only retrospectively identified from the standpoint of an end, as the first of a series of moments or events. To this limited extent, we may conclude that "In the Beginning" was the *word* "beginning" – spoken by a God who could see what would unfold. This is an uncompromised, absolute beginning that knows its end and hence knows that it is the beginning of everything.

The Pentateuch which moves swiftly from an account of how Something came out of Nothing to a story about the first humans and their relationship, initially to God and then to each other, thence to the history of a particular nation's relationship to God and to other nations, mediated by God, runs quickly into the implicit impurity of any beginning, compromised by the rhetorical purposes of story-telling. Philosophers whose ambition is to uncover the *Logos* of the world without *Mythos* (including even in some cases doing without that which comes from the testimony of senses which are deemed to be unreliable) dream of such a beginning – one that belongs to all possible sense-makers – is not tethered to any specific, that is to say contingent, ending, and is not pre-begun.

This is in part expressed in the philosophical dream of standing so far back and adopting a point of view from which all that is may be seen as consequence, or a conclusion of, a general potentiality, of the most fundamental nature of the world and of ourselves in it. The First Philosophy would specify the first kind of Stuff, the properties that characterize its standing state, and the laws that dictate its evolution. The ontologist or metaphysician replicates the act of Creation in an act of re-creation. A dormer window is opened, bringing the hope that human consciousness has found a new outside from which it can see and examine itself and its world – the view from nowhere and no-one that is the asymptote of objectvity. We are promised the sunrise of a higher mode of human self-consciousness. In reality, philosophers find themselves caught up in the threads of the multi-stranded millennial-long conversation humanity has been having with itself rather than discovering a hoped-for, uncompromised Beginning of all Beginning.

The beginning, in which Being and Sense are co-created, and man the sense-making creature is fashioned, is captured by Augustine in this poignant claim: *"Initium ergo, ut esset, creatus est homo, ante quem nullus fuit"* ["Man was created so that there could be a beginning"].[27] There are many ways of interpreting this striking thought. Eternal God, Who is without end, is also without a beginning. He therefore creates man so that there shall be a beginning – the first moment in a story of unfolding sense, which in virtue of being a story must be driven by a sensed incompleteness that furnishes it with its forward momentum, opening the space of possibility, of not-yet, of the unknown. The act of creation separates: that which is from the sense it has; the sense-making from that which is made sense of; and (connected with this) the sense that is hitherto made from the sense yet to be made. Without the discontinuity, the interruption, the delay and (implicitly) the incompleteness of sense, there is no act of sense-making, no explanation, no understanding, no revelation. So, at the moment of creation God might as well have said "Let there be half-light" in order that humanity, living by the mind-sweat behind its furrowed brows, may undertake a journey from greater to lesser darkness.

There is another aspect of the Beginning captured in the numinous, poly-semous Greek term *arche*. As well as "beginning" *arche* means "origin" and, importantly, "source of power". In Presocratic philosophy, it meant both the first principle or element, the formless stuff out of which the differentiated world arose, but also the divine order which informed and hence shaped it. In short, *arche* is primordial stuff, *and* the order which shapes it, *and* the power that drives it towards order: it is initial Chaos and subsequent Cosmos and the transformation of the former into the latter. *Arche* was not only "the ultimate underlying substance" but also the "ultimate undemonstrable principle", as if *arche* for Aristotle provides the conditions of the possibility of things – thus uniting creation and shaping, actualization and *forma formans*.

Which is a cue for a return to the Creation myth echoed in the Old Testament background of St John's enunciation of Salvation and what we might charac-terize as the battle for priority between *Logos* (and uttered, and hence Sound) and Light, between the Word and what it commanded into existence:

> And the earth was without form and void; and darkness was on the face of the deep. And the Spirit of God moved upon the face of the waters.
> And God said, "Let there be light"; and there was light.
>
> (Genesis 1:2–3)

And so it came to pass that the Word brought the void to its, and eventually, to our, senses. Nothing(ness) was told what to do and obediently it became Something. God's first command switched on the light, poised between Stuff and Sense. And, although darkness was on the face of the pre-creation deep, He switched on the darkness as well. The light highlighted the dark and the dark "highdarked" the light.

Leaving aside the strange notion that the void should understand Hebrew (or English in the received pronunciation of educated Jacobeans), or whatever Ur-Language God spoke (or spake – because His antiquity demands antique grammatical forms) and that it should be inclined to obey the command to cease to be void – the priority given to light is thought-provoking. For while the association of light with our lives and wakefulness, which begins when we open our eyes and finishes with our lids being sealed for ever, places light at the centre of our sense of the world, there is something deeper. Light is the proto-revelation that precedes the Word in which the world is spoken, and the world knows itself and is gathered up as one. The visual field is the proto-world revealed in a proto-picture.

In Genesis, light being commanded into existence must, however, be preceded by words. It was the Word that brought into being light and all that succeeded the Great Flash with which the universe began. And thus we have another case of horse and cart disorder. The command as to what ought to be the case must issue from and be addressed to what is already the case, even if that is only an attentive and obedient void. The notion that (non-)existence could be commanded into existence, that the utterance of words can bring about things, is therefore problematic, although it helps in seeing how Being and Sense co-emerged.

Of course, words make things happen. Our common human worlds, our lives lived and led, chosen and inflicted, are woven out of words. Speaking is acting and speech acts are the very fibre of our social being. Words are the means by which we extend our agency through acting on others who are agents like ourselves. You do as I say. I do as you say. We do as they say. They do as we say. Word-mediated agency, however, requires, operates through, other agents. Words must be manufactured by existing beings, arising out of an existing culture, and travel through existing spaces. They are thus far downstream of any First Act that brings the Universe into being.

God, alone, can bring things about directly through words. And he brings about, rather than merely shapes, things. His throat is the ultimate 3- (or indeed 4-) D printer. "My word ... shall not return to me empty; but it shall accompany that which I purpose" as Isaiah (55:11) said, ventriloquizing God. God's thoughts create what they think in virtue of creating the truth conditions of his thoughts. God furnishes the world; we only rearrange the furniture. Things are ordered into existence and, existing, they are ordered. The initial command that brought Nothing into Something also imposed order on disorder. And it did so through bringing darkness into light.

Light – that luminous beginning of everything – is the First Effect of the uttered First Cause. Or closer even than that: God's very existence is identical with light, as reflected in the evocative phrase of Aramaic St John, who refers to "The I am" that "illuminates the world" (1:4). So, the Light and the Word jostle for position as the beginning of the beginning. If the light seems to have priority, it is because the Word of God may not seem like a word at all; rather a translation of unimaginable power into a language that does not (yet) exist: an anachronism; a pre-equine cart. The words spoken by God belong to a space that precedes language; they share the already noted impossibility of philosophy that begins before the beginning and speaks where there is no medium of speech and locates the philosopher outside of himself and humankind, exploiting the impossibility of language that transcends itself and says "language", the temporal being who discusses "time", the conscious individual who puzzles over "consciousness", the material object that speaks of "matter". Even so, the notion that the word marked the beginning of the All is compelling: it reflects our sense that the world acquired its identity when someone said "World"; when This, That, and the trillion-trillion-fold Other, were gathered into a unity, by means of language that from the beginning had the capacity to outreach its grasp.

The capacity of language to reach beyond its grasp – and paradoxically to seem to pre-exist its own existence – is thus evident in the Genesis story. It is instantiated also in the *notion* of there being a Universe, a Creation, a Totality, notions which must themselves be children of language. In this sense, the Universe began when speakers began to speak of "The Universe". This may make sense of the claim that language reaches back through billions of speechless years before it came into existence; a long, overwhelmingly silent backward shout. Words can envisage a time when the very universe in which they were spoken and heard, and that of which they spoke, lay in an unimagined and indeed unimaginable future.

Herein, too, may lie the deep link between the word and the light; why they are rival versions of that which occasioned the universe. The command "Let there be light!" gives priority to words; but light itself is the first substance of the creation. What light and language have in common are that they are the weft and warp of a grid of coherence gathering a world together, collecting what has been separated in visible space and the invisible realm. Words and gazes, thinking and looking, both collect multiplicity into a unified field.

The story of how it is that the world makes sense to us will be incomplete so long as it does not also account for the incremental process of sense-making – quite different from the all-at-once matching of the *Logos* of the universe and the *Logos* of the human mind. We therefore need a complementary account of how the Light became mingled with darkness, became half-light: of the Cognitive Fall into a world of incomplete sense, ironically arising out of a desire for Divine Knowledge.

One early consequence of the Fall was the decline, described in Genesis, of the Word, no longer underwritten by the Divine mind, into a babble of mutually unintelligible languages. Things had begun well with creation and discourse coordinated in a pre-established harmony of matter and meaning:

So out of the ground the Lord God formed every beast of the field and every bird of the air; and whatever the man called every living creature that was its name. The man gave names to all cattle, and to the birds of the air, and to every beast of the field. (Genesis 1:19–20)

Thus the prelapsarian linguistic paradise, when words were co-indexed with things, language with Being. Each word was the name of a thing, or type of thing, and each thing had a name. The world made sense and that sense could be spoken, perhaps even spoke itself, with things speaking prose or at least nouns: "And the whole earth was of one language and of one speech" (Genesis 11:1).

So what went wrong? Adam wanted to *know*; to trace the meaning of the world to its source. To know was to know what God knew and so become god-like: to close the gap between the Creator and his creation. Hence the expulsion from Paradise – a Paradise of good-enough understanding as well as of unearned material goods. After The Fall, the dream of becoming God-like and returning to Heaven was forever renewed. The Tower of Babel was built to bridge the earth and the heavens: a pre-scientific attempt, perhaps, to know the mind of God. The punishment was precisely calibrated to the crime: it was for the minds of men to be even more curdled by a multiplicity of languages. The Word was shattered into smithereens of sense: not only was it broken up into names, it was further fragmented into separate cultures and minds that did not comprehend one another. Speakers emitted bits and pieces of meaning from their separate vessels of flesh. There followed misunderstanding between individuals, connected and separated, linked but more deeply divided, by their common needs and their common sense. Mutually opaque discourses, a thousand languages, tens of thousands of dialects, millions of idiolects – thus humanity shouting across a network of large and small divides, constituting the million-stranded conversation it had with itself. *Logos*, harvested into imperfectly communicating vessels, was contaminated with nonsense and senselessness. Primordial Understanding was darkened by Blunderstanding.

There was another consequence of the Fall: knowledge brought its own punishment; as it got larger, so the knower, by comparison, got smaller. Man was gradually displaced from the centre of the universe, the mid-point of boundless space, the top of the tree of life. When he felled God, man brought himself low. Fortunately, it was only as an *idea* that the universe was a whole with a centre; and being expelled from that idea was less important than retaining our position at the centre of a room or of some other sphere of attention.

The invention of writing gives an interesting twist to the rivalry between Light and the Word. Written words, which do not immediately fade like utterances bleached by silence, are both closer to vision and are at the same time woven in with a new kind of darkness. Inscription is visible – as in markings on bark and bone and in the sand and ultimately on parchment and paper – but also encodes invisible meanings. The use of ink imports shadows into the heart of light: the absence of what is made present only through reference is made explicit. Ink "highdarks" the light of the mind, the counter-light of memory and thought, of abstraction, argument and reason. The God of the written – of the religion(s) of The Book – is an absent God; there is an immeasurable distance between the words on the page and the deity in His Heaven. Even so, the stability of the inscribed confers a lasting, transcendental, even eternal significance, on the conflict and separation of discursive communities. Meaning arrested on the Sacred Page is pre-dogmatized by stability (even if susceptible to many conflicting interpretations). Such meaning may be unforgiving, coming not with Peace but with a Sword. Or bringing the promise of Divinely-authorized Peace by means of the Sword.

The Fall awoke the need for a new beginning, expressed in the Christian tradition in the New Testament, in the birth of Christ, in Whom the Word was present not absent, in the flesh not in the form of *Deus Absconditus*, a deity eternally Hidden.

> In the beginning was the Word, and the Word was with God, and the
> Word was God. (1:1)
> And the Word became flesh and dwelt among us, full of grace and
> truth. (Gospel According to St John 1:14)

The Word that brought the universe into being was echoed in a second word bringing hope for Creation's favoured child. The language that had led us into the paths of death also brought salvation.

So, the Word returns to the beginning, and yet not at the beginning, and not entirely as Word. This time the Word is flesh, not at the proximal end of a creative command, but dwelling in the Creation. The Word is both God, who is always at the Beginning, and his Son who is and is not Him, who is and is not at the Beginning, who is and is not part of the Creation, who walks the earth and is not of it, who is in time but of Eternity, who moves to the left and to the right, was born in Bethlehem and killed in Jerusalem, and yet is everywhere, and because everywhere, is not anywhere, or not anywhere in particular, and moves not as we move but mysteriously. The Word made flesh is the Word gathered up in the flesh; by this means, the divisions that come from the flesh, the needs, the powers, the exclusions and inclusions are healed.

Thus, some secular thoughts about the relationship between light and words, evident in the Old Testament Genesis Creation myth, and in the New Testament where the characterization of Christ as both *Logos* and The Light of the World[28], is profound. The luminous mystery of light is wonderfully celebrated by medieval philosopher Robert Grosseteste: "[Light] is more exalted and of a nobler and more excellent essence than all corporeal things. It has, moreover, greater similarity than all bodies to the forms that exist apart from matter, namely, the intelligences. Light, therefore, is the first corporeal form."[29] This intuition lies at the centre of the nexus of metaphors that connect knowledge, understanding, cognition with the light in so many ways such that we even report ourselves as *seeing* what someone means.

Even so, it would be surprising if the idea of the intelligibility and the origin of the world – or that in virtue of which the world both is and is intelligible to us and in itself – were confined to one sense modality. Some creation myths allocate *sounds* the role of Philo's First-Born. There is an obvious association of sound with the Word. God's commands would, one might expect, be audible, notwithstanding that, in the absence of ears to hear, they would not be heard.[30]

In the Rigveda (written before 1000 BCE) and in the early Upanishads (800–500 BCE), there is speculation about a sonar origin of the universe. This grows out of the utterance of a single primal word or syllable: "Om" or "aum" was thought to capture this because, when uttered in the correct way it contains all the vowels. The primal word was pregnant with meaning – "sphota" (or "bursting out"). The grammarian and philosopher, Bhartrhari (*c*.450–510 CE) brought together these doctrines of the cosmic primal word, the Vedas, and "sphota" in a synthesis of language, of an idea of the nature of the world, and of salvation. In the beginning, therefore, the primal Sound burst forth as the primal Word or primal Meaning, giving rise to a universe whose nature was destined to be meaningful vibration.

"In the beginning was the Sound" reconnects us with the Old Testament story of God's act of creation effected by means of shattering the silence (and curdling the purity of the void with Being), in the utterance of the command that there should be light. Paul Valéry plays with this idea in his commentary on Edgar Allen Poe's prescient cosmogony:

> The problem of the totality of things, and of the origin of this whole, arises from a very simple state of mind. We want to know what came before light; or perhaps we try to find whether one particular

combination of ideas might not take precedence over all others and engender the system which is their source, meaning the world, and their author, who is ourselves.

Whether we dream of an infinitely imperious Voice, somehow shattering eternity, its first cry announcing Space, like tidings that grow ever more pregnant with consequences as they are carried towards the uppermost limit of the creative will, and the divine Word making a place for essences, for life, for liberty, for the fatal contest between law and reason, between law and chance ....[31]

A quieter form of the imperious shout is the Stoic's *pneuma*, a concept we have already touched on. It means many things but its origin in the observed closeness of life and breathing is entrancing. *Pneuma* is an organizing principle, evident in both individual objects and the cosmos: it is a combination of air and fire.[32] At its highest level, as "constructive fire" it is indistinguishable from *Logos*. We can imagine the animist thought that *pneuma* is active in the day-wide breathing of the open, when a breeze animates all it passes through – making clouds race across the sky, trees swish, leaves hurry, curtains billow, and the philosopher's manuscript rise and fall.[33]

CHAPTER 3

Deflating the mystery 1:
Putting the world inside the mind

If the eye were not sun-like, how could it see the sun?

Plotinus[1]

Mysteries are an affront to reason. One response is to deflate them. In the case of the "eternal mystery" of "the comprehensibility of the world", such an approach may take the form of collapsing the distance between the comprehending mind and that which it comprehends. That this merely displaces, rather than solves or dissolves, the mystery will become clear; but it is worth dwelling on this way of dealing with Einstein's mystery because it has played an important part in the history of thought and of our sense of who and what we are.

The gap can be closed in either of two ways. According to idealistic philosophy, the comprehended natural world is internal to the mind that comprehends it. I shall examine this view, through its most influential exponent Immanuel Kant, in the present chapter. The opposite view is that our minds are internal to, through being the product of, nature. Our capacity to comprehend the world, the argument goes, is not in the least bit surprising because it is a necessary precondition of the existence and survival of those organisms that have minds. This view, most explicitly developed in evolutionary epistemology, will be the subject of the next chapter. The two approaches can be seen as opposite responses to Plotinus' luminous question. For idealism, the eye sees the sun because the sun is eye-like; while for naturalistic (materialistic) epistemology eyesight is sun-like, being fashioned out of the same material and subject to the same forces as the sun.

Before I address the first option, the eye-like sun, I need perhaps to defend my choice of philosopher. Why Kant? There are, after all, purer versions of idealism, most notoriously that of George Berkeley the eighteenth-century empiricist philosopher for whom reality consisted solely of minds and their ideas. Such idealism however removes, rather than addresses Einstein's mystery: the comprehended world is dissolved without remainder into the comprehending mind. This generates two problems: the origin of a common world distinct from individual minds (to be solved only by appeal to God-the-Perceiver who upholds such a world); and accommodating the process by which the knowing mind comes to acquire (only) partial and progressive knowledge and understanding of its world. An alternative port of call to Berkeley would be industrial-strength or Absolute Idealism exemplified by Hegel which (according to the nineteenth-century interpretation) "included both subjective life and objective cultural practices on which subjective life depended within the dynamics of the development of the self-consciousness and self-actualisation of God, the *Absolute Spirit.*"[2] This view of Hegel has recently been contested, with some interpreters denying that he espoused spiritual monism or even that he had wanted to advance the kind of dogmatic metaphysics Kant denied. It does not, however, make his writing any more amenable to incorporation into our inquiry, especially as most of it lies beyond the cognitive pay grade of the present writer. Kant, as we shall see, at least seemed to be aware that there was an outside reality to be somehow acknowledged beyond the experience of our senses. What is more, he is a pivotal figure in Western philosophy of the last 500 years. Like Bach in Western classical music, he took account of all that preceded him and has influenced, to a unique degree, all that has followed him.

At the heart of Kant's vision is what he characterizes as his "Copernican" revolution that locates objects of experience inside, rather than outside, the mind:

> Hitherto it has been assumed that 'all our knowledge must conform to objects' but since this assumption has conspicuously failed to yield any metaphysical knowledge 'we must therefore make trial whether we might not have more success in the tasks of metaphysics, if we suppose that objects conform to our knowledge.'[3]

As for the knowing mind, it has two primary faculties: the *sensibility* and the *understanding*: "Our knowledge springs from two fundamental sources of the mind: the first is the capacity of receiving impressions (receptivity for impressions), the second is the power of knowing the object through their representation (spontaneity in the production of concepts)".[4] The object of knowledge is consequently the product of a) "the forms of sensible intuition" – space and time – in which it is located; and b) the understanding that places it under certain categories – such as a causal relation to other objects. By this means, the object is unified and itself forms part of a unified world, whose diverse contents are ordered, connected, and brought into relation.

Kant's most radical suggestion is that "space and time belong only to the forms of intuition, and therefore to the subjective constitution of our mind, apart from which they could not be ascribed to anything whatsoever".[5] The categories of space and time are the condition of the possibility of our having any experiences at all; they are not properties of things in themselves but only of appearances: "[I]f the subject, or even only the subjective constitution of the senses in general be removed, the whole constitution and all the relations of objects in space and time, nay space and time themselves, would vanish".[6] The forms of sensible intuition are the condition of coherent experience, necessary to call delirium to order.

The world of experience coheres because it is brought together in the mind – a thought that leads to Kant's boldest claim: "the synthetic power of the mind is the lawgiver of nature".[7] This power does not merely happen to be a contingent characteristic of experience: it is a necessary condition of experience. It follows from this that the way the world holds together, its unity, is underwritten by the unity of the mind, more specifically of the self: "I" and "it", the one who comprehends and that which is comprehended, are mutually dependent.

The second notion, fundamental to Kant's "transcendental idealism", is that the world of experience is not, however, the whole story of what there is. Comprehension, pure reason, (contrary to the assumptions of the metaphysicians whom Kant opposed) do not reach all the way to the heart of reality. Beyond the things-for-us that populate the phenomenal realm there is the noumenal realm of the thing in-itself. While all our knowledge begins in experience, there is more to reality than what we can experience. This distinguishes Kant's "transcendental idealism" from the phenomenalism of philosophers such as Berkeley for whom, as we have mentioned, there is nothing other than perceptions and perceivers – the latter including God necessary to maintain the existence of objects when they are not being perceived – such that the sum total of experience is the sum total of reality. Because the noumenal realm is purely an object of the understanding – an inferred something – it has no experiencable content. It is, however, that which is ultimately real and ensures that phenomena are not just free-floating illusions; that appearances are genuinely appearances of something real.

Kant's system is immensely complex and developed with vision and ingenuity. It is, however, possible to bypass the detailed working out when assessing what, if anything, it has to offer in making the comprehensibility of the universe less mysterious by closing the gap between mind and nature.

A critique of his *Critique* could begin by focusing on his conception of the mind to which the world is internal and which generates the phenomenal realm out of the noumenal reality. Mind as we know it, as it is usually understood, is not a single, seamless, item – a category like "space" – but is distributed between an indefinite number of individual consciousnesses, more or less independent of one another. The human minds that comprehend the world are intimately tied to the trajectory and fate of individual bodies that occupy particular locations in space over a particular stretch of time. It would seem to follow from this that space and time are prior to, rather than underpinned by, minds. This explains how it is that I experience some parts of the world and not others; more specifically, how I can experience myself as being surrounded by certain objects rather than by others, as being here rather than elsewhere, now rather than some other time. And this is how it is that you come to experience different things from me and in a different way. I see the keyboard in front of me but not a keyboard in America or one that was destroyed twenty years ago. And while I can have awareness of items in distant places and times this awareness still has to be mediated by signs and representations that are in my vicinity, experienced here and now. I must sit in front of the computer screen to see you via Skype. If space were imposed by me, it would be difficult to understand why I have little control over the contents of my vicinity, indeed, over the way such items are disposed in the space around me and elsewhere. It does not lie within my gift to determine which bit of earth is beneath me and which clouds are above my head. Most inexorably, it is not in virtue of the properties of my mind that this body is my body spatially related to certain other bodies and experienced as mine. If it was in virtue of my mind that my body occupied a certain portion of space-time, then it would seem that the mind would have to take on the job of locating itself, with nothing to justify its locating itself in one place rather than another. Without a viewpoint already located in space and time, embodied in an object among objects, there can be no basis for experiencing one part of the world rather than another.

The opening sentences of the *Critique*, perhaps inadvertently, flag up this problem:

There can be no doubt that all our knowledge begins with experience. For how should our faculty of knowledge be awakened into action did not objects affecting our senses partly of themselves produce representations, partly arouse the activity of our understanding to compare these representations, and, by combining or separating them, work up the raw material of sensible impressions into that knowledge of objects which is entitled experience?[8]

"Objects *affecting* our senses" to "*produce* representations" gives the inescapably unKantian impression of a relationship, an external relationship, even a causal relationship, between an object and an (embodied) subject that is made possible by the spatiotemporal connection between the former and the latter. The image is one of encounter or impingement: it seems to suggest, even to presuppose, spatial and temporal relations in the world beyond, or prior to, experience, giving the latter its specific contents.

Kant's own understanding of space, time, and causation does not allow this. Let us focus on "causation". It is not an intrinsic property of the noumenal world, or a feature of the interaction between the noumenal realm and the mind. Since causation is one of the categories of the understanding it must be internal to the phenomenal realm. It cannot operate outside the sphere of experience in order to justify the subject having one set of experiences rather than another. Causation is, as it were, a horizontal relationship between experiences, or objects-as-experienced in the phenomenal realm, not a vertical relationship between noumenal reality and the phenomena experienced by the mind. In short, if causality is really a mind-imposed property of the phenomenal realm, we are not permitted to think of things-in-themselves *causing* the representations that constitute the experienced world.[9]

There is another, common-sense, reason for denying ourselves the idea of a causal relationship between the noumenal and phenomenal world. Causes and effects are typically proportionate to one another and they belong to the same fundamental kinds. Neither of these could be true of putative noumenal causes of phenomenal effects: nothing in either realm could be commensurate to anything in the other realm. Even though, Kant argues, we cannot know anything of the noumenon because it is not accessible to experience, we may safely conclude from his general position that it is not differentiated in the way that the objects of experience are differentiated. There is consequently nothing in the noumenal realm to "ground" the specifics of the multi-coloured phenomenal realm: it does not contribute anything to the form and content of experience. Indeed, since there is neither space nor time to separate items, there is nothing in the noumenal realm to underpin the multiplicity of distinct identities that populate the world we know. After all, for Kant the difference between unity and multiplicity belongs to the categories of the understanding.

In summary, concerning the noumenal realm, not only is there nothing to be said about its intrinsic properties, there is nothing intelligible to be conceived of its relationship to, in particular its role in the genesis of, the phenomenal realm, either as a totality or as regards the particular dispositions of its contents. Without causation, or any other power of "becausation", it does no work at all and, indeed, it *must* remain idle if it is to serve the purpose for which Kant introduced it.[10] Its job is to save Kant the embarrassment of being regarded as a Berkeleian idealist. As such, it seems little more than a "placeholder" to reassure us that appearances are not disconnected, free-floating, and unjustified and that our knowledge has grounds outside of knowledge. They do not, however, deliver much reassurance because the phenomena are appearances of things (noumena) that have no intrinsic properties relevant to the appearances. As objects of (purely) intellectual intuition they would be available only to God who would think and create them in the same instant.

It might be argued in Kant's defence that when he says that there is nothing that can be said about the noumenal realm (or reality behind appearance), he means exactly what he says. So we cannot even discuss its having or not having specific causal properties to justify the specific experiences that our minds order according to the forms of sensible intuition and the categories of the understanding. That, however, is to evade the question and also to be inconsistent in the application of the limits he places on metaphysical explanation. His claim, for example, that space and time are forms of sensible intuition that are not inherent in reality seems to transgress beyond his self-imposed limitations in two ways. Firstly, it gets outside of experience (admittedly using reason rather than experience) to look behind it to its workings. Secondly, it defines the noumenal realm at least privatively by asserting that many things are not true of it – such as spatiality, temporality and causal connectedness.

At any rate, it is evident that minds in the plural, actual minds, your mind, my mind, minds of subjects embodied in bits of flesh, cannot each, individually, be the bearers of space and time which for Kant are unified, connected totalities (as they are in common sense) in which all things are located. Their specific experiential contents *presuppose* spatial and temporal locations conferred upon them through living bodies that are themselves located in space and time. What we experience depends on where we are and where we are is anchored in the location of our bodies – in a pre-existing, objective, shared space-and-time – that could not themselves be synthesized, nor located through, the activities of our minds since the latter would lack a *point d'appui*.

This is not to reject the Kantian notion of the spontaneous activity of the mind. There is a sense in which our minds are active inasmuch as we can, of course, adjust our experiences by redirecting or resetting our attention. That, however, is a liberty we exercise within the constraints of a pre-given sensory field. I can look to the left or to the right, focus on the colour of something rather than its shape, or on the voice of the person talking to me rather than the background bruit. I have no discretion over seeing unaided a village in another continent or the back of the moon. I cannot hear a whispered conversation ten miles away or observe George III ascend the throne. In short, I have – or in some sense *am* – a viewpoint that is in the first and last instance located in, and both enabled and constrained by, the location of a body itself occupying a certain location in space and time. Collapsing the gap between mind and world by locating the primordial outsides even of physical space inside the mind, in "us", cannot accommodate this fundamental aspect of experience.

It has been suggested to me that this is no more problematic than the recognition that many features of the world are both mind-generated and constrained by extra-mental reality.[11] These may be gathered under the general heading of "secondary qualities" that Galileo drew attention to and Locke made central to epistemology. Tomatoes are not red in themselves: they become red only to conscious beings with a particular kind of nervous system; their redness is not an intrinsic property but a disposition to induce a sense of redness that is realized only when they fall within a particular kind of visual field. This does not, however, palliate the scandal of Kant's gathering space (the source of *primary* qualities such as size, shape and location) and time into the mind. The idea of mind-dependent secondary qualities at least presupposes distinct objects and minds, located in space and time, and causally interacting. Kant's mind-dependent space and time takes away all of this, folding all the constraints on objects into the mind. That is a fundamental difference between Lockean (and comparable forms of anti-realist) empiricism and Kantian transcendental idealism.

The fact that I find myself in a particular region of space and over particular stretches of time cannot therefore be reconciled with the (seemingly disembodied, de-situated) Kantian mind as the *source* of space and time. Viewpoints are populated with the objects and events located in the portion of space in which they are, courtesy of living bodies, located. More precisely, they are populated with objects and events seen from a certain perspective, without which there would be no appearances. Think of the (non-) appearance of a rock from no perspective, observed at no scale.

If the human body – an object located in space and time – owed its most important features to the activity of the mind, there would be no basis for the token world that is the cognate object of an individual consciousness. More specifically, space and time would appear twice: as, according to Kant, that which any viewpoint (or mind) must generate to order its experiences; and that, according to common sense, in which the viewpoint is already located, and more broadly individuated, courtesy of the body of the subject. The viewpoint has to be found a place in the very view he/she upholds and thus lay claim to his own patch of space-time.

Making sense of this becomes even more difficult when the *self* undergoes Kantian treatment.[12] Kant agrees with Hume that the self is not an object, an item, that can be encountered in perception. It is sustained by an *activity*: the apperception of perceiving and unifying one's own perceptions. The self is the product of the "synthetic unity of apperception", in virtue of which I ascribe my experiences to myself, and which also unifies the objective world.

The connection is lucidly expressed by P. F. Strawson:

> What is required for a series of experiences to belong to a single consciousness is that they should possess precisely the rule-governed connectedness which is also required for them collectively to constitute a temporally extended experience of a single objective world. The burden of the entire argument is thus shifted to the necessary unity of consciousness.[13]

And this is amplified by Gardner: "The Copernican strategy of explaining objects in terms of our mode of cognition amounts to explaining objects in general in terms of one privileged real object, the self, which has the role of providing a fundamental *ontological* condition for all other objects."[14] The self is not merely the epistemic underpinning of our knowledge of objects but the condition of there being (discrete, stable, unified) objects at all.

Kant speaks of the self as having the capability of accompanying each perception with "I think" and in virtue of this claiming ownership of those perceptions.[15] The transcendental self is the necessary condition of perception. It is, however, difficult to see how the self could identify itself as the same self – the thinker as the same thinker – without a spatiotemporally trackable body tagging it.[16] And it is the body, of course, that ensures that the experiences are valid and relevant to a person's life. Kant's claim that the synthetic unity of apperception is secured by a transcendental subject belonging to the noumenal realm, simply compounds the difficulty of a) securing the intersection of mind and noumenal world, and b) of explaining how our experiences are about or of individual worlds bespoke to our individual lives and minds. The body that seems to be necessary to secure the life of the (empirical) self that has, or is, a viewpoint on the world, and synthesizes that world into a unity, is an ill-matched partner for the transcendental self, given that the former is located in space and time and is an object on all fours with, moving among and interacting with, other objects, denizens likewise of the phenomenal realm. The body appears to be required to sustain that in virtue of which the self has a particular world – namely, the sensorium that delivers particular sense experiences and the mind that allocates sense experience to spatiotemporally located objects and places them under the categories of understanding.

It may be argued that the synthetic power of the mind or self merely orders what is given but doesn't itself give anything.[17] We have already noted the problems that arise if we think of the noumenal realm serving itself up to individuals: what would it serve up, to whom, and how? If there were intrinsic "givenness" in the noumenon that was harvested by minds or empirical selves, the latter would seem to be superfluous to requirement or as idle as the noumenal realm in the more conventional interpretation of Kant that we discussed earlier. If the mind was not idle and did have the role Kant assigned to it, then what is served up would lack spatial location and temporal order, location, or duration, which would not be much of a constraint on the operation of the mind. At the risk of mixing metaphors, we might say that the mind, imposing primary qualities (and presumably secondary) qualities on the noumenal offer, had a pretty free hand.

There is another defence of Kant; namely that identifying the self with a viewpoint as it is usually construed is to miss the entire point of his analysis of the subject, by reducing the latter to the empirical self. Kant postulates that there is a transcendental self which is itself divisible into the self as transcendental subjectivity (the condition of there being objects), and the self as a thing in itself, as a noumenon. But this distinction only displaces, without resolving, the problem of how to connect the individual, empirical self situated in, or relating to, a particular, bespoke, world with the self as a category that transforms the noumenal realm into the phenomenal one. The doubling of the self into transcendental and empirical realizations simply highlights the paradoxical notion of undifferentiated noumenal items grounding individual differentiated phenomenal realities, and by so grounding them providing the basis of a distinction between veridical perceptions and hallucinations.

There is another challenge to the Kantian system – opposite to the mystery that is driving the present inquiry. It is not that of how we understand so much

– the mystery of the comprehensibility of the world – but how we understand so little: how our knowledge is so far from completeness. If knowledge arises out of experience and experience is shaped by the mind – even to the point where the synthetic power of the mind is the lawgiver of nature[18] – how are we to account for cognitive growth – both in individual lives and over successive epochs of humanity, even if we are careful to distinguish between law-governed nature and the laws that are extracted by the non-natural means of scientific inquiry? And how are knowledge and understanding developed to such different degrees in different people, and different cultures, or at different times in the same person?

It would be a fundamental misunderstanding of Kant to suggest that he imagined that he believed that science advances by introspection; or that we arrived at the field equations of general relativity by turning our gaze on the forms of sensible intuition and the categories of the understanding.[19] After all, he maintains that nature is "not a thing in itself but merely an aggregate of appearances".[20] Even so, there is no way of engaging with the partial comprehensibility or the progression towards more complete understanding. We are either omniscient from the start – since what we know is internal to us and the synthetic power of the mind is the lawgiver of nature; or – since the noumenal realm has the monopoly on reality and is inaccessible to experience – we are and remain totally ignorant of what is real, although, through the power of reason, we are somehow apprised of our ignorance. There seems to be no place for the gradual, painstaking uncovering of the laws, and even the nature, of nature in his system according to which "the order and regularity of the appearances, that we entitle *nature*, we ourselves introduce".[21]

Thus, Kant's transcendental idealism would seem to turn our mystery upside down: it is no longer the fact that we know *so much* but that we know *so little* that demands explanation. We are at a loss to explain the influence of location in space and time, and our personal and collective history, on the growth of our knowledge, and the constraints on what we individually and collectively know. We cannot give an account of why advances in understanding nature do not merely amount to an advance in self-understanding or an understanding of our understanding. If the laws of nature are intrinsic to *all* possible experience, Kant may as well concede that they belong to nature herself, a nature independent of any particular mind and hence of "mind".

Moreover, Kant does not begin to address the character of something that lies between the individual mind and "mind" as a category; namely the community of minds in which knowledge, understanding, intelligibility is progressed and held in store – though it has to be realized in individual minds

– and which is reflected in the individual self that grows in, and makes sense of itself and its world. The problem presented for Kant by the community of minds, consisting of separate individual viewpoints with distinctive histories, but profoundly interdependent, further highlights the fundamental weakness of his account of the relationship between mind and world: namely, its failure to distinguish between mind-in-general and mind realized in individual consciousnesses. This failure makes it impossible to account for, or even conceive, the individual configuration of our experiences and of the individual scope of our ability to act.

That these questions do not figure as large as they should perhaps may be because Kant and the Kantians do not clearly specify whether the mind is a general category or, on the other hand, a collection of individual consciousnesses that are indissolubly caught up in individual living bodies, and which can be extinguished by fatal damage to those bodies. This ambiguity makes it possible to avoid the obvious question of how the space and time that constitute the forms of (sense) experience are differentiated into specific insides and outsides, particular "heres" and "theres", specific "nows" and "thens", my world and your world. If individual minds were constituents of an undifferentiated "mind-in-general" supporting a unified phenomenal realm – "*the* world" – there would be no way of explaining the multiplicity of distinct worlds, the difference between a private and a public realm, and even the vulnerability of those worlds to a particular bash on a particular head. Even less would it explain how the mind, as a shifting viewpoint, would be able to travel in space.[22]

A direct consequence of this ambiguity – whether mind is a non-located category or is distributed through independent embodied subjects that are themselves located – is that Kant can seem to get away with giving no clear account of the relationship between the transcendental, ideal, space and time imported by subjects and the empirical spaces and times in which objects are located and subjects live and objects are encountered by people. Accepting that space and time could not be discovered through experience but must be presupposed in it leaves conspicuously unexplained our individual descent to the particular spaces and times in which we and the things we live among are experienced. The particular "outsides" and "insides" remain unexplained if we gather the General Outside into the subject, and subject and object underwrite each other, and we do not assign a key role to our (non-transcendent) bodies. Or if, as Gardner has expressed it, "self-consciousness [is]… viewed … as the encompassing ground of the world of objects".[23] This leaves token worlds that are the cognate objects of individual subjects conspicuously unexplained if the living body, that would seem to provide the basis for the individuation and coherence of consciousness, itself owes its unity to the unifying power, the transcendental apperception, of the mind.

As we have seen, the problem this presents is no way alleviated by invoking the distinction between the transcendental and empirical selves; it simply moves the problem on from minds to selves. The transcendental self is merely the unifying principle accompanying all perceptions and other mental phenomena. Its relationship is an internal one: the self-consciousness of the self identifies its ever-changing contents as belonging to the same individual. It clearly contributes nothing to the localization of mind or minds within the world or in its own world. What is more, the Kantian transcendental self or subject is unnervingly impersonal, being over-and-against the experienced world and the empirical self. It is not clear how it interacts with the latter; or how the two aspects of the subject – transcendental and empirical – are united such that the mind that underpins space and time is able to locate itself within a portion of space over a stretch of time.[24]

Could Kant defend himself by arguing that, while subjects or minds are independent, they are not spatially or temporally located in virtue of their being associated with an individual living body? I think not, for it would leave unanswered the legitimate question as to what confers their individuality upon individual minds? A mind is a viewpoint, a "take", on the world and such a take would not be possible without an indissoluble relationship to a body located in space and time. Such a relationship must be more intimate than a (dualist) partnership: it must be *em*bodiment. The body in virtue of which actual minds are embodied is (among other things) an object among other objects, located in space and time.

In short, by collapsing the distance between the mind and its experienced world, Kant seems to remove any basis for the way we experience what is out there, for our experiencing a particular "out there" – and *a fortiori* for being ourselves in that particular "there", for being given in experience as well as givers of experience, being that in virtue of which there is objective, empirical knowledge and objects of that knowledge. The real outside is moved to an unknowable margin, the noumenal realm, and particular experienced outsides (and the contrast between outside and inside) seem groundless. The phenomenal realm of appearances from nowhere-in-particular would be of nowhere-in-particular. Timeless, locationless, noumena, not in a causal relationship to phenomena, can hardly stand surety for the validity of appearances that have specific spatiotemporal features and which are not hallucinations. Kant, it seems wants to retain an independent external reality to avoid pure

(Berkeleian) idealism and yet cannot grant that outside any features to justify its appearances as appearances "of". There is neither a causal nor intentional relationship between the phenomenal and noumenal world.

What we have lost is the fullness of the idea of an objective world. Such a world, as we know and suffer it, is not simply an aggregation of objects like mountains and cups and human bodies whose unity and relationships are imposed by the mind. It is much more. It is a mind-independent law-governed, spontaneously active domain, within which our lives are regulated, our destinies enacted and, with some significant margins of freedom, determined. The noumenal realm that lacks all the properties of that world could not supply this. It is not the kind of "outside" into which we are plunged, into which we are born (without being consulted) and out of which we fall as we die.

For these reasons, the Kantian collapse of the distance between mind and world does not help us to address, or in any way diminish, the mystery of the comprehensibility of the world, even less the kind of hard-won progressive comprehensibility that we associate with the advance of science.[25] And Kant may well have accepted that, as a consequence of his commitment to a more modest mission for philosophy than the metaphysician's traditional ambition to make the world intelligible. It was, however, not surprising that some of Kant's successors, notably Hegel, saw the Kantian explanation of the world's making sense as an unsatisfactory half-way house to a full-blown idealism and that understanding could be understood if we saw it as a progressive replacement of matter by mind and individual minds by an Absolute Spirit. In short, they rejected his transcendental idealism in favour of a pure idealism that allowed nothing outside of the realm of the mind.

We have entered upon vast territory and it will be wise for this writer not to advance any further. However, it is worth noting that subsequent philosophers who have dismissed Kant's approach to collapsing the distance between the comprehending mind and the comprehending world have often done so by sharing his objections to the way the problem has been framed. The original sin, it is argued, has been the Cartesian error of a dualism which begins with a mind that is directly available to itself but must somehow get outside of itself in order to acquire reliable knowledge of the material world set out in space. Locke denied that the mind had intrinsic properties separate from the experienced world: it was built up out of experiences. For Kant, however, this would not deliver the coherent unified world of causally, interacting, enduring objects set out in space and time for a consistent and coherent self. It seems too haphazard. Self and objects would be exposed as "logical fictions" or "logical constructions" as arch-sceptic Hume pointed out.[26]

Kant thought that he had found the way of addressing the "scandal" of philosophy that it had not found a rational proof of the existence of an external world. His response – that the external world, insofar as it appears to us and is set out in space and time is in fact internal – simply moves the problem to a different place. An alternative response is the second-order scepticism of those who feel that there is something deeply fishy about a scepticism that questions the reality of the external world. Prominent among these meta-sceptics is Martin Heidegger and it is worth glancing at his hugely influential dissolution of the problem that Kant endeavoured to solve.

In *Being and Time* Heidegger argued that the "scandal" of philosophy "is not that we lack this proof [of the existence of an external world of which we had certain knowledge] but that *such proofs are expected and attempted again and again*".[27] Such proofs would not be needed if philosophers did not begin in the wrong place – the Cartesian place of a mind (or a self, spirit, or soul) divorced from a world assumed to be of an entirely different (material) nature, accessed through the mediation of a consciousness that had to piece it together.

What is primordial, Heidegger asserts, is being-in-the-world and this is where we should begin our philosophical investigations. We are not therefore minds attempting to contact an utterly other reality to which we have only mediated access. On the contrary, as beings "whose being is an issue for itself", we are thrown into, rather than sealed off from, the world: our very being – or Being-there or *Da-sein* – is to be engaged with, caught up in, caring for, the world, as an inseparable part of our caring for ourselves. The world, in the first instance, consists of entities that underpin a network of significations, not the inert objects transfixed by the "rigid staring" that characterizes the stance of the philosopher. The world of *Da-sein* does not therefore have to be discovered, constructed, unified: it is something deeper than all this – it is "the clearing of Being". The work done by the Kantian mind is not therefore required because we do not begin in an inside that is trying to piece together an outside. Our very being is already out there and if we cannot see this fundamental fact of our existence, it is because of the intellectualist Cartesian spectacles through which we see our being in the world. Placing "disclosedness" – which is not *of* the world but *is* the world – at the centre of being-in-the-world bypasses the need for an interaction between the conscious subject and the world of which he or she is conscious. Kant's unsatisfactory solution was to a non-existent problem.

Unfortunately, Heidegger's rejection of Kant's problem itself generates problems analogous to those we have identified in relation to Kant's internalizing the outside world; namely, that of explaining the parochiality of our being, our lives, our knowledge, our viewpoint, and the fact that our understanding is partial and capable of growth (and contraction) with the passage of time, that certain things and not others are disclosed to us and that they vary from person to person and from time to time.

Just as Kant exploits an ambivalence between Mind as a category and minds corresponding to individual consciousnesses, so Heidegger's *Da-sein* is neither entirely a general category or an indefinite number of individuals. If it were a general category, then we would be unable to explain our individual lives and viewpoints (and their limitations), account for how the Open disclosed to us is closed off or limited, its being limited by an horizon. If on the other hand *Da-sein* were allocated to, or distributed between, individuals, the consciousness localized by its body (as opposed to being-in-the-world) returns, along with the problem of access to the world.[28]

In contemporary thought, idealistic notions about collapsing the gap between mind and world have come from what might seem to be an entirely unexpected source: hard physical science, specifically the Copenhagen interpretation of quantum mechanics. According to this interpretation no physical parameter – at least at the fundamental level – has a definite value, indeed a reality, until it is measured. Mind seems to permeate the physical world at the atomic level.

This is an illusion but it is worth dwelling on at least briefly because quantum idealism is widely discussed and taken seriously by many thinkers.[29] One of its most flamboyant exponents was John Wheeler who developed the idea of a *participatory universe* arguing that "IT" (the universe) came "from BIT" – that is bits of information. We shall return to this in Chapter 8 but for the present we note that this form of idealism would not address the inadequacies of either Kant's transcendental idealism or Heidegger's existentialism. If mind was everywhere – and we were able to access the universe because we had a crucial role in its creation or determination – it would be difficult to understand: a) how it would be gathered up into localized minds such as yours and mine that are aware of, perceive, or know, or understand, some things rather than others; b) the dependency of knowledge on the viewpoint of an *embodied* subject; or c) any form of liberation from cognitive limitation. Another way of putting this is that the entangled single wave-function universe of quantum mechanics does not seem to be able to accommodate the multiple, distinct, conscious viewpoints of the community of human minds – although it depends on such minds to make those measurements that impose determinacy on an indeterminate world.

"It from Bit", physics-based, metaphysics is a striking confirmation of Thomas Nagel's astute observation: "Scientism is actually a special form of idealism, for it puts one type of human understanding in charge of the universe and what can be said about it".[30] The type of understanding in question grants ultimate authority to measurements, denies the fundamental reality of qualitative experience, and reduces what there is to "a system of magnitudes".

This, notwithstanding, "It from Bit" is a further illustration of the hopelessness of trying to account for the comprehensibility of the world by theories that deny the independence of our understanding minds and the understood world. Even if Kant's *Critique* did not have the problems we have identified, it would not address our question at the right level: it is too fundamental for the higher-level inquiry into how it is we can have a general, and advancing, understanding of the universe that takes different forms as the natural sciences advance. Kant's solution – or non-solution – addresses a question that is wider, and deeper, than that of our progressive cognitive advance to its present almost miraculous level of attainment. There is also the point (that we shall discuss in Chapter 6) that the parties to the relationship must of necessity be distinct and indeed independent for there to be the kind of knowledge that we are trying to explain.

Even so, it is worthwhile examining another, currently more popular, approach to the comprehensibility of the world that also collapses the distance between mind and world. The opposite of a transcendental idealism that argues we can know the world because the world has been constituted by the mind, this other view maintains that the material or natural world is comprehended by the mind because the latter is a product of the former, having been shaped by evolutionary imperatives to deliver (reliable) knowledge. This is the theme of the next chapter.

Addendum 1
The harmony of world and mind

I have focused on Kant – as the exemplar of philosophers accounting for the comprehensibility of the world to our minds by enclosing in our minds the world we have to make sense of – because of his extraordinary depth of thought and his huge influence. In this brief note, I want to illustrate the kind of approaches to be found in the space between idealist and materialist explanations of our being attuned to the world in which we find ourselves.[31]

Aquinas highlighted the harmony of the relationship between *esse natural* of the world and the *esse intentionale* of the thinking mind. What makes my thought of X is the very same thing that makes an X an X; namely, the *form* of X. Unfortunately, while this may help to identify what it is about mental contents that makes them be about the world, it does not address the question of why or how there are such truthful mental contents, such that thought can be "adequate" to things. What is more, precisely what is meant by "a common form" between thought and its objects remains obscure. We do not have a clear idea of what the form of a thought is – other than the thought itself – or what aspect of its object it captures – other than that specified in the thought. The thought "The cup is on the table" seems to have little in common with the state of affairs it asserts. "Logical form" delivers very little: it is empty of anything that would specify the scope of its applicability to bits of the material, even if it could itself be defined. And it would be difficult to apply the notion of common form to most of the statements that express the sense we make of the world, even lean scientific assertions such as "$F = ma$".

Behind Aquinas there is an extensive scholastic tradition of the notion of "inexistence" in virtue of which one object (such as a referent) can be inside another (such as a thought). This has a direct line to the nineteenth-century German philosopher Franz Brentano who revived philosophical awareness of the distinctive feature of mental phenomena, namely that they include an object intentionally within themselves; they have aboutness or intentionality. For Brentano's contemporary, Gottlob Frege, who shifted the focus from consciousness to language, it is because words express a sense that they are about anything at all. The word is *about* the object in virtue of the sense of the word being identical with the or a sense of the object. Since Edmund Husserl's "noemata" (objects or contents of thought at the far end of the intentional relationship whose origin is in the "I") and Frege's senses cannot be reduced to something individuated perceptually, they seem attractive as mediators between mind (concepts) and the world (objects). They lie on the path between sense experience and sense-making that involves intelligible abstractions. On closer inspection, however, the problems unresolved in Aquinas are equally unresolved in the phenomenologists' objects of the consciousness and the analytical philosophers' accounts of the senses and referents of words: the principle of underlying the mapping of mind and world seems impossible to specify.

I mention these as examples of approaches less radical than Kant's as to how the mind can comprehend the world. They postulate a world that is, as it were, partly soluble in the mind. They are all, in a sense, piecemeal and do not offer a global solution to what is a global problem. For Aquinas, of course, that solution is already available – provided by God who ensures that the world is sufficiently intelligible to the favourites of his creation.

Addendum 2
"The outside"

One way of characterizing the gap between mind or self and world is to describe the latter as "outside" and the former as "inside".[32] This is, of course, vulnerable to criticism since the world is not outside the mind as items in the world are outside each other – in the way, for example, the garden is outside of the house or the matchbox is outside of the matches contained in it.

Trying to deal with the "outsideness" of the experienced world is what in part motivates Kant's endeavour to internalize the outside by making space simply one of the forms of sensible intuition. Space is not genuinely "outer" but sustained by the "outer sense". So, when Kant speaks of "the starry sky above and the moral law within" – the twin miracles engraved on his headstone – the distinction between "above" (or "outside") and "within" is not as we would normally understand it because the starry sky is also within, since it does not belong to the noumenal realm.[33] Indeed, his Copernican revolution would place the starry sky (or its being "above") within and the moral law without – in the noumenal realm.

We seem, however, to require a genuine, subject-independent, outside in order to differentiate that which belongs to ourselves and that which belongs to the world. Kant himself seems to admit this when he says that there must be "a *thing* outside me" not "the mere *representation* of a thing outside me".[34] It is difficult, however, to characterize the boundary between that inside and that outside without borrowing boundaries that belong to the outside world – for example inside and outside of the body, or parts of the body such as parts of the brain. These are clearly the wrong kinds of boundary because they separate regions of the (phenomenal) outside. The boundary, for example, between the cerebral cortex (for some deluded individuals, the primary locus of the mind) and the rest of the world clearly does not delineate the border separating what we might call the metaphysical inside and outside. We are naturally inclined to think of the mind as "metaphysically" rather than empirically "inside".

So why does Kant internalize the outside in his metaphysics of experience? He gives various reasons. For example, he says that we can imagine space without objects occupying it but not objects or events that are not located in space or filling some of it up. Our idea of space, therefore, must precede any experience of items in space. The weakness of this argument, surprising in view of Kant's astuteness, suggests that it must have undeclared intellectual motivation commending it. I suspect that it may lie in the puzzling nature of intentionality, particularly evident in the case of the most explicitly spatial of the senses – vision – but present throughout our experience of an external world. This warrants brief examination.

My awareness of something "over there" reaches across, and hence seemingly overcomes, the intervening space but also maintains that interval. The glass on the table, and the interval between me and it, is incorporated in my mind as an object of perception. If the glass were truly separated from me, then I would not seem to be able to reach it; but if it were not separated from me, it would not be other than me: it would not be (a freestanding) "it". So, Kant's intuition is that the space in which the perceived object and the perceiving subject are located is separate from the object: the space belongs to the perceiving self as the form of sensible intuition which permits the object to be "out there". Space becomes a kind of "ghost" presence between, or containing, things that are present: that in virtue of which there is, or can be, presence *to*.

This ingestion of the outside into the experiencing mind, is as we have noted deeply problematic. It is difficult to see how the self could sustain, even less contain, the multi-loculated, multi-layered, physically limited, space that is available to ourselves as viewpoints; the outside of fresh air and domestic spaces; of packet, cupboard, field, and landscape; outsides that are abuzz with intimations of insides that encompass outsides. Kantian space would not support the nearness and remoteness, dappled hiddenness and disclosure, ignorance and knowledge, the light and dark, of the space in which we pass our lives; nor the fact that while it is shared between consciousnesses, access to it is bespoke to individual viewpoints; nor explain the work that is required to move our bodies or in some other way extend our acquaintance with the contents of space. It does not answer to our sense of being "thrown" (to use Heidegger's term) beings, cast into space (and time).[35]

It seems as if we cannot do without a genuine outside – object-object externality in which the body of the perceiver is side-by-side with the material of the perceived item – if we are not going to lose the difference between self and that which is other than it. Even so object-object externality is not in itself sufficient to create the contrast between self and other, given that no (material) thing is of itself outside (nor, of course, inside) of another thing. Placing "outsideness" inside the mind would seem to collapse the difference between the self and the other; in short lose "otherness" altogether.

We may be seduced into overlooking the need for a true outside because much of the time we are intentionally related to abstract, absent or merely possible items in our thoughts and memories, that is to say, to items that are not in any sense outside. However, such higher-level intentional relationships, which make connections within the self, are possible only because of the ground floor of perception; perception, that is, of truly outside objects that we may bodily take hold of, bump into, or steer or squeeze past. What is more, truly experiencing a material object is not just a matter of "entertaining" it in the way that thinking of something general, absent, or possible is. In the case of the latter, there is an inside-outside, in that what is thought of is both inside of the mind ("economic trends" are not self-bounding) and outside of it (there would be no such trends were there not a true outside).

The transcendental standpoint which "considers things *in relation to* our mode of cognition … from the standpoint of an enquiry into the conditions under which objects are possible for us"[36] cannot ultimately ignore or bypass the most fundamental of these conditions – namely that a) these objects exist and that b) we are in their vicinity. The noumenal realm – offered as the ultimate, transcendental outside – is not a particularly promising location for such spatially localized objects if only because it does not seem to be able to house objects in the plural, given that Plurality belongs to the categories of understanding and hence are applicable to the phenomenal realm.[37] If anything, the noumenal realm seems to be like the Eleatic One of Parmenides: undifferentiated, single, and unchanging, although Kant may not have seen it like that, given that the One/Many distinction applies only to the phenomenal realm. Be that as it may, it is difficult to think of multiplicity in the absence of the divisions made possible by space and time or even to think of the possibility of change, given that these seem to take time and are localized in space.[38] If this is the case, then (of course) the noumenal realm offers no underpinning of, and hence justification for, the subject having one experience rather than another.

Kant's claim that "representation in itself does not produce its object insofar as its *existence* is concerned"[39] is self-evident: that which is represented must first exist in order to be a) presented and b) *re*presented. But it is problematic. Noumenal, stand-alone, existence(s) would seem to be "bare existence(s)" or existence(s) not only without properties but also without spatiotemporal location. How would such existence have individuality? We need space and time to distinguish objects. And without individuality how could it have existence? They simply are, without being anything.

Addendum 3
Kant and the pre-human past

One of the most influential critiques of Kant in recent years has come from Quentin Meillassoux and the "speculative realism" that he had a major role in inspiring. In *After Finitude*,[40] Meillassoux argued that the incorporation of space and time into the condition of experiences and his denial that they are features of (noumenal) reality makes it impossible to accommodate the idea that there can be true facts about the temporal order of events before there were human minds. How can we say (for example) that the earth was formed *before* the origin of life, that life emerged *before* conscious life, and conscious life *before* self-conscious human life? There is no "before and after" before there is mind; and mind appeared only after, say, the origin of the earth. We seem to be arguing that there is "before and after" before there were experiences conferring temporal order on events – in short before there was "before and after"![41]

At first sight, Meillassoux's argument seems unanswerable. If we accept the deliverances of the natural sciences, in particular physics, chemistry and biology, we must accept that there was a series of events that had a definite order before human minds occurred. That order is not merely a contingent fact but has an element of necessity built into it: life must have preceded conscious life; the Big Bang that created something out of nothing, must have preceded the emergence of minds out of a mindless universe.

A response to this is that Kant is not pretending to describe the nature of reality in itself: that would be the aim of *transcendent* metaphysics. No; his aim is to develop a *transcendental* metaphysics which is a metaphysics of experience determining the *a priori* framework of the conditions of empirical knowledge.[42] So when Russell pointed out (against Kant) that:

> I accept without qualification the view that results from astronomy and geology, from which it would appear that there is no evidence of anything mental (e.g. transcendental categories) except in a tiny fragment of space-time, and that the great processes of nebular and stellar evolution proceed according to laws in which the mind plays no part.[43]

Kant might argue that he (and Meillassoux) were "conflating the empirical and the transcendental, collapsing the latter into the former".[44]

This defence does not, however, seem to work because we cannot shake off the idea that the mind emerged at a particular time in the history of the world, while Kant makes "particular times" and "histories" contingent on mind already being in place. The seemingly stronger argument that the temporal ordering of events occurring prior to the emergence of mind is retrospective unfortunately does not seem to work either. While it is true that "being before the event of the emergence of conscious minds" is not a constitutive property of the event of "the emergence of living beings", the ordering in which they occur must be true before their truth is established. Mind is required for this truth to supervene on their being; what makes it true must be settled before mind emerges.

Behind this is a larger issue: that of (to use a phrase of Quine's) "reciprocal containment".[45] The history of conscious beings is located in physical time (they are latecomers) and physical time is in fact located in conscious beings; that time contains mind and mind contains time. There seems, however, to be a difference between the time that mind shapes to house and order its experiences and the time that is found in the physical world, according to which the natural world unfolds. There is clearly an important (and difficult) job to be done specifying that difference. In doing so, it will be necessary to take account of analogous examples of reciprocal containment – as when, for example, I see myself located in the visual field that I uphold, or make statements about the universe of which I am a small part. We are talking about a capacity to be outside of ourselves and to locate ourselves in the outside – hugely amplified by knowledge – which we uphold. We are close to Husserl's question: "What is the status of the paradox of humanity ... as world-constituting subjectivity and yet incorporated in the world itself?".[46]

CHAPTER 4

Deflating the mystery 2:
Logos as bio-*logos*

So much, then, for the notion – in its most powerfully worked out form of Kantian philosophy – that the power of mind to make (at least partial) sense of the world is explicable because the world is in some, admittedly difficult to grasp sense, inside the mind. What of the opposite view, currently more fashionable, at least in anglophone philosophy, that the world is intelligible and the mind makes accurate and truthful sense of the world because it is shaped, even created, by the world of which it is making sense? Instead of the "outside world" being inside the mind, the mind itself is outside in sense of being part of nature.

It is difficult to grasp this directly as a metaphysical thesis. The troubling ambiguity of the relationship between "mind-in-general" and "individual minds" which we identified in Kant's transcendental idealism remains unresolved in the naturalization of the mind and its knowledge. "Mind-in-general" in "the world as a whole" sounds dangerously like panpsychism; and if we are talking about individual minds, they seem to be located in an outside that they have not themselves constructed. The problem of how their sense-making capacity exceeds their, presumably organic, basis, returns. Even so, it is instructive to examine the form the naturalizing thesis most commonly takes in contemporary philosophy: evolutionary epistemology. Evolutionary epistemology is anchored in the individual experience and needs of the living organism.

The central claim is that even the kind of high-level sense-making that we are concerned with boils down to a form of awareness that shapes and guides behaviour necessary for survival. What astonished Einstein, so the claim goes,

is less astonishing because it is ultimately an expression of a necessary biological function of the organism. The world *must* make sense to sentient creatures
like ourselves otherwise we would not survive. Getting things right is a matter
of life and death; and creatures that did not get things right simply would not
exist. If we did not make moment-to-moment sense of what was going on
around us, there would be no "us". Inhabiting an entirely unintelligible world
in which nothing could be understood, anticipated, or acted upon with reliable
consequences, would be incompatible with life.

There are many closely connected reasons why there is no "of course" here.[1]
As we noted in the Overture, not all organisms – and more importantly not all
successful ones – are even conscious, never mind capable of making the kind
of sense that we are concerned with in our present inquiry. It is not necessary
for the world to be "got right" by an organism serious about survival because
it is not necessary to be "got" at all.

Noting this brings us up against something more basic – the supposed
function and evolutionary value of consciousness. It is always assumed that
being conscious gives an organism "an edge over the competition". It is not,
however, clear that (for example) seeing light confers an advantage over mere
possession of a chemical photosensitivity that is wired into appropriate behavioural outputs. Heliotropic organisms can maximize their intake of sunlight
without being aware of light, its distribution, its source, or its fundamental
nature. It might be argued that experiencing and valuing sunlight may make
sun-seeking organisms more successful in their quest but this does not consider the hazards of the quest which may offset the benefits. In short, there
is no need to be aware of light in order to respond to it in a way that has biological utility. It is not evident that natural selection would favour actions that
were driven by true beliefs as opposed to automatic responses.

Self-replicating organisms that depend on making sense of the world to
ensure, or maximize, replication, are very recent entrants into the story of
life. Until comparatively late in the story of evolution, it has been enough for
the replicator simply to incorporate an insentient collection of mechanisms
that will give it a reasonable probability of delivering more of itself. Moreover,
given that replicators have themselves come into being as an expression of the
laws of nature and given also that those laws are unbreakable and, therefore
unlike conscious decisions, entirely reliable, becoming conscious would seem
to be a foolish move – or not self-evidently a wise one by an organism serious
about maximizing replication.[2] The last we would expect of insentient living
matter would be to become conscious as a means of increasing its probability
of survival and replication. Besides, it seems entirely unclear how the blood

bath between competing (material) organisms could give rise to something as different from matter as sentience, even less objective knowledge of the properties of matter; something that can clamp inverted commas round "matter".

Since this argument seems fairly straightforward, it is worth pausing to consider why the idea could arise that consciousness at *any* level between dim sentience and higher-level knowledge (never mind at the level of explicit sense-making) is "explained" by evolutionary pressures; that a smidgeon of sentience would confer a survival advantage and a more elaborate mindfulness would confer a greater advantage; that the brighter the better.

The idea seems compelling if we start in the wrong place: at the end (or the end so far) not the beginning of the evolutionary process; at where we are now – with animals that are smart because they are conscious and are engaged in a competition where the prize goes to the smartest; a world of know-how and know-that. The right place to start is the natural world before there was consciousness: at an imagined fork in the unfolding of the biosphere whose two branches are marked "sentient" and "insentient". Starting this far back will prevent a retrospective application of the fact that if you are a conscious organism, you may indeed have the advantage over one that is unconscious. However, in many cases it is scarcely an advantage. In the battle of higher organisms against parasites, for example, consciousness has until the last few thousand years only a minimal part to play; and knowledge of what parasites are, and how they can be defeated, even less.

While certain modalities of consciousness may seem to give an extraordinary advantage in the most potent driver to evolution, namely competition from one's own species, it is again not true at the beginning of the long journey to animals with present modes of consciousness. For example, vision enables one to foresee what is happening and, what is more, to take in an entire field at a time. But this is a late development, useful only for recently evolved creatures. Most organisms are blind (and deaf, numb as well as dumb, etc.) and the overwhelming majority of the most flourishing ones are insentient.[3]

Of course, if you are already a conscious organism relying on making sense of the world in order to function in such a way as to increase the probability of survival it is clearly a good idea to remain conscious. A conscious organism – guided by awareness – rendered unconscious will be helpless and unlikely to last very long. This does not alter the fact that all but a few successful organisms do without consciousness and rely on automatic responses to enable them to flourish and ensure their replication.

Extraordinary things can be achieved in the absence of consciousness. The growth of most organisms – which are unimaginably elaborate even at the cellular level – is a good example. And the prenatal development of all organisms is another striking case. The intra-uterine growth of the human brain (said by their proud owners to be the most complex object in the world) occurs without conscious intervention and intention. How even conscious organisms continue from day to day is also overwhelmingly unconscious. The complex homeostatic mechanisms that control a thousand parameters in my body – blood pressure, ionic concentration in the blood, temperature – do not involve conscious judgements or deliberate action on my part. I would be doomed if they did. And the entire evolutionary process likewise took place of its own accord, without anyone being in charge. This is the sense in which it is true that (as Samuel Butler famously complained) Darwin "banished mind from the universe".[4] Mechanisms don't have to get things right because they cannot (even) get them wrong: they don't have to "get" them at all. Anticipating the preoccupations of a later chapter, we note that there is no need for something called "truth" which is hard-won stuff at the best of time.

Evolutionary theory, therefore, does not help to explain even sentience, even less the unfolding of the Great Chain of Being from insentient Gunk to Oxbridge graduates, a journey from an Original Darkness of Basic Stuff to the mind-lit world of the everyday life of human beings. Even if an organism that had a smidgeon of sentience of stimulus X had the advantage over one that simply unconsciously reacted appropriately to X, this would not account for the emergence of sentience in the first place or its elaboration into the kind of awareness evident in human beings that entertains general laws. Differential survival and reproductive rates can only select between a menu of variations that already exist. As Thomas Nagel has put it:

> [Evolution] may explain why creatures with vision or reason will survive, but it does not explain how vision or reasoning are possible. [...] The possibility of minds forming progressively more objective conceptions of reality is not something the theory of natural selection can attempt to explain, since it doesn't explain possibilities at all, but only selection among them.[5]

In short, natural selection can work only with what is already available.

The direct and indirect, or mediated, intentionality that lies at the heart of sense-making consciousness does not seem to be the kind of thing that unconscious organisms can manage to requisition as a weapon in the struggle for survival, given that those weapons have to be forged by unconscious processes out of existing materials.

The attempt to deflate the mystery of our ability to make sense of the world by seeing this as being explained by the capacity to survive in nature thus cuts no ice. The higher-level sense-making we are concerned about has – at the very least until recently – nothing to do with survival. The cognitive gaze of Newton or Einstein would hardly seem to be an obvious elaboration of the consciousness necessary to steer us safely through the leafy jungle of nature (or even the concrete jungle of the cities). Only very recently has it been true that the geek shall inherit the earth. For most of its history, scientific inquiry has been driven by a curiosity that from the biological point of view is unacceptably idle. Knowing that the earth is flat or round, or that the earth goes round the sun rather than vice versa, have hardly given individual humans an edge over the competition from fellow humans or afforded added protection from predators.

These criticisms have, of course, been anticipated by those for whom evolution is the key to explaining how we understand the world to the degree that we do and how we are able progressively to advance our understanding. The most common ploy is a) to take sentience as a free given that somehow emerged in an insentient universe; and b) to assert that there is a continuity between sentience, or at least the sense experience of our animal selves, and more advanced cognition, including the procedures of science. The cognitive capacities that give us an edge in escaping from predators, we are assured, are at bottom the same as those that are mobilized when humanity progresses from hunting and gathering to farming and which, modified by the experience of farming, subsequently become of use for flourishing in cities, and that, further modified, they enable us to engage in the kinds of inquiries that result in the great body of knowledge whose most developed form is natural science. Thus, the capacity to discover that $E = mc^2$ (in the case of Einstein) or to understand what it means or to apply it (in the case of a few more of us) is a natural extension of traits that were adaptive, of value to the human organism, in the unmodified wild. The curiosity of the physicist is simply an extension of the curiosity of the squirrel.

Thus the article of faith of those for whom Darwinism provides the only kind of explanation of what we are and how we came to be what we are. It will already be obvious that what is offered is a mere description of successive phases of our collective consciousness and not an explanation. It does not even offer much of an account of how the basic capacity to avoid predators progressed in the way it did, so that it no longer depended on the ability to react nimbly and fast. The emphasis in prudent human life is on not having to react at all, in virtue of looking ahead in a way that does not involve literal looking. It requires to be demonstrated, and cannot be assumed, that the cooperative activity of building a city wall paid for out of taxes raised on an equitable basis is simply an extension of the strategies of running away or hiding from predators or burrowing behaviour.

The cognitive discontinuities become even more striking when we compare the modes of awareness of other species – so far as they can be inferred from patterns of individual and collective behaviour – with the most common-place aspects of human cognitive activity; for example, the deliberate acqui-sition of (factual) knowledge, tested and then stored in propositional form, having a general scope, which may or may not prove to be of use. I am talking particularly of know-that rather than know-how (although in our cognitively advanced state know-how will draw on many layers of factual know-that).

It is not necessary to ascend to Einsteinian levels of sense-making to find items that are resistant to evolutionary explanation. There is much that we know, and actively acquire through memorization, which is of no practical use or whose practical use is dependent on circumstances that are not amenable to reduction by biological re-description. My knowledge that Adelaide is a city in Australia, which I probably acquired before I was ten years old, was not caught up in any action until I was invited to be a visiting professor there decades later. The knowledge was disconnected from any biological purpose.[6] The fact that Adelaide is in Australia is not something that can be understood in organic terms. It belongs at least in part to the collective, the community of minds; indeed, to the Space of Reasons, which we shall discuss in Chapter 6.

Some evolutionary epistemologists acknowledge this and have invoked the notion of an "extended phenotype", incorporating amongst other things, bodies of knowledge, institutions, and so on, and of elements of the collec-tive mind that are envisaged as circulating through the culture at large. The analogy is with the organism whose functions and organs are shaped by genes selected for by their success in enhancing viablity.[7] This – the appeal to so-called "meme" – is manifestly an ad hoc remedy designed to close the embarrassing gap between the programmed responsiveness of the animal organism and the knowledge-based decisions to act or not to act taken by the human person. It fails even at the level of analogy, given that its key concept – that of a meme – seems to correspond neither to the elements of the genotype nor the phenotype. In short, it does not work even in terms of the echoes of the biology that is invoked.[8]

While it is evident that evolutionary epistemology, and the endeavour to understand the origin and increasing power of human cognition in entirely biological terms, looks unlikely to succeed, it warrants careful examination not only because it is popular among philosophers but also because it is a manifestation of a wider intellectual trend. The endeavour has many different strands but they include:

1. *Behaviourism.* Human beings are organisms that have sensory inputs or stimuli and behavioural outputs or responses. There is nothing significant, or significantly different, in between. For behaviourists, even something as abstract as understanding the meaning of a word or a sentence amounts simply to an increased propensity to exhibit a particular type of behaviour. As many philosophers have pointed out, the vast majority of mental contents – the knowledge, thoughts and memories I have and even what I see "out there" – do not prescribe specific behaviour. Indeed, it would be difficult to know what would count as an appropriate response to many types of mental contents such as thoughts or memories, were they defined by their capacity to prompt particular kinds of actions. To put it another way, there would seem to be little congruence between the classification of the contents of thoughts or memories and the classification of types of behaviour supposed to be made more probable by them. Behaviourism runs into trouble even with quite basic mental contents. What sort of behaviour would correspond to the entirety of a visual field cluttered with clouds, trees, pavements, shop fronts, facial expressions, and so on? The argument that we are obliged to respond only to *salient* contents has some traction but the fact remains that we are nonetheless fully conscious of many things that are utterly irrelevant to behaviour. They cannot be assimilated into the flow of inputs translated into outputs.

2. *Functionalism.* This is superficially a more sophisticated form of behaviourism. The contents of the mind are not defined by any internal constitution. Rather they are individuated by the *function* they discharge in the living system of which they are a part: they are what they do. Any intrinsic qualities, distinctively mental, are squeezed out in favour of their supposed external relations. At its crudest, functionalism conceives of mental contents as entirely cashable in terms of their (typically biologically relevant) causal connections: the relations between inputs through sensory pathways and outputs realized in overt behaviour, alterations in the body, or increased probabilities of either of these. The mind is a mere way station in an unbroken causal flow through the organism or person and its contents are not fundamentally different from (say) the events inside an unconscious artefact such as a computer or a robot.

The contrary idea that the very being of, for example, perceptions – never mind thoughts and memories – lies in their being experienced, not in any causal relations or indeed in any putative material basis, is rejected, often as a kind of hangover from Cartesian dualism. The undeniability of the existence of contents of consciousness distinct from the flow of (biological) inputs and (behavioural) outputs should seem decisive. A long cul de sac was opened up by Daniel Dennett. He has argued since the 1960s that, while human behaviour is best understood at the level of "the intentional stance" which ascribes feelings, thoughts and beliefs to others, this should not commit us to accepting the reality of these "folk" psychological entities.[9] Consciousness is still to be defined in terms of behavioural capacities and not in terms of intrinsic phenomenal contents. Dennett's views can be opposed by anyone who happens to be conscious. Those who are not conscious will not be in a position to contradict the phenomenal stance – nor to maintain the intentional stance, as Dennett does. The idea that intentionality is something we ascribe to others makes the very act of ascription of intentionality – in beliefs that we have and express about others – impossible. Dennett, it appears, would have us believe that there are no such things as beliefs because that is what he believes.

More seriously, functionalism falls foul of the objections already lodged against the traditional behaviourism that dissolves mind into the lawlike tendency of organisms to behave in certain ways given specific environmental stimulations. What is often overlooked is that this form of behaviourism, like any other, helps itself to the difference between "input" and "output", between points of "arrival at" and "departure from", that would not seem to be available if functionalism (that wires, indeed dissolves, the individual mind into the world) took itself seriously. Without mind as a point of arrival and departure, the distinction between input and output would require an external view point (a conscious point of view) to supply it. This betrays how functionalism outsources the mentality of the mind to another mind which is in turn outsourced to a third mind and so on – just as Dennett's reduction of the seemingly intentional contents of consciousness to the products of "an intentional stance" simply move those contents on to the individual adopting the intentional stance. Moreover, if mind is reduced to functional connections that boil down to causal relations, causation must operate differently on the input and on the output side. In the case of perception, the effect (for example, neural activity) has, as it were, to reach backwards to the cause, so that the latter can become the intentional object of the former. In the case of action, the direction of mental function is forward from a putative cause (an event or events in the agent) to a putative effect (movement). To say this is merely to highlight how there is nothing in the causal net that would create the basis of arrival versus departure, making a functionalist mind a centre of a world.

These problems are entirely predictable. They are the consequence of embedding the "inner" in the "outer" or of externalizing mind into the world, or collapsing the gap or distinction between mind and world. This has attracted less attention than the fact that, by emptying the mind of intrinsic contents, functionalism also mislays what is distinctive about sensations, perceptions, and propositional attitudes such as beliefs – namely the ineliminable "what it is like to be having them" that could be altered without a corresponding alteration in the causal relations between inputs and outputs. It also makes it possible logically to conceive of a device that looks and acts like Daniel Dennett which is simply a mindless robot and yet would meet all criteria for being the ingenious philosopher. What is more (and this is connected with the wider point), it would, if valid, justify the doubts regarding the (biological) utility of consciousness. If minds boil down to mechanisms, if they are merely conduits for energy passing through bits of matter called organisms, they would seem to be pointless.

3. *Teleosemantics.* The aim of teleosemantics is succinctly summarized by Macdonald and Papineau: "to offer a naturalistic account of mental representation ... to show how the representational powers of mental states fit into the world revealed by the natural sciences ...[I]t explains the truth conditions of belief-like states ... in terms of the biological functions of these states.[10] This approach to the naturalization of the mind shares the endeavour, seen in traditional behaviourism and functionalism, to collapse the distance between mind and (material) world by absorbing the former into the latter. They "wire" the subject so tightly into the natural world that it becomes an indistinguishable part of it. The human subject is identified with certain functions of an organism that is the locus of immediate or delayed reactions to salient contingencies of the material environment. A consequence of this is a reduction of human actions to direct or indirect reactions to stimuli, to responses whose form is ultimately genetically dictated. Mind is replaced with mechanisms whose purpose or *telos* is translated into biological functions.

The endeavour to deny that mind is something distinct from the natural world is never entirely successful. Excluded from places where it should be – in human persons – the mind surfaces in places where it has no place being. The personification of the brain (which "guesses", "believes", "hopes", "calculates", "judges", etc.) is the commonest example. But "the return of the repressed" is observed in even less appropriate places, most strikingly in the case of genes, long judged to be (admittedly metaphorically) "selfish".[11]

Naturalized epistemology overlooks the fundamental character of the conscious subject as someone who *faces* the world and is explicitly surrounded by his or her surroundings. An obvious casualty of teleosemantics is explicit knowledge and the "thatter" – our sense *that* such and such is the case – which we shall focus on in Chapter 6. Another casualty is the source of the (often long) delay in sense-making that distinguishes trying to "suss out" something in the immediate environment from trying to make sense of a phenomenon such as the passage of the sun across the sky. Ptolemy's epicycles and Copernicus' heliocentric theory took a long time to be arrived at and were based on observations accumulated over many hundreds of years. The 600-year journey from the theory of planetary motion via the laws of mechanics, to the general theory of relativity, and thence to GPS devices that have enabled us to move from place to place more confidently, is far too long to serve any biological purpose. The remote, transgenerational future cuts no evolutionary ice. Sense-making in nature is usually a matter of seconds rather than centuries.

The counter-argument that the kind of epistemic foraging evident in natural science is in fact an expression of a curiosity that also has a more direct biological utility in the natural world where survival is more directly at stake seems tendentious. The patient collection of data about something – the relative motion of earth and sun – that has little immediate or medium-term application, hardly seems even remotely connected with the cognitive activity engaged in by the most "inquisitive" of animals. And, given that "by their fruits we shall know them", this probably explains the rate of progress of animal technology. Five million years ago, the height of technological achievement of a chimp was to crack a nut with a stone. Five million years later, the height of technological achievement is – to crack a nut with a stone.

We shall return to the question of utility presently but before doing so, it is appropriate to consider another casualty of collapsing mind into the regularities of instinctive or conditional behavioural responses to material events qualifying as stimuli. Truth, and the possibility of falsehood – ubiquitous in the propositional awareness that comprises so much of our mental life – do not seem to have a place in a world of stimulus and response, however complexly mediated. Admittedly, evolutionary epistemology and the positions we have just listed do not entirely dispense with some residual notion of truth. They are closely associated with extreme pragmatist accounts of truth, which squeeze out the "thatness" or "is the caseness" of truth in favour of "what works". A glance at pragmatism is warranted.[12]

Assertion (or belief) A is pragmatically true if it promotes behaviour that enables an organism O to flourish or at least to achieve its goal(s). It is false if it prompts O to behave in a way that is to its biological disadvantage. Truths, in short, are beliefs that are adaptive and falsehoods beliefs that are maladaptive. They are, ultimately, a matter of the life and death of the organism and of the evolutionary success or failure of the species defined as the type-vehicle of a genetic replicator. In the case of the most spectacular body of truth – natural science – the referent of "what works" is a vast landscape of techniques, and technologies, of material infrastructure and cultural superstructure that have arisen from it and which may assist the primary goal of living long and health-ily – although this may be suborned to the secondary goals (sometimes at odds with the primary goal) of living pleasurably and richly.

The obvious rejoinder to pragmatic interpretations of truth is to turn the aphorism on its head and say that the truth is what works because what works is what is true. If I want to get to Adelaide I have a much greater chance of getting there if my belief that it is in Australia is true. The belief that it is in the Czech Republic won't work because it is untrue. This places *correspondence* between a thought, belief, or assertion and that which is thought, believed, or asserted at the heart of truth. There is no place available for such (explicit) correspondence in a mind reduced to efficient wiring between organism and environment enabling the fine-tuning of behavioural responses to external stimuli. Correspondence is a development whose ground floor is the con-sciousness of a being that *faces a world* rather than wired into a bit of nature. There is equally little place for the *coherence* between truths large and small that is a marker of our sense of what is, or what is likely to be, the case, at both the everyday and scientific level. The coherence between truth A and truth B at the same level or between a particular truth and a higher-level truth (as when an event instantiates a law) assists us to correspondent truths and may be a check on the latter. We shall return to the connection between the idea of truth and the nature of the conscious subject *facing* the world in Chapter 6.

The most telling objection to the extreme pragmatism of teleosemantics and other behaviourist reductions of the truth is that there are many truths (and falsehoods) that are quite unconnected with any behavioural output or anything that touches remotely on survival. Our minds are cluttered with vast numbers of facts that are of no practical use at any particular time and, in some cases, for most of the time. Uselessness does not make a proposition any less likely to be true; and knowledge may guide, even prompt, action but it is not obliged to do so. Indeed, the very impersonality of knowledge, the fact that it is not personally held as beliefs are, is connected with its truth claims and this impersonality is in turn connected with its frequent lack of influence on the probability of action. The difference between the truth that the earth goes round the sun and the falsehood that the sun goes round the earth is not to be measured by their respective contributions to my likelihood of survival. Ditto the more homely difference between the (for me useless) truth that Adelaide is 855 miles from Sydney and the falsehood that it is 830 miles from Sydney. We often acquire knowledge – both individually and collectively – for its own sake. This is an aspect of our sense of ourselves; of a life that has a narrative that strays into a huge territory that is remote from biological need; of a person who lives a life in accordance with a multiplicity of senses made of it.

One argument available to the fundamentalist biologism of teleosemantics is to argue that the value of my capacity to retain the fact that Adelaide is in Australia is a marker of my intellectual reach and this, and the (general) ability to retain many other facts, will in the way things are at present a) make me of outstanding use to humanity and b) by advancing my path in a competitive world will improve my chances of attracting a genetically superior partner. By this means, my ability to remember that Adelaide is in Australia will have biological utility to the point of serving the aims of the genes needing to shape organisms that will flourish in the world that human beings have created.

This is a truly desperate attempt to deal with the shocking uselessness of much that is acquired during the individual and collective cognitive advance of humanity. Unfortunately, it assumes precisely that which must be explained; namely that humans, unlike other species, live in a world in which facts play a central role. How did a reacting machine come to be dealing in facts that are timeless, albeit that they enter time through token assertions? Functionalism and other forms of behaviourism should eliminate these entities. Pragmatism, the existential contingencies relevant to survival, would seem to leave no place for correspondent truth beyond the implicit (pre-factual) truths of the *umwelt* of the human organism.

Critics of teleosemantics see the issue of unexploited mental content as damaging to this approach to understanding the relationship between mind and world. Ruth Millikan, a leading proponent of teleosemantics, addresses the issue of "Useless Contents" head on and her argument is worth consideration.[13] If, she concedes, we are confined by our perceptual systems and biological needs to a world created by our "peculiarly human constitution and abilities … we should be intrinsically unable to represent a truly objective reality. The enterprise of empirical science is doomed to presenting only a warped and truncated vision of the world."[14] If the content of a mental representation must depend in the end on its having *biological* utility, what are we to make of the useless (but true) facts that clutter our minds? Cognitive orphans disconnected from any biological function would seem to lack criteria for truth and even lack content if the latter is defined by, or emptied into, such functions. Millikan argues that, while our conscious goals may be remote from those that can be ascribed to our genes, there is as it were a functional audit trail connecting higher, more abstract, distinctively human cognitive functions with those that are of direct biological utility: "Even the most highly theoretical of beliefs are not excluded from having direct biological utility ... so long as they participate in chains of reasoning that eventually bear practical fruit".[15] Beliefs unconnected with any conceivable practical goal can, the argument goes, be reconnected with biological functions by being part of a coherent system of beliefs that do have such functions. What is more, coherence among beliefs is central to our being able to re-identify items and this is the key to our being able to acquire expertise in negotiating our way round the world.

It is difficult to see this defence as anything other than a restatement of an article of faith: that in the end everything we do is grounded in biology. The conflation of "practical fruit" with "biological function" helps to close the gap between the theorizing human person or community and the reacting organism, the person that speaks and the jelly that responds. Of course, many actions we perform do have practical use even when they are remote from biological function. For example, designing a body-worn cross that is made of plastic will certainly make this more cheaply available to many who wish to wear a cross – it is a practical solution – but it is remote from anything that would promote the replication of the gene. What is more, the appeal to "chains of reasoning" leaves gene-directed behaviour far behind, unless we think of biological material as somehow engaging in "chains of reasoning" of the abstract kinds that would link one bit of factual knowledge with another. Chains of reasoning, on any reasonable interpretation, require the capacity for abstract thought disconnected from any biological programming. This will become even more obvious when we discuss the difference between the Space of Reason and the material world in Chapter 6.

What is more, it is the *uncoupling* of the pursuit of fundamental truths without immediate regard to biological utility that has made human cognition, notably natural science, so powerful. One example already touched on will suffice. If I go into the desert, it might be a good idea to know where I am in relation to my destination. The most powerful and accurate way of locating myself is by GPS. The extraordinary success of the GPS system is in part the result of satellite technology whose accuracy depends on corrections calculated on the basis of the general theory of relativity and the reduction of the mechanics of gravitation to the solution of a single system of partial differential equations. When Einstein arrived at his field equations, they had no practical use. Indeed, it was necessary to look at the bending of light passing through a gravitational field evident at the time of a total eclipse of the sun even to find an experiencable consequence of them. There was at the time no measurement, even less an experience, on earth that could have discriminated general relativity from Newtonian mechanics. So while the truth was arrived at in 1915–16, its application, its use, came many decades later.[16] Biology does not have, nor could it afford to have, that patience: it would be fatal and there are no posthumous rewards in the natural world.

Indeed, it is the *separation* of the pursuit of truth from practical interests, and even greater separation from biological utility, that is a key to the power of science and is also an important element that distinguishes scientific inquiry from the wishful thinking shaping witchcraft or shamanism. The latter, which wants immediate results, cannot distinguish wishes from horses. The separation underlines what is central not only to truth narrowly construed – the separation marked by "that" in "that such-and-such is the case" – but to the whole process of sense-making, acquiring knowledge, and pursuing truth, as a collective enterprise involving people who for the most part do not know and will never know each other personally, and conducted over centuries. It takes place at, and further widens, a distance within us and in the story of our lives. Most importantly, it expresses preoccupations remote from the organism, its needs and its appetites. The distance between the knowing subject and the known world is something unknown to biology. But without that distance there is neither truth nor falsehood – as we shall discuss further in Chapter 6.

The endeavour to eliminate that distance is evident in the use made by some proponents of representational theories of the mind where a) the representation is assimilated to biological function; and b) the latter is reduced to causal interaction between organism and not-organism. In so-called "indicator" or "causal" semantics, the *content* of a belief (or what is called a "belief-like state") "is that condition that typically causes it and which the state therefore indicates".[17] Essentially this amounts to the claim that, if B is caused by A, then it will point to A; that B will *represent* A in virtue of being an effect of it. Because it is profoundly untrue, this kind of view is worth examining further.

Firstly, it misrepresents something central to propositional attitudes such as beliefs, knowledge, thoughts, etc. It confuses the forward-pointing causal relationship – A at t_1 causes B at t_2– with a backward-pointing intentional one – B at t_2 is *of* A at t_1. The stimulus that it is thought to cause the experience is confused with the experience that is "about" the stimulus. Secondly, while merging mind with the material world is the result desired by advocates of teleosemantics, it would have undesirable, indeed absurd, consequences:

every time-slice of the universe would be a representation of the preceding time-slice that caused it and the nexus of causes would be a nexus of indications. The boundless, dense, causal network of unfolding nature would be a forest of competing indications. There is a further consequence: if the causal relationship between A and B were sufficient for B to be a representation of (indeed *a belief that*) A, it would not be possible to get things wrong and for there to be misrepresentation. But the possibility of misrepresentation must be a condition of something counting as a representation.

This last is a common objection to the theory. But there is a more profound objection, which connects with a point made at the beginning of the chapter: representation would seem to be redundant if it were merely input wired to output. Why bother with *re*presentation, or, come to that, making present at all. What's the point of consciousness or, indeed, truth and falsehood? The claim that: "the meaning (representational function) of a perceptual experience is given by the co-ordinated schema that emerges in the coevolution of the detector and effector systems"[18] prompts one to wonder why the evolutionary process didn't cut out meaning and perception; in short, dispense with the (conscious) middle man. Coordination would work perfectly without consciousness, as it does throughout most of the (living and non-living) natural world, where crystals, trees, and kidneys come into being and be themselves. The defence that consciousness permits flexibility of response would entirely undermine the central claim of teleosemantics, that there is a biologically essential, Pre-established (Material) Harmony between inputs and outputs.

This, however, seems a minor objection compared with the metaphysical absurdity already alluded to of having causation as the basis of representation. Every effect would be a representation of its cause; consequently, every time-slice of material world would be an image of the preceding time-slice. Such absurdity is an entirely predictable consequence of what will happen when knowledge and belief and other propositional attitudes are assimilated to the wiring of a (physical) organism to its (physical) surroundings; when the putative cause of a belief (or indeed a perception) doubles up as its content; when knowledge is swallowed up in biological function.

There is an instability in teleosemantic approaches to contents of consciousness. While there is a backward-looking identification of representation with that which causes it, content seems to look forward to a goal. Macdonald and Papineau suggest that teleosemantics "explains the content of a belief-like state, not in terms of its typical causes, but in terms of how it is biologically *designed* to function".[19] This has the apparent advantage of having propositional attitudes pointing forwards to their *telos* or purpose rather than backward to their causes. Moreover, it does seem to create a space for the difference between truth and falsehood: a true belief is one that prompts an appropriate response and a false belief one that prompts an inappropriate one. If I retreat from a real snake, the content of my belief (that the item is a snake) is true. If I retreat from a toy snake, my action lacks biological utility and the content of my belief is wrong. But many other problems remain.

The most fundamental is that it reduces mental contents to the kind of behaviour they prompt. The difficulties associated with this are common to all forms of behaviourism, and we have already touched on them. First, the way in which beliefs and other propositional attitudes (including items of knowledge) are differentiated hardly correspond to general patterns of behaviour that have distinct biological utilities. There are, as we have discussed, no biologically defined classes of behaviour corresponding to the vast hoard of knowledge we have and may or may not use. Secondly, the content, cashed out as behaviour loses its status as a piece of representational content. The latter is an inevitable result of a ruthless pragmatic reduction of the nature of truth that, dispensing with correspondence and coherence, leaves no space for truth itself as a connection between two distinct items. What we have is a portrait of the mind in which representation, and goals, are conflated in the overall idea of causal connections passing through the organism.

Teleosemantics and other attempts to translate the mind into biological functions and its contents into dispositioned behaviour and hence to reinsert it into the natural world, require an almost wilful overlooking of the cognitive nature of the knowing, inquiring, sense-making human creature. Human hospitality to "useless contents" is no minor quirk, but a profound manifestation of the kinds of minds that humans have; minds that have made possible extraordinary cognitive advances, which have often – though not reliably and frequently after a long interval – delivered biological utility. Such contents are, of course, abhorred by the aficionados of biologism because they hint at a mind floating free of nature.

Crude pragmatism is highly popular with thinkers who want to question the possibility of objective truth and, with this, the dignity of man, the Knowing Animal, and to tell us that humans are just organisms. In his wildly successful *Straw Dogs: Thoughts on Humans and Other Animals*, philosopher John Gray challenges the vanity of a humanism that espoused the delusion that "we can free ourselves from the limits that frame the lives of other animals".[20] Clearly, the limits he is talking about are not those defined by technology because we know of no other animal that, for example, communicates with its conspecifics over thousands of miles using mobile phones, travels the world on economy class flights or performs delicate surgical operations using an extraordinary range of tools and techniques. Rather, he is talking about cognitive (and incidentally ethical) limits. Darwin's theory, Gray believes, has cured us of the idea that our knowledge is objective: "[T]he human mind serves evolutionary success, not truth. To think otherwise is to resurrect the pre-Darwinian error that humans are different from all other animals."[21]

By this reckoning, it is a pre-Darwinian error to think that the Darwinist conclusion about truth – the product of the human mind – is itself anything more than a device to serve "evolutionary success" (whatever that may mean). The theory of evolution itself is therefore not true in the elevated, objective sense it is generally accepted to be. Nobody who understands the implications of Darwin's theory and accepts its objective truth, it appears, should accept that it is objectively true.[22] Gray's appeal to the objective truth of Darwinism to demonstrate that it is vanity to think we have access to objective truth makes him a worthy successor to the famous Cretan liar who claimed that all Cretans were liars.

The path from *Logos* to bio-*Logos* and the naturalizing of mind is opened up by a mis-reading of the significance of the argument that *of course* the world makes sense to sentient creatures like ourselves otherwise we would not survive. As noted at the outset of the chapter, there is no "of course". That our survival *requires* an intelligible world simply moves the mystery on to another place. Most organisms flourish without being conscious and the members of only one species locate themselves in a world of which they make general, even if incomplete, sense. The laws of nature – and the very idea that nature is law-governed – appear to be beyond the cognitive reach of all but *H. sapiens*.[23] What's more, many humans flourished before Newton announced his discoveries, Einstein formulated the general theory of relativity, and before the scientific revolution that made these discoveries possible. Their benefits in terms of increased life expectancy have been slow in coming. And many cultural-cognitive advances – the agricultural revolution, urbanization, and the first phases of the industrial revolution – were associated with *increased* morbidity and mortality. The fact that they may ultimately have resulted in increased life expectancy is irrelevant: evolutionary theory does not allow for deferred benefits, or any such mode of group selection in which several generations are sacrificed for their remote descendants. Biology does not deal in vague, promissory notes.

The naturalization of sense-making becomes an even more dubious exercise when it is attached to a wider materialism according to which the world contains only physical events, so that the mind is composed of nerve impulses.

We shall set aside for the present the impossibility of accommodating the intentionality or "aboutness" of sense-experience within neural activity, and a fortiori the sense-making that we are concerned with. Instead we shall examine an especially ambitious attempt to assimilate mind, and its knowledge, to the physical reality uncovered by the natural sciences – namely that of Quine who summarized a lifetime's philosophizing in his short (and final) book *From Stimulus to Science*.[24] It attempts a scientific, empirically testable, account of how we can advance from sense experience to scientific knowledge of the world.[25] He aims, in short, to anchor his account of this journey to science in science itself, using the fruits of science in investigating its roots. This is central to his naturalism – according to which epistemology should be or aim to be a branch of the psychology of a primate *H. sapiens* – that (in a passage already quoted) he characterizes as the:

> rational reconstruction of the individual's and/or the race's acquisition of a responsible theory of the external world. It would address the question how we, physical denizens of the physical world, can have projected our scientific theory of that whole world from our meagre contacts with it: from the mere impacts of rays and particles on our surfaces and a few odds and ends such as the strain of walking uphill.[26]

In tracing the journey from the sense experience humans share at its most basic level with animals to the formulation of scientific theories that endeavour to represent and explain the world imagined or at least conceived as a whole, Quine identifies several early stages: the global stimulus, observation sentences, and reification. On close inspection, none of these stages looks like manifestations of an organism whose capacity to be aware of the world is identical with brain events or irritation of nerve endings – and this remains true even if we overlook the issue of the origin of intelligibility and its place in the natural world. His account of the cognitive ascent of man is, however, worth examining if only for its boldness and (for the most part) clarity.

For Quine, as for John Locke, *nihil in mente quod non prius in sensu* – nothing in the mind that is not first in the senses. Hence the platform from which the journey to science begins is "the global stimulus", the subject's total sensory experience at a moment. Its "physical analogue" is: "the class of all sensory receptors that were triggered at that moment; or, better, the temporally ordered class of receptors triggered during that specious present".[27] This notion sounds like an unexceptionable start, with the surroundings of the organism being transformed into the proto-world of a subject. Unfortunately, this is not so. We are offered nothing to account for that in virtue of which the distinct and multiple deliverances to, and of, the various senses are totalled to the contents of a globe. As Kant was aware, something must secure the uniting of certain visual experiences with other visual experiences (to create a visual field) and visual experiences with experiences from the other senses – distance senses such as hearing, proximate senses such as smell and taste, and the experience of the body itself. Something in addition has to integrate this registration of physical impingements on the body with memories, thoughts, and other elements of consciousness that make sense of what is present. As if that is not difficult enough, something has also to prevent this union of diverse impingements becoming mere "merging": the distinct elements have to converge while at the same time retaining their separation in space and time and their distinct qualitative identity. The rain of impingements has somehow to be united in the conscious moment of a subject while at the same time retaining its multiplicity.

Whatever one might think of Kant's response to this problem and his appeal to "the forms of sensible intuition" (see Chapter 3), he at least noticed it. Quine seems to have overlooked the fact that a proto-world could not be built up out of a kaleidoscope of tingles and flashes and bangs, without something to tether them to; at the very least an array of objects set out in space and time. What is more, if the sense experiences are to mark the beginning of sense-making, they must be recognisable in the light of previous experience. This implies a temporal depth which sensory experience *at a moment* – a physical instant – or even a specious present does not possess. This last point carries more weight when it is recalled what is central to Quine's naturalism: namely, that sense experiences are identical with neural discharges (which he calls "neural intake") or, more broadly, with a present passive physical state of the nervous system, such that each state of the mind corresponds to a state of the brain-in-the-body. Such physical events could not unite while retaining their identity nor have temporal depth.

Quine correctly highlights the early crucial role of joined attention in creating an intersubjective world, en route to objectivity. There is "a public harmony of private standards of perceptual similarity"[28] – guaranteed to be the same in all parties by their being shaped by the shared forces of natural selection – so that the individual can externalize what is a private experience. This, however, takes us further into a mode of shared sense-making than is warranted. Quine claims that the human mode of sense-sharing – "observation sentences" – are analogous to apes' cries and bird calls, being like them "in holophrastic association with ranges of neural intake".[29] Observation sentences are basic, in that their truth does not depend on another assertion. They are taken from direct observation, and can therefore be understood without further knowledge. Examples would be "The man is standing up", "the sky is dark". The dubiousness of the idea of such a sentence making a direct and discrete connection of the realm of nature with that of discourse is something we shall further discuss. For the present we note that Quine seems to retrofit the grammar of referential discourse to the grammarless reactions of beasts – reactions that do not have referents, or not of the kind or in the way that sentences do. An animal's cry is not an assertion of a matter of fact. While Quine does not ascribe the subsequent developments – "observational predication" ("That lion is dangerous") and "observational categoricals" ("When it snows, it's cold") – to non-human animals, his smooth passage from ape calls to human discourse, stitching together a shared world, is effected only by slipping past the fundamental difference between animal squawks and observation sentences. With this free gift, it can seem as if the next steps – predication and general statements – are as good as already taken.

Behind the specific flaws in Quine's *legerdemain* is a broader failure to appreciate how human language belongs to a subject *facing* the world – much of which is either absent or, if present, is so in general form – not an organism neutrally wired into its material surrounds. What is more, sentences do not arise individually; nor are assertions stand-alone in this sense. They belong to a network, just as beliefs belong to a network – something that on other occasions he seemed very much aware of, when he shared Donald Davidson's notion of the holism of belief.[30] We shall return to both these points in Chapter 6.

Hereabouts we encounter a greater challenge to a naturalism that tries to incorporate sentences and the utterances that use them into the material world of causes, effects and stimuli. There is no adequate naturalistic account of the contents of propositions and even less of those elusive parts of nature or the human world that are scissored out to be the contents of propositions. Even if there were sufficient correspondence between the referents of a (spoken or written) sentence – namely, what propositions propose – and a piece or aspect of the material world that would make a sentence true, the latter would not be simply a self-defining slice or fragment of nature. If I say "It was chilly yesterday" it is easy to determine the conditions under which this is true but not, except via language, pick out that which makes it true – even less what makes it true as I say it today. Yesterday's chilliness does not have sharp boundaries and, more to the point, even if it did, it would not be available to be picked out by non-linguistic means

We can see this profound *dis*connection between on the one hand propositional and on the other bump-into-able reality – the kind of items that animals,
too, could take hold of – between the referents of sentences and that which is
experienced through our senses, most clearly when we think of assertions that
turn out to be true but are not (yet) true at the time that they are asserted. I
am referring to so-called future contingents. The content of the proposition
"There will be a sea battle tomorrow" is both more and less than any actual
sea battle that occurs the day after the assertion. It is more, inasmuch as it
postulates a general possibility which a whole class of sea battles could realize. It is less in that (the other aspect of its generality) it lacks all the countless
specific features any actual sea battle must have – ranging from the outcome
to the facial expression of Able Seaman Jones at 10:01am during the battle.[31]

There are, of course, obvious problems with attempting to "naturalize"
statements about abstract objects, future- and past-orientated propositions,
and general, conditional, and normative statements. In short, with pretty well
everything we say, from the homely remark that it is chilly for the time of year
to the claim that the universe began 13.8 billion years ago. We reach knowledge fundamentally different from sense experience – the supposed reference
of Quine's "observation sentences" – long before we reach high-level assertions. This is connected with something essential to the most basic assertions,
such as "The man is standing up": the mode in which their contents are shared.
While I may keep what I know to myself, knowledge is intrinsically public. It
can be known by any number of people. It lacks the fundamental, intrinsic
privacy of experience, including the experiences that form the basis of observation. The reason for this is important: it is connected with the difference
between animal experience and human knowledge, a difference that Quine
elides by talk of "observation sentences". The experiences of animals may be
complex but they are fundamentally different from that which is asserted in
"observation sentences".

The ability to share knowledge is reflected in the fact that it is expressed in
type words; the inability to share an experience, by contrast, is reflected in the
fact that it is composed of tokens rather than types. While I can share the fact
that I have a pain, I cannot share the pain. When I say "I share your pain", this
is only metaphorically true. The pain in my back remains in my back, irrespective of my having communicated it to you by groans, grimaces, or utterances.
To put this another way, the actual pain I feel at t_1 is not available to be experienced by anyone else; the piece of knowledge corresponding to the fact that I
feel a pain in my back does not "occur" at t_1 or at any other time. All that occur
at particular times are events such as grimaces, groans, and verbal complaints.

It is this difference that lies at the heart of the possibility of weaving together a shared body of knowledge and forms the fabric of the community of minds that underpins and maintains the human world. To revert back to our earlier discussion, it forms the "semantics" in "teleosemantics". While we may share a *telos* with animals (such as not dying, or eating enough, or finding a mate), we do not share the semantics.

Quine's third step, reification, seems to be entering the scene rather late. He claims that at the stage of observation sentences (and even at the stage of "observation categoricals" that express general expectations of connections such as "When it snows, it is cold"), there is no reference to bodies or other objects. Observation categoricals simply assert concomitance or close succession of observed phenomena and reflect the (testable) expectation that arises out of this. Surely, one would think, they should come before, rather than after, observation sentences; objects must be presupposed in observation sentences – "The man is standing up" – and their like. Quine at least acknowledges how remote the idea of an object is from the experience of a stimulus and the inadequacy of a phenomenalist approach to building up objects out of "neural uptake".[32] He argues that objects are "posits" and the "leap to reification" is based on a linguistic shift:

> We can almost get [reference to objects] with the observation categorical 'Whenever there is a raven, there is a black raven'. But not quite. The crucial leap to reification of ravens can be achieved by changing 'there' to 'it': 'Whenever there is a raven, *it* is a black raven'[...] 'It' posits common carriers of the two traits, ravenhood and black.[33]

The carriers are bodies – full-blown objects – and the pronominal construction achieves objective reference.

It seems highly unlikely that the transition from the experience of the clustering of phenomena to the sense of an object as the substrate underpinning those phenomena and accounting for their coherence and stability, could be captured by something as specific and far down the cognitive track as the creation of a pronominal hinge – it – to link the features of an object. The verbal cart is being placed before the thing-like horse. Equally topsy-turvy is this characterization of the role of reification: "We [see] reification at work forging the sameness of reference between clauses. That is what it is for. The function of identity is recurrence in discourse".[34] Things, surely, must be the other way round. Sameness of reference *presupposes* sameness of identity, rather than establishes it. A pebble was enduringly itself long before a speaker made repeated reference to it and put it in inverted commas, referring to it as "that pebble".

Reification, is a serious business, not easily, even less reliably, built on the stimulation of nerve endings such as gives rise to sense impressions. At the heart of the notion of an object is of something that exists in itself and has properties distinct from, or at least not exhausted by, our experiences. It is an enduring entity that is available for any number of observers: it is a public body that is enduringly available to be experienced and re-experienced because it continues to exist even when I or indeed anyone else is not sensing it and persists over time.

Quine focuses on persistence over time and imagines the human race – represented by an emblematic cave man – discovering objects when he realizes that the bear he and his friend are chasing is the same bear as the one that killed their friend last year. This primal scene seems entirely fanciful. More damagingly, it overlooks the need for a prior establishment of, at the very least, the objecthood of the reifier and of his or her conspecifics for there to be a community in which (enduring) things become a shared or common currency of reference. A world picture that already includes bears, friends dead and alive, and "last year" surely presupposes that of enduring public, objects, existing independent of those who encounter them. My sense of there being a "last year" in which my friend was killed seems to require the prior existence of that which Quine supposes to be established by communication about it.

We shall return to objects in the next chapter. For the present we note they lie at the heart of the human intuition of the world as "out there" in the sense of being other than our selves; and this is a fundamental, global intuition that is inseparable from the full-blown "aboutness" or intentionality of our conscious experience. Objects are the cornerstone of our public world, and the godfather of all the different kinds of shared spaces that characterize that world. It seems difficult to imagine them being delivered by neural activity that is the mere effect of the impingement of energy on an organism. It seems not unreasonable, therefore, to conclude that Quine's endeavour to collapse the gap between mind and nature creates: a) an insuperable barrier to explaining our everyday ontological commitments, from material bodies upwards; and b) his need to overlook intentionality even in cognitively advanced items such as "observation sentences". Reification which "proved indispensable in connecting loose ends of raw experience to produce the beginnings of a structured system of the world"[35] eludes Quine's explanation. It is certainly indispensable but there is nothing in the rickety structures of his naturalized epistemology to begin to account for it.

Undaunted, Quine presses bravely onwards on the journey from tingles to theories and arrives at science which he characterizes as "a biological device for anticipating experience".[36] The most fundamental aspect of science is the scope and robustness of its general assertions, facilitating such anticipations, although that which is anticipated may be something as esoteric as the conditions under which we can technologically exploit certain mechanisms in natural processes or the outcome of an experiment. Quine's jump from the global stimulus to observation sentences seems to smuggle in the capacity for generalization – predication and categorization – as a faculty not requiring explanation, rather as with Millikan's "chains of reasoning" referred to earlier. Seen clearly, however, the human capacity for generalization is an extraordinary faculty that cannot be taken for granted and if understood correctly cannot be naturalized.

General assertions allocate objects and events to *classes*. True classification involves seeing an entity X as *both* its (token) self *and* as belonging to a type. This duality of cognition is linked with many other capacities or operations. They include:

a) distinguishing two levels of identity of an entity – type or qualitative and individual or numerical identity – such that an object may be both an instance of a class and a particular occupant of a location in space and time;

b) reclassifying an entity under more than one type – seeing that item over there as a chair, a piece of furniture; an obstruction; a fire-hazard on account of its being inflammable; a treasured heirloom; and so on, without apparent end;

c) separating the entity from its meaning or significance on a given occasion – as when we realize that something that is a nuisance is also a chair;

d) on the basis of this, communicating intelligence about the entity.

If it is worth spelling out these rather obvious points, it is because they highlight the fundamental difference between human classification of the contents of the world and what is called "classification" as something carried out by animals. The capacity to classify items is ascribed to animals on the basis of the *failure* to discriminate between items that share key general characteristics. A male robin may respond with aggression to all objects that have a combination of a large red spot on a brown background – a stuffed red breast, for example – as if it were a rival male.[37] This is called "stimulus generalization" and is seen as a primitive or even primordial form of classification. In fact, it is a mistake to see such *failures* of discrimination as evidence of the presence in the creature's mind of a broad class of items called "aggressors". Moreover, the classes identified in the case of so-called animal classification – which seem to aggregate items that elicit the same responses – are not distinct from the objects or events that fall under them. Humans separate the classified members from their class. It is this distance between individuals and the classes to which they are ascribed that permits *re*classification, most evident in full-blown predication that explicitly predicates the class of the entity seen as a subject: "Socrates is a man", "Socrates is a bore", "Socrates is a Platonic myth". Indeed, I can refer separately to classes as I do when I use common nouns such as "table", "cloud", "tree".

A truly classifying animal – and there seems to be only one of these – is a consciously *re*classifying animal that sees items as existing in themselves independently of any class to which they may be allocated. The capacity for reclassification is also evident in the extent to which encounters with items are only loosely connected with patterns of behaviour, in contradistinction to animals where what is called "classification" is defined by elicited behaviour. Our relationship to objects is not defined by a disposition to respond to them in a certain way. Chairs do not automatically elicit sitting behaviour: they may be used to block doors or as weapons (as in so many Westerns); gazed at with pleasure; or put up for sale to realize their value in times of hardship. We use items, yes; but we use them *as* such-and-such and the "as" reveals an uncommitted space between object and behaviour. The loose connection between classification and action – how we see or interpret things – is a central aspect of our agency and of our inhabiting a world that is at least in part a chest of tools or, less formally, of handles and levers. Genuine tool use is a relationship between a subject and its world that is remote from that between an organism and an array of stimuli. Even where tools and other objects are expropriated to biological ends, the relationship between tool and tool-user, object and object-user, is unlike that seen in the quasi-tool use of animals.[38]

It is revealing that Quine actually accepts the independence of classes from the objects that fall under them. Indeed, he goes further – too far, I believe – and assigns them a stand-alone existence. His avowedly physicalist ontology includes "physical objects, plus all the classes of them".[39] We may doubt that classes, which after all are not located in space and time like objects and do not "occur" like events, belong to such an ontology as usually understood. Perhaps we should be grateful for his acknowledgement that classes are not merely the implicit internal accusatives of types of behaviour.

Quine's endeavour to provide an account of how we get from sense experience to scientific knowledge is worth examining a little further because, by virtue of what is missing in it, it inadvertently draws attention to a key aspect of the challenge of understanding our sense-making activity.[40]

As we have seen, Quine believes that the ultimate source of the body of knowledge and theory that is science is the stimulation of our sensory surfaces. Unfortunately, our theories are cast in propositional form – as are the observation sentences that would provide the link between them and the tribunal of experience. "Neural intake" does not have such a form. There is a gap, therefore, between, sense experiences, understood as Quine understands them as "neural intake" and observation sentences that provide a test for everyday and scientific theories. It is a profound gap that should not be glided over for many reasons. Here are a couple. Firstly, we lack explanation of how we get from particular experiences to general statements. Biological mechanisms such as stimulus generalization do not even deliver common nouns, even less the other parts of speech necessary to cobble together a sentence. Secondly (and linked with this) observation sentences are connected in relations of implication and contradiction which are unknown to neural intake (this is the coherence dimension of scientific, indeed of any propositional, truth). If it is true that Socrates is a man, it cannot be true that he is a goat. If it is true that all men are mortal, Socrates being a man cannot be immortal.

Quine attempts to close the gap between aconceptual, non-propositional sensations on the one hand and observation sentences that test scientific theories on the other by mobilizing the notion of the "stimulus meaning" of such sentences. Meaning is defined as the neural activity corresponding to a stimulus that would prompt assent to it. I see a bee, and say "There is a bee". You, who are familiar with the language, think "there is a bee" when I utter this sound. Thus, I communicate to you the fact that there is a "bee". The connection between the observation sentence whose truth would support a theory and neural intake is a causal one.

There are surface and deep reasons why this does not work. The surface reason is that there is no simple mapping between a sentence (never mind one advanced with the aim of testing something as complex as a scientific theory) and a pattern of neural discharges. In short, it is impossible to imagine a congruence or isomorphism between what is happening in the observer's brain when she experiences the sentence as true and what is happening in the brain when that which makes it true is observed. This is evident, even in the case of seemingly basic observations. I am looking out of the window of the café at which I am now writing. There is a busy scene and I observe a couple in deep conversation hurrying past. Nothing plausibly neural would seem to correspond to that which is picked out from the background – from the pavement, from the crowd, from the street – of the couple, the depth of their conversation, and their hurry.

There will be those who stubbornly adhere to the neural theory of any element of consciousness – so let us move to a deeper reason for rejecting the idea of "stimulus meaning". They are connected with the illuminating flaws in the causal theory of knowledge. The idea that the relationship between an observation and assent to an observation sentence predicting the observation could be causal would, if true, collapse the complex, many-layered intentionality connecting scientific observations with, on the one hand, the theories which they test, and, on the other, the experience that makes true the sentence capturing that observation. That is why Quine's aim to reduce epistemology to "an improved understanding of the chains of causation and implication that connect the bombardment of our surfaces, at one extreme, with our scientific output at the other"[41] is to bypass pretty well everything that is distinctive about knowledge.

It also removes the basis for the distinctive power that knowledge, particularly scientific knowledge, confers on us. If knowledge were simply another means by which we were causally wired into nature, it would hardly enable us to operate, as we do, at such a distance from the natural world, so that we can shape nature in accordance with goals that nature does not envisage and in a timeframe that is not evident elsewhere in nature. The extended powers of *Homo scientificus* would be entirely inexplicable. Closer to home, there would seem to be no place for *judgement* – of truth or falsity, of validity or non-validity, of observation sentences, never mind higher-order theories.

What kind of material effect is it that judges its material cause to be true (or false), valid (or invalid)? The effects we are familiar with in the natural world do not hark back to their causes and hardly ascribe truth values to them. And what of the propositions that are so judged? The world does not naturally divide into discrete items corresponding to what is proposed in propositions. Referents are on the far side of a double intentionality – the aboutness of the experience of a heard or read sentence (my hearing what you have just said, or seeing what I am reading), and the aboutness of the token sentence (what the utterance or written sentence meant). The boundaries of those referents, what is more (even when they are singulars such as "the Battle of Hastings"), scarcely correspond to nature, or the physical world, self-carving at the joints. At any rate, the causal theory of knowledge – perhaps the original sin of naturalized epistemology – involves taking the idea of causation to places where it has no right to be.

What is, perhaps, most fundamentally missing from Quine's account of the passage from "stimulus to science" is that it overlooks the profound difference between the passive sentience of the recipient of a stimulus and the active sense-making of *Homo scientificus*. Indeed, this contrast is present at much lower levels in the contrast between (passively received) sense "impressions" and (active, proposing) "propositional awareness". From a basic level upwards, humans are not merely subject to experiences but actively shaping, organizing, interpreting them and generalizing them so that even experiences that are not directly connected may be sorted according to their putative origins. If Kant overstates the activity of the mind in putting together a world, Quine understates it, in his desire to build an account of our world-picturing out of neural events in which the fundamental mental activity of positing intentional objects is somewhat bypassed – even in his employment of the notion of "reification". His term "neural intake" overlooks the fact that what is taken in reaches out; the light that gets into the eye is the basis for the gaze that looks out. To reiterate a point made earlier in relation to the lack of a basis for the input-output reference in functionalist and other forms of behaviourism, "intake" would not, simply as part of a causal chain, even count as *in*take because there would be no basis for the contrast between "in" and "out". It is the "outreach" that locates the organism as a point of reception and the centre of its world.

Quine's attempted rational reconstruction of the journey from stimulus to science, from tingles to theorems, only highlights, therefore, the failure of the larger project of naturalizing knowledge. Ernst Mach's earlier naturalizing project is, if anything, more ambitious. He spoke of his "profound conviction": "[t]hat the foundations of science as a whole, and of physics in particular, await their next greatest elucidations from the side of biology, and especially from the analysis of sensations".[42] In some respects, this may seem less radical than Quine, if only because Mach did not seem to be a consistent hard-line physicalist. Indeed, he wasn't even a hard-line anything-ist. He is often associated with a monism that saw mind and matter as aspects of a single stuff. However, he regarded monism "as provisionally a *goal* after which we [he and his closest intellectual allies] all strive, but ... scarcely anything fixed or sufficient".[43] That goal was in part to be pursued by a Quine-like tracing of the connections between basic sense experiences and scientific theories; between itches and the theory underpinning the pharmacology of treatments for scabies.

The guiding assumption was also the Quinean one that the world we experience is a construct of the nervous system whose (biological) function is to enable us to respond effectively to a changing world. One aspect of this is that we don't perceive things directly but rather the relations between the stimuli that are associated with them. This may sound like a Kantian domination of mind in the shaping of the experienced world but it is not; for the mind, according to Mach (as with Quine), is not the manifestation of a transcendent self but the (physical) activity of a brain shaped by evolutionary processes.

This shaping is evident at a very basic level in a phenomenon associated with Mach's name: the intensity of changing stimuli is exaggerated while the intensity of constant stimuli is underplayed. Change, novelty and boundaries, are privileged, something that is clearly of adaptive value. New messages are more important than "messages already received", and occurrent events more important than their standing background. This a priori that shapes experience is emphatically not a Kantian a priori but one formed by experience, being imposed on later experiences by earlier ones. Since it is mediated by the evolutionary process, "earlier experiences" are not confined to the life of the individual organism but have arisen out of the experiences of ancestral organisms forged by the processes of natural selection. For Mach, scientific inquiry is also child of adaptive behaviour guided by adapted perception: "Scientific thought arises out of popular thought, and so completes the *continuous series of biological development that begins with the first simple manifestations of life*"[44] (emphasis added). However, science, as Mach admits, has been "the most superfluous offshoot" of biological and cultural development.[45] For the greater part of the history of humanity, power – and the opportunities to replicate one's genetic material – has hardly lain with those who advance the cognitive capacity of humankind. It has more often been the privilege of the most successful fighters, foragers and predators. Even at a collective level, conquest and triumph have depended more on social organization than cognitive superiority. Science remains a biological mystery to which biological science offers little to help us solve.

Our cue for a return to Quine's attempted rational reconstruction of the path between stimulus and science. I have argued that it proposes steps for which there is no clear biological mechanism. The unification of the sensory field into a moment-to-moment proto-world, the metaphysical intuition of enduring, public objects-in-themselves, and the emergence of explicit classes to which items in the experienced world are allocated – none of these seem to yield to a neural or neurobiological explanation. Even if these steps brought biological utility, this would not explain how they are biologically generated.

It might be argued that there are many evolutionary developments that we cannot even begin to explain. The origin of life, the emergence of multi-cellular organisms, the development of organs such as the eye – these are some of the targets those who wish to cast doubt on the theory of evolution, have fixed on. There is, however, a plausible gradualist story for much of what happens in evolution. By contrast, the passage from insentient mechanisms to conscious behaviour is difficult to account for – at least at its origin – in terms of competitive advantage; and so too is the capacity for the kind of cognitive advance seen in humanity. At any rate, it is impossible to see that kind of advance as being driven by, as well as conferring, biological utility.

Naturalism therefore does nothing to demystify our extraordinary capacity to comprehend the world by claiming that we are part of that which we understand and that there is consequently no gap between the world that is comprehended and the mind that comprehends it. To makes this idea seem plausible, it is necessary to glide Quine-like over the real discontinuities – such as between stimuli and our large-scale ideas of the world. By the time we have reached scientific theories, we have long ceased to be (just) material objects in a material world or organisms in nature. These discontinuities are evident, as we have seen, at a level far below that of scientific hypotheses about how the world works with their apparently limitless range. Naturalistic accounts of human knowledge are given seeming plausibility only by a confusion between a) demonstrating that something may conceivably have a biological advantage and b) proving it must therefore have been generated by, and is therefore explained by, the kind of processes that gave rise to wings and kidneys. There are many capacities that might confer biological advantage – for example the ability to become entirely immaterial for a period when a predator is circling – but this does not mean that they are there to be requisitioned: their value does not explain their genesis. We should not confuse why science takes the form that it does such that it "works" with the question of why there is science. That potential biological utility is not sufficient as an explanation of a desirable capacity such as this ability to make higher-order sense of the world is evident from the fact that much higher-order sense does not translate – and certainly not directly or immediately – into replicative advantage for the genes of the organisms that are blessed with such sense.[46]

There is a more fundamental reason why the naturalization of sense-making – which aims to close the metaphysical gap between that which makes sense and that which it makes sense of – is misguided. It is this: the gap is *necessary* for the (undeniable) distinction between the two to be maintained. The sense-maker who "faces" the world, and tries to understand it, must be *offset* from it in a way that is different from the way two pebbles are offset from each other or the separation between an insentient organism and "its" environment. We shall return to this issue, central to the present inquiry, in Chapter 6.

If we set aside the lens of evolutionary theory and ask whether the very fact we are part of something could help to explain why or how we can make sense of it, we can see the difficulty more plainly. A pebble is not granted insight into matter simply in virtue of being a piece of matter – or of course granted insight into its own nature in virtue of being a pebble. Nor does it have a *world*. The biological approach to knowledge and understanding that identifies these faculties with neural activity – minute events in a minute part of the universe, scintillations miniscule compared even with our pin-prick heads – does not seem to be able to accommodate the kind of difference from pebbles that would reveal to the world its own nature. If nerve impulses are understood as physical events, they seem highly unlikely to rise above the small patch that they occupy to view and make sense of a world that vastly outsizes them.

In short, the very claim that comprehension of the material world is a biological, that is to say a material, part of the material world – and which consequently collapses the gap between knower and known – makes our knowledge *of* or *about* that world seem *less* not more comprehensible. Our being exquisitely tuned to our ecological niches, so that we are square pegs in square holes, hardly explains how it is we make sense of the holes, the pegs, or the world into which the hole is drilled – even less of the universe compared with which our world hardly figures as microscopic patch of light.

In the present chapter and the last, we have examined two approaches to dissolving the mystery of our making such large sense of the world. They both endeavour to collapse the distance between the mind that does the sense-making and the world that is made sense of. Kantian idealism gathers up the experienced world into the mind. The various forms of naturalized epistemology embed the mind in the natural world: our sense-making capacity is a necessary feature of an organism that has been forged by natural selection.

Both views are anti-realist in that they accept that what we make sense of is not something "in itself", entirely independent of our sense-making minds. This is obvious in the case of Kantian transcendental idealism but perhaps less so in the case of evolutionary epistemology. The latter appears to be tough-minded, connecting the sense we make of the world with the conditions under which we *qua* organism can survive. But the difference is more apparent than real. The world we make sense of is a world in part defined or constructed by our senses. More importantly, it is a world defined by our material needs and the vulnerabilities and opportunities connected with them. It would be going too far to describe evolutionary epistemology as "organic idealism" because much that is relevant to the welfare and fate of the organism is unknown to it – remote from any ideas it might have, even from its experiences, indeed from "mind" even in the broadest sense.[47]

Organisms such as our own bodies are largely mindless but our human lives are wall-to-wall mindful. So, while we must engage with the natural world because that is where we have come from and, as organisms, we are part of it, we do so from an increasing distance. We are increasingly insulated from natural forces not only because nature inside and outside of us is to some degree pacified but also because we interact with it via numerous mediators and are separated from it by many layers of the human world. The layers of insulation can be lost at any time. We can trip over and be broken like any other material object. We are fastened to a living organism and share its fate. Such salutary reminders of our lowly estate make the fact that knowledge and understanding – sense-making – which are central to our distance from the natural world and the life of the organism, are precisely what we need to account for. Naturalism highlights, rather than defuses, the mystery of "Man as the sense-making animal". The efficacy and hence apparent validity of the sense we make is particularly extraordinary in view of the kind of creatures humans are: metaphysically chimeric and epistemologically messy embodied subjects.

It is to the human subject we shall now turn.

Addendum 1
The anthropic principle

There is an alternative approach to internalizing the relationship between the sense-making mind and the world that is made sense of that seems yet more tough-minded than evolutionary epistemology because it originates not from biology but from physics. Its key notion is the anthropic principle (AP).[48]

The AP is succinctly defined by Brandon Carter, with whom it is most closely associated: "What we can expect to observe must be restricted by the conditions necessary for our presence as observers".[49] The strong version of this principle is that "The Universe (and hence the fundamental parameters on which it depends) must be such as to admit the creation of observers within it at some stage".[50] The principle is a response to the startling fact that the conditions under which life – and hence conscious life, and the sense-making mind – is possible are highly restricted. If certain physical constants were different by an order of 1 in 100 billion, matter would not dominate over anti-matter and elements such as carbon (which are essential for all forms of life that we are aware of) would not have been possible. We should not, however, so the argument goes, be surprised at this fine-tuning of the universe because it is precisely what we would expect. If the universe were *not* so ordered as to support life, including the life of physicists who observe it, there would be no observers. That the observed universe is one in which observers are possible is hardly astonishing. If there are physicists, the universe, therefore, must be so constructed as to enable physicists to emerge, flourish, go to university, and make sense of the universe.

The fine-tuned universe becomes even less surprising – so the argument continues – if we accept a particular interpretation of quantum theory, which proposes vast numbers of universes parallel to the one in which we live. All possibilities are realized but the one we observe is the one in which observers are possible.

This endeavour to deflate the mystery of sense-making has many flaws. It leaps over the specific conditions that not only make life possible, but also human life possible, and the intellectual history of mankind leading up to making physicists possible. To connect this very particular history with the fine-tuning of the universe through the specific values of constants is as absurd as (for example) the argument:

$F = ma$ therefore *magna carta* was signed in 1215

The laws of nature, with their finely tuned constants, are a necessary condition of the kind of world we live in and the kind of "we" that live in it but they are not a sufficient condition of either.

The anthropic principle is not so much an absurdity as a tautology; or an attempt to get a result – humanity – out of a tautology; out of the assertion that if the universe, characterized by its constants, were not such as to enable life in the form of physicists to emerge then the universe would not have been disclosed to physicists. Given that it has been disclosed to physicists, it must be such as to be able to sustain the form of life called "the physicist". But this does nothing to close the gap between the picture of the universe as an almost boundless waste composed largely of insentient matter, energy, fields, space and time and the scientific mind that can conceive it and seem to make progress in comprehending it. It says nothing that bears on the fact that the universe seems to be disclosed in, or to a minute part of the universe – namely humanity represented by the community of physicists. Even less does it illuminate the mystery of the *partial* comprehensibility of the world and the gradual apparent progress towards more complete understanding.

In summary, while the universe we observe necessarily has a history that led up to observers and that history must have been regulated by fine-tuned laws that ultimately delivered observers, this does not delegitimate surprise. Our surprise simply widens from the truism that the observed universe has properties that permit the emergence of observers to the fact that there is a universe that is observed.[51]

Addendum 2
A note on Russellian monism and panpsychism

At the heart of Quine's endeavour to naturalize knowledge is the assumption that our understanding of the world ultimately arises from stimulation of our nervous system giving rise to sense experience. The latter is essentially identical with neural activity in certain parts of the brain.[52]

The problems with this view begin at the ground floor – with sentience, perception, and ordinary everyday knowledge – long before we get to understanding the world. Neural activity supposedly associated with consciousness does not look like the elements of consciousness. As has often been pointed out, there is nothing like the experience of red in certain discharges in the visual cortex. The gap seems greater when we think of objects that are experienced as being "over there", distinct from ourselves as subjects, distinct from experiences. And the gap is greater still when we come to memories of things that are past – things that are present to us but explicitly no longer present – or knowledge of facts, such as that the Battle of Waterloo took place in 1815.

These problems are compounded by the fact that neural activity that is supposed to be identical with consciousness (such as in parts of the cerebral cortex) is not fundamentally or even strikingly different from neural activity that most certainly is not (in most of the rest of the brain and spinal cord). Nevertheless, the variant forms of neural theories of consciousness seem to some to be the key to the naturalization of knowledge and to closing the gap between world and mind and (apparently) making the mystery of our capacity to comprehend the world less mysterious.

Russell argued that the difficulty of understanding how something as apparently utterly different from experiences as nerve impulses could be in reality identical with them originates in the fact that objective observation does not give us the nature of material events.[53] We can get to know the causal relations and the mathematical structure of matter but not its intrinsic nature.[54] And this restriction applies equally to those instances of matter that are brain states. What we learn of them through neuroscience does not tell us what they are in themselves. To know what they are in themselves you would have to *be* them. And we *are* our nerve impulses (or at least some of them). Since we are them, we find they are experiences; or we experience them as experiences.

It is this that justifies Russell's seemingly counter-intuitive claim that a physiologist observing a brain is seeing not the activity in the examined brain – which is observed from without – but his own experiences, that is to say his own nerve impulses, which are experienced from within. What we directly know is our own brain activity which gives us only mediated access to external objects and hence to the objective knowledge that ultimately leads to the science of the brain.

For Russell, the argument opens the way to a broader neutral monism in which mind and matter are simply aspects of a more fundamental stuff that is neither. It does not, however, help us to solve the epistemological problem of cognitive advance and science or even the less ambitious problem of understanding the relationship between neural activity and consciousness. If all stuff has mind as one of its aspects, what is special about the brain such that it – and not say rocks and trees – is aware of a world in virtue of being aware of itself? The mind-like aspect of things seems to be spread too promiscuously to require something as specific as a brain to manifest itself.

There is also another danger: neuro-solipsism. If all that I know is activity in my brain, then the sense that I know a world out there populated with things and people, must be an illusion. This conclusion has been drawn by several contemporary philosophers who have denied the reality of intentionality. Alex Rosenberg, for example, argues that, if it is neural activity, "consciousness is just another physical process. If physical processes cannot by themselves have or convey propositional content [i.e. aboutness], then consciousness can't either."[55] All we know is our own neural activity and so there are no true (or false) perceptions, beliefs, or thoughts. It should be obvious that, if Rosenberg's theory were true, it could not be stated because nothing, including Rosenberg's arguments has "aboutness" or propositional content. Even if it could be stated, there would be no point in doing so. In fact, it is of course a belief "about" something, putatively based on knowledge of stuff outside of Rosenberg's own head, and propagated to minds other than his own.[56]

According to neutral monism "mental" and "physical" are two ways of presenting the fundamental stuff of the universe, or in which the fundamental stuff of the universe may present itself. The stuff is in itself neither mental nor physical. This is a half-way house to panpsychism, which has recently had a revival. It, too, has arisen as a radical response to the difficulty of understanding how material events such as neural discharges can underpin or be conscious experiences, once their distinct and different natures are acknowledged.[57] Panpsychists claim that consciousness is present throughout the natural world so that the smallest things have very basic kinds of experiences. As an advocate of the theory Philip Goff puts it, "an electron has an inner life."[58] The macroscopic consciousness of organisms such as birds and beasts and people like you and more is built up out of these elementary constituents.

What the consciousness of these constituents would amount to and how the consciousness of each of a vast assembly of such constituents would throw in their lot with billions of others to generate an agreed upon continuous, world-supporting viewpoint of a macroscopic conscious being is entirely obscure. This is the so-called combination problem.[59] Equally, or even more, obscure is why this happens in some beings and not others; in people, for example, and not pebbles, mountains, toe nails or kidneys.

This objection applies with particular force to a variant of panpsychism termed "cosmopsychism", proposed to address the combination problem.[60] Cosmopsychism argues that it is a mistake to begin with the "smallist" assumption that the primary components of consciousness are to be found at the level of microscopic constituents, so that we have to account for how they throw in their lot with each other to make up a macroscopic mind, a viewpoint. Rather, it is the universe as a whole that is conscious: "the one and only fundamental individual is the conscious universe".[61]

While this may address the problem of tiny bits of conscious stuff working together to produce macroscopic conscious entities, it does not explain a) how it is that some entities are conscious and others are not; b) how among conscious entities, some (e.g. philosophers) are more conscious than others (e.g. oysters); c) and how conscious beings such as you and me have distinctive viewpoints on the conscious universe and particular contents of consciousness. As regards c), it looks as if the combination problem has been replaced by the "disaggregation" problem of how Mind becomes minds. It is reminiscent of the challenge that Kant's transcendental idealism faces in accounting for individual minds and their specific contents, which seems crucially dependent on the spatiotemporal location of a particular (organic) body.

The consciousness of a conscious universe would be either a consciousness of everything (impossible to imagine) or a consciousness of nothing given that there would be nothing outside of its consciousness to be conscious *of*. In either case, cosmopsychism overlooks the fact that the intentional relationship is local and has to be justified – otherwise it has no target and amounts to mentality without object.

If standard panpsychism responds to the problem of getting a full-blown conscious subject together in a world that seems largely insentient, cosmopsychism makes it impossible to understand how the world is divided into seemingly conscious and unconscious bits and how consciousness is distributed between many distinct and largely independent conscious individuals. Panpsychism ironically falls foul of the danger that, if the relationship between mind and body, or more specifically knower and known, were too cosy, then there would be no objects of knowledge and no painful, laborious process of acquiring knowledge. Either everything, or nothing, would be known already.

Goff's defence of Panpsychism – that no other theory can account for the relationship between mind and brain, and can take the reality of experience seriously – is rather analogous to the "God of the gaps" argument. An "ontology of the gaps", perhaps. Some advocates of panpsychism also argue that, not only is there no other plausible response to the mind-body problem but that ideas that have once been thought crazy are now conventional science, so they should be taken seriously. I am reminded of Groucho Marx: "They said Newton was mad and he was a genius; they said Einstein was mad and he was a genius; and they said my Uncle Louis was mad – and he was".

CHAPTER 5

The escape from subjectivity

We have set aside two explanations as to how we can comprehend (at least in part) a world that so vastly outsizes us. The first (Kantian) explanation is that this is possible because the comprehended world is folded inside the comprehending mind. This, however, leaves the problem of accounting for the sense of a world outside of the mind of which we have incomplete knowledge. If extra-mental reality is a featureless noumenon, then we must find within ourselves the difference between what we feel we are and what we feel we know. The experiencable Other loses its opacity and, indeed, its otherness. It is difficult, moreover, to understand how the Kantian transcendental subject fails to be all-powerful, if it creates the context (the world) in which it both exerts its power and experiences its limitations. The opposite explanation that the mind is attuned to the world as a matter of biological necessity – the mind is wrapped in the natural world – proves equally flawed as an attempt to deflate the mystery of the comprehensibility of the world. There is nothing in biological processes that seems able either to generate mind or to account for its putative value as a condition of enhanced replicative power. Besides, if there is only nature, then the fact that mind is "about" nature remains unexplained. Organisms, as part of nature and subject to its laws, do not seem to have the wherewithal to generate the kind of distance explicit in intentionality. The determined attempts to eliminate intentionality by many philosophers committed to naturalism is striking testimony to this. Moreover, in both Kantian idealism and the various forms of naturalism, the gradual, laborious acquisition of explicitly incomplete knowledge is equally without explanation. The problem of the intelligibility of the world returns with an added force when we consider the nature of the being – the fallible human subject – that comprehends the world.

The cognitive progress of humanity is typically presented as being characterized by, and dependent upon, progressive escape from the subjectivity of the knowing subject. Minds, it seems, understand the world only by overcoming some fundamental aspects of themselves. The very idea of objectivity is rooted in subjects' insight into their own unreliability. The "merely subjective" gives place to the coolly objective. The path to objective truth is opened up when individual human beings and mankind "get themselves out of the way". By this means, we access a new kind of reality which not only lies beyond the world construed according to wishful thinking, or even as the thwarting, obstructing stuff out there that requires our will to shape or lies beyond our scope to do so – but also beyond immediate or even delayed or mediated appearances. As individual subjects, we see what-is from a certain, necessarily partial, necessarily limited viewpoint – the front of the house not the back, the table not its atoms, the locality not the totality. And even collectively, everything we experience is ultimately mediated by subjects, with their quadruple lenses of sense organs, biological needs, historically determined interests, and symbolic systems.

It would be absurd to attempt to do justice to our (partial) awakening. Here, however, are a few steps in any story of our emancipation from individual, cultural and species subjectivity:

a) If we ever start out as a bubble of sentience or a cloud of sensations we soon rise above this. At the heart of "objectivity" is the sense, acquired early in development, that the world is populated by items, notably objects, that have an existence independent of our experience of them. Objects have intrinsic properties, and modes of interaction with other objects, that belong to them not to us. There are things about objects that are there to be found out: they have a hiddenness, that the infant enquirer reveals by lifting them up, turning them round, shaking them, banging them on the side of the cot, dropping them on the floor, tearing them apart. Such are the modes of primitive interrogation of the material world.

b) The intuition of the object "in its own right" is the first hint of a detachment from the perspectives through which things are encountered, and the needs – with associated value judgements – that they might serve. This is an essential first step towards the deindexicalized vision of science. That objects are available to all and everyone reinforces the intuition that they have an existence in themselves. The developing awareness that others have different (literal) points of view revealing different worlds and that these have equal validity extends our sense of the world – as a public, shared realm.

c) The transcendence that is implicit in experience of objects, such that the basis of perception is exceeded by the perceived object, is made explicit in shared knowledge. For example, the items in the visual field are more than the seen.

d) Our awakening out of sentience, and a widening sense of an ontology of items beyond our subjectivity, is accelerated by discourse. We are able from our earliest years to draw on others' knowledge, taking much of our intelligible outside world "off the shelf". We get to know of vastly more than we could ever experience first-hand and about things and states of affairs that are only distantly related to experience.

e) Associated with this headline truth about discourse are a couple of other consequences that have particular relevance to escape from subjectivity. Word-mediated knowledge belongs to no-one, not even to the person who discloses it to us. While possession of knowledge may enhance personal power, true knowledge, unlike experience, is impersonal. "The fact that x" is not owned by you or me but is part of a world outside of any of us; only mistakes, misinterpretations, and lies have personal ownership, although they ape the impersonality of true knowledge. Knowledge is not "held" in the way that a belief is and while facts may change their character as they pass from person to person, at the heart of knowledge there is the assumption that its content is independent of the mental soil of the knower.

f) Knowledge is not directly translatable into subjective experience. Facts are invisible, inaudible, tasteless, cannot be smelt, or fingered. The testimony of others, that is, not only liberates us from the confines of our sensorium, but liberates us from the confines of *any* sensorium. Every fact is part of a view from nowhere. This is connected with the general nature of the object of knowledge – a chair, a tree, etc. – even when the referent of any proposition in which the knowledge is expressed is a particular – "that chair", "the tree outside the window".

g) If this is less obvious than it should be, it is because we are conscious that factual statements are the product of judgements and the latter have had a toe-hold in viewpoints, based on sense experience necessarily bound to a perspective. But facts transcend the perspectives which generate or underwrite them. This is true at quite a basic level.

It is a subjective experience to see an object a long way away. When, however, I *say that* an object is a long way away, I have made that perspective explicit, and created the context in which it can be overcome. A cognitive space is opened up in which other perspectives can be accommodated; for example, in which the object is "near" to other subjects or, indeed, to other objects.

h) The liberation from the subjective viewpoint afforded by making the viewpoint explicit is evident in any mode of representation. A painting, for example, may show figures in a distance. That "distance" – which can be seen close-up by the viewer in the gallery – becomes itself an object. The figures are lifted from the landscape in which they are located and their distance is revealed as relative to the viewpoint of the painter or (more precisely) the viewpoint the painter wished to depict. To see perspective is no longer to be in thrall to it.

i) At the root of shared knowledge – the testimony of others that liberates us from our subjective viewpoint – is the joining of attention. In a communication even as primitive as pointing,[1] there is a faith in a common awareness of a shared reality which is susceptible to being encountered by anyone and everyone. This is the vital first stage in the passage to the scientific "view from nowhere". The speech-mediated testimony of others is built on our sense of an objective reality which we only minutely sample through our own experiences. The intersubjective joining of attention, directly to things that are present, or through the mediation of speech to things that exist but are beyond the circle of presence, is equally, or more, potent as a means of awakening us from our own viewpoint when there is no agreement regarding the object of attention, such that parties have to defend their beliefs as to what is the case. While animals may be dimly aware of viewpoints other than their own – as when a predator sneaks up on its prey or the latter hides from the former – there is limited consciousness of the other's awareness of other objects, of a sensory field anchored to a different centre.

j) We see a path of gradual awakening from the naked moment of experience, to stretches of experience checked for internal consistency, layered critical self-consciousness, participation in corrective dialogue exercised in a polyphasic and polyphonic fabric of meaning, teased out in discourse, in arguments, shared and unshared practices, in conflict and cooperation, and in a dozen modes of agreement and disagreement. All of these processes are accelerated by the preservation of speech, and the knowledge transmitted in it, in the written word. Writing is central to epistemic sharing within and across moments, within and between individuals, within and across communities, generations, and epochs.

k) Written sentences extend our cognitive reach beyond our meat-enmired sentience, taking further something that is implicit in all discourse; namely, liberation from the "here and now". What is referred to on the page is not located in the place where the record is set down or read. With this comes a vast amplification of the sense that the world – of people, places and things – is bigger than any one can experience, know, know of, or even understand.

l) The pre-scientific expansion of knowledge-by-description,[2] the testimony of communities, and cultures, and the accumulated intelligence of the ages, opens up a world from which we are largely absent and in which our individual preoccupations do not count, or are not central. The other aspect of this is awakening out of the magic thinking which spreads our minds, our individual or communal subjectivity, and our needs and preoccupations, sometimes located in spirits and deities, into the universe. With the (comparatively recent) "disenchantment" of what is out there, a world picture develops in which agency is overwhelmingly displaced by impersonal forces and causes and we acknowledge a material reality whose behaviour is largely deaf to our wishes and indifferent to our fate.

m) At the very least, intuitions imported from everyday life, flavoured with meaning, significance and purpose, are no longer regarded as a reliable guide to the nature of things. The Copernican revolution that challenged the most universally and continually visible feature of our days – the movement of the sun round the earth; the basic laws of mechanics according to which there is no fundamental difference between movement at uniform velocity in a straight line and the state of rest; and the relativization of "up" and "down" to the direction of the centre of massive bodies – are ubiquitous manifestations of the distance between how things seem and how they are.

n) The acknowledgement of a disconnection between our judgement and reality culminates in an evolving sense that we neither are, nor are at, the centre of the world in which we find ourselves. The accepted world picture is no longer arranged around the collective ego of humankind. We inhabit a world – first intimated in objects that have intrinsic reality independent of our experience of them – that must be understood on its, not our, terms. Those terms are ultimately expressed in hidden laws that science eventually uncovers. The sense of those laws lies in their interconnectedness rather than any direct connection with the immediate meaning of our experiences and needs.

Thus, a very sketchy sketch of some of the steps in the path – taken uniquely by humans – out of the putative starting point of the sentient subject awake only to his or her own sensations towards a full-blown picture of the world. The experimental science that has been so central to the cognitive development of humankind is a relatively recent phenomenon. Most of the steps described above are pre-scientific; indeed, they provide the necessary ontological or epistemological platform for scientific inquiry.

At the heart of science, building on observation and the disciplined imagining of conjecture, is of course measurement. That this is a key to the escape from our individual and collective subjectivity hardly needs spelling out – although there are anti-realist accounts of science that will contest this. However, the nature of measurement deserves more detailed attention. We have become so used to it – it is after all ubiquitous in technology and all aspects of our daily life as well as being the lifeblood of science – that its astonishing nature is usually concealed from us. We also take for granted its crucial role in liberating us from the constraints of subjectivity. Measurement decisively marginalizes the perspective of the subject and subjective impressions of size, extensity, distance and intensity. Sense experience with its secondary qualities is demoted to (merely) "subjective experience" which has diminishing authority on what is taken to be the nature of things, on how they truly are, what they are like. Measurement lies at the heart of science – our most spectacular source of intellectual advance and of the globalization of world pictures.

Measurement reduces what is there to quantities and consequently to what can be agreed upon. "How much?" is clearly less contentious than, for example, "How good?", or even "What kind?". The consensus moreover seems to be true to the object rather than merely a reflection of herd behaviour: it appears (at least to those who are not of a conventionalist or operationalist persuasion) to generate knowledge about what the object would look like even if it were not being looked at. Notwithstanding jibes about "lies, damned lies, and statistics", measurement settles disagreements because it seems not only to be objective but also, as it were, on the side of the item being measured. *You* may think the table is big and *I* think it is small but both of us – and indeed strangers we have never met across the globe, and across the ages – must agree that it is 2 feet by 2 feet – leaving aside variations, irrelevant to the present discussion, that may result from frames of reference in relative velocities that are a significant fraction of the speed of light. Measurement, in short, seems to be uniquely liberating from individual or even collective subjectivity. The quantities it generates are contrasted with the (merely) secondary qualities delivered by direct sense experience. This is in part due to the healthy suspicion that drives the ever-increasing sophistication of measurement: the concern for reliability, for repeatability within and across observers, and for control of any measuring instruments, expressed in calibration and recalibration. Our sense of what is the case is grounded in a sense of what *anyone* would find to be the case: the intersubjective passes over into the objective. The escape from subjectivity in testimony which is authenticated through being put to the test is taken to a new limit, as the measurement is subjected to quality control.

The instinct or appetite for *consensus* has deep roots. We do not set out as monads whose sensory windows are blacked out by the fact that experiences cannot be directly shared. The starting point for the journey from experiencing subject to objective knowledge is not a stand-alone "I". Even at an early stage in development, "I" grows through interaction with other "I"s. The sense we make of the world (including ourselves) is joint and several from the start. "We" is as profound as "I". The journey from meaningful experience to shared sense-making is shorter than may be typically described by philosophers who envisage as a starting point a torrent of sense data presented to an isolated individual consciousness.

Long before the rise of quantitative science, consensus in measurement played a major role in social coherence – in regulating the exchange of goods and services, assessing productivity, determining and apportioning just reward, and drawing up and delivering on contracts. In this respect, science as we now know it was a relative late development in the exploitation of the possibilities of measurement. The story of the origin of the geometry that ultimately delivered the general theory relativity – namely that it provided a way of assessing areas of land when they had to be reapportioned after boundaries had been erased by the annual Nilotic floods – may be apocryphal. It is, however, a reminder of how measurement was woven into the fabric of our lives long before it was crucial to the advance of natural science. Even when it was tied to solving local practical problems and addressing homely quarrels over quantities – how much is mine and how much is yours – the principles underlying it had universal application.

Measurements stand outside of the flow of experience in which we are immersed. This is especially true of scientific measurement. It is, first of all, active: it is the culmination of a journey from (relatively) passive seeing to more active looking, to deliberate scrutiny, and thence to expert observation.[3] The latter is closely prescribed as to its topics (which will have emerged from the history of a discipline) and its methods. What we seek and how we seek it is remote from what we happen to see. What is more, individual measurements explicitly stand for a whole class of observations, apt to be incorporated into general laws. That is one of the reasons why the discrete actions that are scientific measurements may be very complex and have a vast background of assumptions and concepts and scholarship. Not only may they require the requisitioning, setting up, and employment of instruments of varying degrees of sophistication, in more recent scientific inquiry, they may also involve travel to facilities and cooperation with others. At any rate, a measurement is *an experience by appointment*, even when the appointment is with an instrument that is sought out, picked up, and used, rather than another person. While there is no right and wrong way to have an experience, there most certainly is a right and wrong way to have, or more precisely carry out, a measurement. The run-up to the moment of measurement may include instruction in relevant techniques and broader training in the surrounding disciplines. There are rules governing, and standards of, measurement; quality controls that ensure reproducibility within and across individuals, and within and across disciplines and cultures. (Such standards developed in science feed back into everyday life via the bureaux and other institutions of "weights and measures" that uphold those standards.) Measurement and theory are braided together both historically and conceptually. Theories are tested by measurements and the instruments that make measurements possible are themselves built according to a nexus of theories that pick out the parameters that are measured and underwrite the connection between what is seen on the dial and what is being measured. The distance between direct experience and measurement is further extended by the processes of calibrating devices against standards and checks for accuracy and precision. Behind these norms is the idea of an asymptote in which quantitative observation is entirely congruent with the size of that which is observed.

These characteristics underline how remote scientific measurement is from the mere receptivity of gawping or the happenstance of everyday experience. It is to a greater or lesser degree independent of the circumstances under which it takes place and the rest of the life of the individual making the measurement − the journey to the lab, the lunch-break, the contractual requirement of the job. Of course, experience is still key; but the kind of experience that is generated by measurement is as distinctive and as remote from the sensory impressions of moment-to-moment daily life as the methods by which they are acquired. We position ourselves to make measurements: a measurement is something that is done, a completed measurement is an achievement. Its outcome is a *result*, a *datum* or *data-point* that may or may not confirm expectations, predictions, or correspond to a desired value. The result "fits", or importantly does not fit, with what is anticipated or aimed at, having a place in an entire network of findings coordinated by concepts, the latter being in part implicit in the units in which the measurement is expressed.

Measurements are typically pure quantities expressed in a *number* – a location in a scale or a quantity of units. Numbers have no properties or none that are salient. They are without qualities and location – except within a scale or an order of magnitude – and do not belong to the experiential flux of the person who obtained the result or the place in which it was obtained. Their home is within the data set to which they belong and, in the case of scientific measurements, the laws, or nexus of laws, which they confirm, illustrate, or express. Results, or findings, in short, belong to no-when, no-where and no-one. Measurements flatten difference: they homogenize. All units are, by definition, identical: six feet of flesh and six feet of rock are identical in terms of the measurement made. They are (importantly) without evident perspective or phenomenal appearance, except that necessary for them to be made visible and shared. Any phenomenal appearance – for example the colour, size or font of the numbers on the dial – is irrelevant just as anything specific to the person who obtained the result is a contaminant. The irrelevance of the phenomenal characteristics of any representation of a "data-point" is underlined by the fact that analogue results can be digitized. Equally irrelevant are many of the specific details of the process generating the result; for example, my entering a room, picking up a detector at a particular time in a particular place and putting it down ditto. Whatever sense experience is associated with obtaining or experiencing the measurement – the act of measurement – is stripped off in the "result": it is as irrelevant as a coffee stain on a page in a physics textbook. A measurement is (to borrow a term used by Heidegger in another circumstance) a "de-experience".

Measurement extracts numbers from objects, events, or intervals. Such extraction is predicated on, and perhaps justifies in an iterative way, a prior abstraction, whereby material is reduced to a quantifiable aspect or a concatenation of parameters. Even in the case of something as basic as size, measurements are made on abstractions. We may approach a body of liquid as something that has (say) depth, volume, weight, density, transparency, temperature, viscosity, solvency, temperature-dependent expansion and so on. We quantify these separately, though they cannot be separated in the material itself or as it is directly experienced. When we jump into a swimming pool, we cannot jump separately into its depth, its volume, its temperature, its viscosity, etc. The use of instruments tuned to these individual parameters introduces another gap between measurement and the flux of experience.

The outcomes of measurement are located in a space increasingly remote from that occupied by the objects and events that are directly encountered, including those that have been subject to measurement, and indeed from the lived space of the measurer. This is an important foundation for the most fundamental Copernican revolution: namely, one that displaces the subject from the centre of her world and relocates her as a small item in that world. As a mode of encountering the world that is ultimately answerable to experience but at the same time outside of it, measurement starts the process that has taken us to a remarkable place from which we could look at our world from the outside. It is an important element of our awakening from the *umwelt* granted every organism to a world-picture that only humans entertain. While experience remains the ultimate foundation of objective knowledge, the latter stands to the former as the roots of a tree in the soil to its leaves spread out in space.

These fundamental differences may be lost sight of when measurements – even those undertaken in advanced science – are characterized simply as "experiences". Describing science, as Quine does, as a direct descendent of experiences and identifying the latter with "neural intake" overlooks the chasm between the informality and passivity of daily experience and the formal activity of scientific or any other disciplined observation, whether it is physics or ornithology. In this gap lies the basis of our awakening out of our subjective point of view to a widening intersubjective reality whose imagined asymptote is an appearance of the world as a reality that would be common to all actual and possible subjects; to an ideal or non-subjective subject, something that Arthur Eddington expressed when he said of general relativity using tensors that it "symbolized absolute knowledge" because "it stands for the subjective knowledge of all possible subjects at once".[4]

Convergence on a number is a process both of waking out of our private or personal view and, on this account, reaching a seeming approximation to the intrinsic properties of the object. Size, which is most closely identified with number, is apparently an intrinsic property of an object. This is connected with Galileo's distinction between what were later to be called "primary" and "secondary" qualities:

> I feel myself impelled by necessity, as soon as I conceive of a piece of matter or corporeal substance, of conceiving that *in its own nature* it

is bounded and figured in such and such a figure, that in relation to others it is large or small, that it is in this or that place, in this or that time, that it is in motion or remains at rest, that it touches or does not touch another body, that it is single, few, or many; in short, by no imagination can a body be separated from such conditions; but that it must be white or red, bitter or sweet, sounding or mute, of a pleasant or unpleasant odour, I do not perceive my mind forced to acknowledge it necessarily accompanied by such conditions; so that if the senses were not the escorts, perhaps the reason or imagination of itself would never have arrived at them.[5]   (emphasis added)

To discover what, in colour, is intrinsic to objects, we need to translate them into wavelengths, so they, too, acquire the status of primary qualities. The agreement in numbers – the replacement of perceptions by agreed quantities – is thus a passage from secondary (subjective, mind-based) qualities to primary (numerical object-based) measures and an awakening out of ourselves to a nature whose language, as Galileo famously said, was that of mathematics. While we may assume that primary qualities are experienced by animals, they are not experienced as encoded in numbers, nor stripped of secondary qualities. This is the path to the notion that the world-in-itself is mathematical, a system of magnitudes; that if things spoke for themselves, they would speak in some dialect of mathematics. The subnumerate experience of sunbathing is relegated to a cognitively inferior place compared with knowledge of the physics and physiology of the impact of light and heat on the body. From Parmenides' notion that sense experience is a source of erroneous opinion rather than truth, to Descartes's idea of sensations as muddled thoughts, and beyond to the idea of the universe as (seen aright) a system of magnitudes – thus the gathering prejudice against sense experience.

The universal appeal to measurement – to empirical data drained of phenomenal or subjective experience – to reveal what is out there has accustomed humanity to the idea that what is "out there" may be entirely different from the way it appears to us as we go about our daily business. This was accepted wisdom long before relativity theory and quantum mechanics seemed utterly to discredit the folk ontology of daily life. The distinctive authority of natural science is expressed in the assumption that truth (even the useful truths of applied science) is beyond what is, or even can be, lived or subjectively experienced: impressions of size or intensity, never mind importance, or value, are displaced by numbered quantities. The corollary of this is that the truth about the material world is equidistant from all subjects and, beyond this, the reinforcement of the conviction that what is truly real can be accessed only by getting ourselves as subjects out of the way. This reinforces a view, established early in the Western intellectual tradition by Parmenides and Plato, that we need to look past the deliverance of our senses, and our subjective experiences, to access reality. The important difference, however, is that it is measurement, rather than reason guided by intuitions and logic, that is the means by which we rise above our subjectivity.

It is a story that is difficult to evaluate. It has been told both as a tale of triumph – the cognitive conquest of mindless nature – and as one of spiritual impoverishment and disenchantment. The ambivalence has been captured succinctly by Erwin Schrödinger:

> [A] moderately satisfying picture of the world has only been reached at the high price of taking ourselves out of the picture, stepping back into the role of the non-concerned observer ... while the stuff from which our world picture is built is yielded exclusively from the sense organs as organs of the mind ... yet the conscious mind itself remains a stranger within that construct, it has no living space in it.[6]

The very possibility of conscious subjects becomes increasingly difficult to explain in a world of objects and when the advance of understanding is measured in terms of a progressively more objective viewpoint. The self-undermining of a world-picture based upon objective science becomes more evident when it is appreciated that the first-person is not merely a perspective but the very possibility of a perspective from which alone knowledge can be acquired. There is no third person without a first-person. The givenness of things has to be given to *someone*.

And there have been profound consequences that go beyond the loss of the authority of the phenomenal content of experience and the manifest image of the world. The privileging of quantity over quality has gone hand in hand with the focus on mechanisms over meaning. W. T. Stace, writing in the wake of the Second World War, highlighted the consequences of developing a world-picture that, except insofar as it enhanced our capacity to control and pacify nature, was void of human significance:

> The founders of modern science – for instance, Galileo, Kepler, and Newton – were mostly pious men who did not doubt God's purposes. Nevertheless, they took the revolutionary step of consciously and deliberately expelling the idea of purpose as controlling nature

from their new science of nature. They did this on the grounds that inquiry into purposes is useless for what science aims at: namely the prediction and control of events. To predict an eclipse, what you have to know is not its purpose but its causes. Hence science from the seventeenth century onwards became exclusively an inquiry into causes. The conception of purpose in the world was ignored and frowned on. This, though silent and almost unnoticed, was the greatest revolution in human history.[7]

The material rewards brought by this self-denying, or subject-marginalizing, ordinance have been immense. Science, after all "works" in several senses of that word. It has extended our capacity to predict aspects of the physical world to an unimaginable degree in terms of both reach and accuracy and it has vastly amplified our ability to manipulate that world to achieve our goals, including ones that pre-scientific man had not even thought to entertain – such as talking to a friend 10,000 miles away, to take a relatively trivial example. Equally impressive are the kinds of achievements we discussed in Chapter 1; for example, assembling a coherent account of the material world in which lower-order laws are subsumed under higher-order ones and all that happens can be presented as an expression of a handful of forces that might one day be reduced to a single force or a unified field. What we can know, and what we can do on the basis of what we know, has been extended beyond anything humankind for most of its history could have imagined.

In the light of such achievements, it is difficult, and would even be perverse, to resist the conclusion that natural science, while beginning with the experiences of the individual subject and being ultimately "cashed" in such experiences, uncovers a fundamental reality that transcends our subjectivity and shows the latter to have been in some sense cognitively deficient. An anti-realist interpretation of science would make its efficacy and coherence – and its obvious progress, notwithstanding regular revolutions in thought – inexplicable.[8]

However, resist we must. Nagel's cautionary note is relevant. It is the case that: "a view or a form of thought is more objective than another if it relies less on the specifics of the individual's make up and position in the world, or on the character of the type of creature he is".[9] However,

> Although there is a connection between objectivity and reality – only
> the supposition that we and our appearances are parts of a larger real-
> ity makes it reasonable to seal understanding by stepping back from

appearances in this way – still not all reality is better understood the more objectively it is viewed.[10]

At the very least, we need a certain constitution – quite narrowly defined – in order to be able to access or contribute to the objective view. This is not, however, as compelling a critique of claims to objectivity as it sounds. After all, the majestic vision of the universe delivered by Newton's laws of motion owes nothing important to the scientist's personality, era, cultural context, even his species. Such a world-picture does not belong to an *umwelt*, even less to the parochial concerns of a bewigged seventeenth-century member of the middle classes. Newtonian science is not contaminated by Newton-the-man. $F = ma$ is not merely third-person; it is no person.

There is, of course, no shortage of ways in which the subject can push back against those successive Copernican revolutions by which we have expelled ourselves from the various centres of the world and have come to see ourselves as smidgeons of cognition located in a place that does not even count as "remote", given that remoteness is an anthropocentric notion. Every moment of our lives – whether we are in love or just in a hurry, worrying about a crying baby or our reputation, or fretting over the future of humanity or looking forward to our lunch – is charged with meanings that the natural world as described by the most powerful science cannot accommodate. What is more, the technology that science has delivered is deployed in lives that rest on unreconstructed common sense. The invention of the laptop computer, on which I am typing this, drew on the same quantum mechanics that denies the self-identity of the elements of matter, and replaces stuff with probability waves. And yet the device is safely situated on my desk and was transported thither by movements that could be captured by Newtonian, even Galilean mechanics. Science itself must be conducted in the everyday world of rooms with floors, doors and windows, using macroscopic bits of equipment and involving cooperation rooted in a shared "now" of embodied subjects experiencing an everyday world in an everyday way. Both inside and outside the laboratory, it is the world of Monday, Tuesday and Wednesday. In this world, reality consists of the objects that surround us, stones we could kick in Johnsonian fashion if we were inclined to defend the folk ontology of daily life. The chairs we sit on exist in defiance of the non-local, probabilistic, entangled world of quantum mechanics, and we eat our breakfast before we set out on our journey to work, however relativity theory may throw into question a fixed order of events, unless they are connected in a causal manner that quantum theory cannot accommodate.

It could be argued that this is not evidence of the fundamental truth of unre-constructed folk ontology. Rather, it exposes the incorrigibility of the human animal: humanity is simply unable to live at the level of its highest cognitive achievements, to imagine, never mind live within, the reality its collective brightest self has discovered. Our falling short of living in the objective reality we have uncovered through measurement, that is, is itself a measure of the extent to which we are hostage to that part of ourselves which is engaged in our daily life, a recitative of the mundane to which we return after brief arias of intellectual space travel. We are always going to return to the places where our habits of reaction and the needs that shape them are formed – to something not far from "where all the ladders start / In the foul rag and bone shop of the heart".[11]

The reason for the resistance of our immediate world-picture to be reformed by what we have learned through measurement-led science is that our knowledge has got ahead of our condition as living organisms. The manifest image is what we need, as both Locke and many contemporary philosophers have argued. Consider Locke:

> The infinite wise Contriver of us and all things about us has fitted our senses, faculties, and organs to the conveniences of life, and the business we have to do here … If by the help of microscopic eyes … man could penetrate further than ordinary into the secret composition and radical structure of bodies, he would not make any great advantage by the change, if such an acute sight would not serve to conduct him to the market and exchange, if he could not see things he was to avoid at a convenient distance, nor distinguish things he had to do with, by those sensible Qualities others do.[12]

James Ladyman, who has argued that reality is a mathematical structure in which there are no things only relations – in particular those weird ones that are revealed by quantum mechanics – deals with the fact that we do not see the world like this in a way similar to Locke's; however, he substitutes for the God of religion the God of evolution, namely survival: "[P]roficiency in inferring the large-scale and small-scale structure of our immediate environment, or any features of parts of the universe distant from our ancestral stomping grounds, was of no relevance to our ancestors' reproductive fitness".[13] This meta-epistemological explanation of the difficulty we have in seeing, accepting or even conceiving the truth about what is real, actually presupposes the reality of the items – namely medium-sized, self-identical human beings (and their "stomping grounds") who have knowledge derived from negotiation with a world made of medium-sized self-identical objects – to which his ontology denies reality.

There is clearly much work to be done in reconciling our everyday image of the world around us and the scientific image that has had such colossal, and largely beneficial, consequences. It remains true that the employment of the fruits of cognitive advance is inevitably anchored in unreformed every day or direct experience. Even when, as is necessarily the case, science goes beyond experience – as when general laws are guessed at – it will be subject to testing by experience. If experience seems to have the first word, it also has the last word. Not only are the claims of science tested in (to use Quine's phrase) "the tribunal of experience" which they face not one-by-one but "corporately".[14] The entire quest for scientific truth is immersed in the sea of individual experience and its fruits enjoyed likewise.

We have already alluded to another way of capturing the miracle of the apparent escape from "mere subjectivity": the passage from *umwelt* to world-picture. Jakob von Uexkull introduced the term *umwelt* to capture how different organisms experience the same environment differently.[15] Each species is attuned to an outside, according to its needs and the sense organs and active structures that serve them. It is this that defines the environment or surroundings with which the organism engages. The same meadow will be differently experienced by a bee rooting in a flower (part of its *humwelt* perhaps), a grazing cow, and a farmer harvesting hay. Each organism – insect, herbivore, human – is enclosed in the closed bubble of a world defined by the systems that secure its survival.

That the notion of an enclosing *umwelt* does not apply to human persons should be sufficiently obvious. The world we live in is *not* defined by the properties of our body, even those of our sensory systems. We participate in a community of minds creating, modifying, utilizing, sharing, and challenging "thatter" or knowledge, which we shall discuss in the next chapter. We are self-conscious, even at times self-narrating, creatures; embodied subjects at a distance from our environment, engaging with absences and not just presences, acting as well as reacting, responding to entertained possibility and not just to actualities, filtered through passive senses, that are around us.

We need look no further than Uexkull's own theory to be forced to acknowledge that it would be self-undermining if it was thought to encompass our own species. If we were truly closed off like bees in our own *umwelt* we could not recognize that bees have a different *umwelt* from ourselves or that cows have a different *umwelt* from bees. We would not be able to access a viewpoint from which these profoundly different *umwelten* are perceived and under-stood – sufficiently to be compared. Significantly, our ability to imagine the world of other organisms as being different from our own is not reciprocated: bees do not apparently busy themselves about our mode of experiencing the world. Most importantly, we would not be able to form the very idea of an *umwelt* and of our being confined to it.

The same point applies to the suspicion that our consciousness is not only *perspectival* but irremediably so, such that we are imprisoned in viewpoints (ranging from literal angles of vision to personal, national, or cultural interests that frame cognition). If we really were thus imprisoned, we would not be able to form the complex notion of "perspective" that we have. As already noted, the intuition is explicit even at the ground floor of our perception, when I not only see a scene but see that I see it from a viewpoint and see also that what I see is bounded by what I cannot see; and that you see it from a different viewpoint and can see and not see different things. The very fact that I am con-scious that I perceive things from a viewpoint shows that I am not deceived into thinking that the item that I perceive is identical with my perception; the *idea* of perspective is a marker of a liberation from perspective. My seeing that I see something from an angle means that my seeing is not entirely hostage to that, or any other, angle.

This is not to say that the suspicion that I must always see things from a per-sonal or shared (say, cultural or disciplinary) perspective, is entirely without foundation. To the contrary, every correction confirms the underlying notion. Even so, the idea of our subjectivity, and of experience, as being a kind of prison, even an open prison, is not upheld. While we cannot think ourselves as ultimately entirely escaping the intersubjectivity of our shared humanity, our being embodied subjects should not be seen as a barrier to our gaining access to a putative reality – indeed to reality itself – beyond appearance.

In support of this, we note that the very idea of the "real" borrows its mean-ing from the opposite: "unreal". Austin characterized "real" as a "trouser-word": "it is the negative sense that wears the trousers":

> That is, a definite sense attaches to the assertion that something is real, a real such-and-such, only in the light of a specific way in which it might be, or might have been, *not* real ... the function of real is not to contribute positively to the characterisation of anything, but to exclude possible ways of being *not* real.[16]

If we were permanently denied access to reality, we would have nothing with which to contrast our experience, or the world we experience, to justify the notion that we have access only to unreality, to "mere" appearance. "Reality" would become an idea without content or the possibility of content; rather like Kant's noumenon, an intellectual intuition, lacking any features or specific content. The global possibility of getting things (locally) wrong does not imply the certainty of getting things globally wrong.

There is, however, a deeper argument against the idea that we are denied access to reality by being imprisoned in subjectivity. It is the necessity of a conscious subject for there to be anything answering to the concept "reality". Basic stuff, matter, what-is, substance, Being – whatever you call it – does not of itself count as real (or of course unreal). A pebble may be part of my reality but it is not in itself real (or unreal). We need something – more precisely some*one* (individually or as part of a community of minds) – to turn what-is into The Given so that it is available for judgement as real or unreal. It is the subject that transforms, upgrades, Being into reality. There is no Given without the Taken, no Givenness without Takenness. To say this is not to espouse either a realist or anti-realist view of objects: without the subject the very idea of "reality" (as well as, more obviously, "unreality") is impossible. Whatever one thinks of Kant's transcendental idealism, it would be difficult to deny this, one of the fundamental assumptions that motivated it. The natural world is not self-given; so the idea of reality is on the borderline between ontology ("what there is") and epistemology ("what we know or experience of what there is").

The idea that the subjectivity of the subject is a mere obstacle to cognitive progress is therefore sheer ingratitude if we think of reality as that which would be evident not merely to an undistorted view but to no "mere" view at all. This would locate reality beyond Nagel's "view from nowhere"[17] to a view from "no-one", a view without a viewpoint, without a viewer; in short, a view that isn't a view at all. The nearest we get to this is the mathematical portrait of the world, drained of phenomenal content, of time and place, and of course of any inhabitants. There is nothing in a mathematical equation that guarantees that anything exists: it is not enough to secure actuality, only the form of possibility. Furthermore, the variables in the equations have to be given values, and of course meaning, from outside. The mathematical view is, at best, an abstract structure without content. Such a view is not even a glint in a glass eye.

It is not surprising that mathematics is void of content, given that it attempts to be the view from an (actual) everywhere rather than (possible) anywhere. Such a view would have to harvest, add up, and reconcile all appearances. The impossibility of doing so is best appreciated if we start on the epistemic ground floor and imagine a gaze that saw what-is simultaneously from all possible angles. Take a homely example. What would a rock look like if it were seen from the front, back, underneath, inside, and outside at once? No such look would be possible. But this is what we would require if we were to demand the appearance of the rock in itself, as opposed to its specific and distinct and mutually exclusive appearances to you or to me – or to the dog running past it or to the insect crawling over it. The idea of an (unmediated) appearance that corresponds to the reality of the rock, to its intrinsic appearance, is clearly contradictory, since appearance is "appearance *to*".

The epistemic ascent from the perspective of individual subjects is not towards say "the correct appearance" or "the canonical view" or "aperspectival view" of the rock – a hypothetical view that gives their appearance when they are not being seen, how they would look as they intimated themselves in the absence of a canvas, mirror, lens, or conscious subject. As we proceed from direct perception to verbal description and from the latter – via measurement – to mathematical characterization, appearances are not replaced by ever more truthful or ideal appearances. Rather, appearances are *shed* and the rock loses its place in space and time and its individuality. Atomic or quantum reality is faceless. We overlook this because space, time and individuality may seem to be recovered in descriptions. This is an illusion. "Six miles from London", "2 feet from Rock 2" and "2, 3, 4 in coordinate framework x, y, z", are not places comparable to the real place occupied by a real rock when it is in front of me. As explanation ascends, so it becomes de-localized as well as drained of phenomenal content. The highest vantage point is not a point or a view from a point. Nothing could be further from a world-*picture* than an equation, although the laws expressed in equations do form the skeleton of a world-picture.

We should therefore discredit the idea that "reality" is an asymptote we can arrive at by entirely disinfecting our cognition of any (subjective) viewpoint; that there is an end-point of intelligibility at which we reach the immediate language of Being, its self-portrait, so that we can tune in to the auto-pandiculation of the universe, somehow expressing its true appearance to no-one and nowhere, unmediated by an aware subject, the look of a world not being looked at, in the absence of the distortion of sight-tinted spectacles. I express it in this way in the Wittgensteinian spirit of passing "from a piece of disguised nonsense to something that is patent nonsense"[18] to expose it more clearly to critical examination.

Sense-making requires a distinctive "other" as its object or substrate. The theme of the next chapter will be the necessary gap between the knower and the known, between the two that is the quorum for the cognitive tango. In

Chapter 7, I will focus on the necessary insolubility of the known in knowledge for there to be an *object of* knowledge. What we may conclude for the present is that "what-is" or Being requires something other than itself to become "reality". That other is the subject who is not therefore a mere distorting lens, or just a ladder to be cast aside at a certain stage of cognitive advance. While measurement draws us out of our individuality, this does not mean that the subject is superseded. The idea that reality is "the Given" unpeeled of putative distortions arising out of the experiencing or knowing subject fosters the illusion that those distortions could be removed by – and only by – removing the subject entirely. Behind this is the further idea that, as objective knowledge and understanding have progressed by getting ourselves as individual subjects out of the way we could arrive at complete knowledge of reality by getting rid of subjects. But, to develop an earlier point, reality would not be given (or The Given) and Being would not be Reality without there being a subject to receive what is given and to make Being "real". This remains true, notwithstanding that we progress towards objectivity through the extraordinary action of measurement that delivers a "result", a dephenomenalized data-point, a pure quantity represented by a numerical token whose experiential features are irrelevant and, indeed, are "looked through".

Regarding the subject as a mere obstacle to knowledge and understanding is the end-point of an ingratitude that overlooks the extent to which the subject creates the very framework, "the outside", within which sense is to be found. We cannot entirely wake out of our putatively parochial selves because we would not have anything to wake with or anything particular to wake to. "Reality" is inescapably an image *of* what-is and such an image cannot be perfected by removing all lenses. The knowing subject is not only necessary but cannot be entirely passive, as if it were a transparent Reality-detector. The entirely passive mind would be a succession of experiences that would not be able to transcend itself to ascend towards objective reality. That is the enduring truth at the heart of Kant's emphasis on the active role of the mind in the passage from sense experience to knowledge.

Galileo, and many thinkers before and after him, have thought that there is a language of nature – namely mathematics – in which a truly transparent, undistorting knower would think the world to himself. The native tongue of nature, or of Being, is quantitative and it is composed of geometrical figures, numbers, matrices, and the like. I have elsewhere criticized this notion at length.[19] Suffice to note, for the present, that a purely mathematical portrait of what-is lacks most of its characteristics: phenomenal appearance and temporality for a start. What is more, mathematics itself is an historical accumulation of procedures, methods, results, etc., and it is difficult to imagine nature speaking in this cacophony of tongues.[20] The assumption that there is a point of convergence of all mathematical activity in an ideal *mathesis* is just that: an assumption.

But there is a more fundamental point. Even if nature spoke in a mathematical *Esperanto* that combined (say) all the dialects of arithmetic, algebra and geometry, it would not say anything unless there were a subject facing and making (partial) sense of it. The subject as the point at which the world is sensed, known, and made intelligible, remains indispensable. Nagel's suggestion that "reality probably extends beyond what we can conceive of"[21] seems to misconceive reality, overlooking that it takes two to tango. This alone is sufficient to justify Nagel's fundamental point that "reality is not just objective reality".[22] There is an inescapable sticky reality in the fear experienced when facing a bully, a predator, a threat to one's life and limb. There is an equally inescapable reality in the shame of an individual caught lying, betraying another, or transgressing in some other way. The reality of the justified, or even unjustified, contempt of others, of being stigmatized or discredited, is reflected in the sense that it is out there, inescapable. Such existential realities may be ultimately connected to basic laws of nature via the customs and cultures that have been established to protect the collective from unfiltered exposure to the threats that are inherent in the fragility of the living organism. The connection, however, is established by a long and winding route that places lived reality at a great distance from the properties of objects as they are described by natural science. There is an unignorable sense according to which "reality" is that which has to be taken account of when we are achieving our ends, meeting our needs, fulfilling our duties. It is co-produced by the subject and that which it encounters.

This may seem to be both obvious and misconceived. It is obvious that knowledge requires a subject, so how could this be overlooked? Possibly for this reason: knowledge and understanding can seem to exist "uncurated" by conscious subjects. Because they can lie dormant in documents, between their moments of being consulted, these things seem to be able to continue as knowledge existing independent of conscious beings. But the contents of a sheet of paper or a computer screen are, until they are being read, only potential knowledge: it is a mistake to ascribe the status of knowledge to ink marks or symbols on a screen. It is the same mistake that authorizes expanding the idea – discussed in Chapter 4 – of information until it encompasses items such as fossils and clouds that might be informative to a conscious being able to interpret them.[23] However, the focus on existential realities in affirming the inescapable need to the subject may seem to be misconceived. Surely these are what we should or must or at least try to escape when we pursue truth in the (relatively) disinterested way of science. It is certainly true that the field equations of general relativity, for all that they are indissolubly associated with Einstein, are not mired in the kind of things I have spoken of. They – and indeed more homely pieces of knowledge such as ordinary facts about the time of the Battle of Hastings and the location of Adelaide – do not have subjects, not at least in the way that pains and worries do. They are not dependent on the accidents of the position, culture, and make-up of any individual. The thought "The Battle of Hastings took place in 1066" has a core that is not affected by whether the person who says it is short of breath or not, angry or happy, old or young, in the dark or in the light, and so on. Even so, the knowledge of the knowing subject is to some extent *self-based cognition.* While it is general knowledge, that is available to all, it still has to be realized or tokenized in individual persons, at a particular time in their lives. The field equations may exist in their uncontaminated purity in the text book but as soon as they are incorporated into the life of someone who can understand them, they are like corks bobbing in the sea of his or her preoccupations.[24] The continuation of that life is dependent on the marshy reality of the biology of a largely mindless body – its organs keep themselves to themselves without consulting the person whose daily existence they service. The body – a bag of blood, bone and gristle, hosting urine, faeces and the like – is experienced by its subject in a way that is remote from anything corresponding to the experience of objective biological knowledge.[25]

There is no "what it is like" to have an item of objective knowledge. There is nothing – or nothing relevant – corresponding to "the experience of knowing that the Battle of Hastings took place in 1066". Any associated experience is accidental, a contaminant. A feeling of pride at possessing such knowledge, an image of a falling soldier, a particular light ascribed to the date are not part of the fact that the battle took place on a certain date. Unlike the subject of experience, the subject of knowledge – while owing its cognitive capacity to her body – is essentially disembodied.

We shall return to this in Chapter 8 but a final thought from Philo of Alexandria might be in order, to help us focus on the mystery of the knowing subject who is inseparable from a body that has many functions that do not rank very highly in the cognitive realm: "Now, when we are alive, we are so though our soul is dead and buried in our body as though in a tomb. But if it were to die, then our soul would live according to its proper life being released from the evil and dead body to which it is bound."[26] He is, of course, repeating the view that has echoed down the ages, especially since Plato – Parmenides' footnote – declared the body to be a serious obstacle to knowledge and truth.[27]

We have argued against a too simplistically negative account of the necessary embodiment of the knowing subject. The ascent to pure, untethered, knowledge is a loss as well as a gain; for knowledge truly to count has to be felt on the pulse as well as in the mind. We should be cautious therefore when assessing the putative constraints that the necessary residual subjectivity of the knowing subject applies to the scope and validity of knowledge. One such reason is well expressed by Nagel, where he argues that it is a mistake: "to assume that if any conception has a possessor, it must be about the possessor's point of view – a slide from subjective form to subjective content".[28] The version of this slide we are concerned about is from the (material, biological) conditions under which the conception is formed to the content of the conception. If they were identical, then by the same token, what we would see would not only be *permitted* by neural activity. It would be neural activity, mysteriously seeing itself or, more precisely, seeing itself as a view identical with that which caused it – a position whose problem we have already discussed in Chapter 4.

As knowing subjects, we are in part engaged in building a picture of the sea in which we are at least partly dissolved; or of the forest in which we are a tree – or, less, a leaf. The process is made possible because there is a party other than I, the body of the I, and the outside-of-the-body: namely, the "we". But "we" does not swallow up the "I". Because of the unique trajectory and history of our bodies, we are not liberated from being windowless monads merely to be dissolved in the solvent of our togetherness. While we are intimately woven into the collective world, we are at the same time offset from, and able to think and act independently of, it.[29]

We may conclude that, if subjectivity is a prison, the subject spends its entire sentence on parole. Indeed, it is essential to the very idea of a subject that it is aware of, or knows, that which it is not; that it is aware of objects. It is conscious "of" such and such (including itself as a body and conscious experiences including thoughts); of being surrounded by that which it is not. The subject's egocentric presupposition that "the world is around me" – that I am the centre of what is, that what is happening is happening to me (because it has in some way to happen to me for me to know it) – is redeemed by the knowledge that what is around me is a) not-me; b) largely indifferent to me; c) situated in a boundless extent of not-me, and d) has innumerable other centres. That is why a human world-picture is not a mere organism's *umwelt*.

It is time now to reflect more closely on the subject's breaking out of itself; to consider "thatter" and knowledge – which straddles the subjective and the objective – in virtue of which Being and beings acquire inverted commas and their existence becomes *that which is the case*; on the subject facing, rather than being merely wired into, the world. This is the theme of the next chapter.

Addendum
Subjects without bodies

In recent years, there have been increasingly vociferous claims that it will soon be possible to create or replicate selves that are not attached to the messy, unreliable, and cognitively curdled stuff of the human body. This is a central plank of the "transhumanist" movement that is driven by the fantasy of achieving eternal life.[30]

The fantasy is built on the presupposition that individual consciousness, the self, consists purely of information. While this information is currently confined to the wetware of the nervous system, it can be liberated from the brain, and freed from the death sentence that hangs over all living organisms, in one of two ways. The first involves a 3-D scanner that identifies the way the brain is connected and its typical firing patterns. These can then be translated into computer code and the latter then uploaded on to appropriate hardware where it can be stored forever and replicated indefinitely. The second exploits supercomputers that are powerful enough to emulate human consciousness. Again, the active software can be stored and replicated indefinitely. Both are ways of realizing the idea of "Substrate-Independent Minds". Such entities will be able "to sustain person-specific functions of mind and experience in many different operational substrates besides the biological brain". This is a process "analogous to that by which platform independent code can be compiled and run on many different computing platforms".[31]

This is, of course, nonsense. The notion of "Substrate-Independent Minds" is based on several unfounded assumptions:

a) A human consciousness can lose the body (with its history) that gives it its location and its agenda without being fundamentally altered and indeed retaining its identity.

b) It is possible to identify and extract the essence of the neural activity that reflects the temporally extended individual self of the character who is to be stored.

c) The self or consciousness in question can be stored in a latent or sleeping form in a holding medium. This is an expression of the dubious but very popular idea that there can be information without consciousness. In reality, for information to *be* it has to be in the process of informing something that is not (other) information – a conscious, sentient being.

In addition:

d) It narrows consciousness from a self-concerned openness-to-a-world to a mass of computerizable data. But sunbathing is not information-bathing. Even less is world-bathing, or being actively world-situated, merely a matter of being a conduit for, or a store of, information.

e) It assumes that a string of 0s and 1s – what computerized scanners would extract from brains – would somehow wake themselves up and interpret and organize themselves: they would "come to" – to themselves and to a world.[32]

Such nonsense is an unsurprising consequence of the belief that a conscious subject can be identified with a subset of physical events in the brain that, of themselves, amount to data – that is to say, revealing facts located in a world which surrounds them. Nevertheless, it has licensed fantasies of humanity being "uploaded" and "colonising space": "[W]hat we now think of humanity would be the nucleus … of some greatly more vast and brilliant phenomenon that would spread across the universe and convert a lot of matter and energy into organized form, into life in a generalized sense".[33]

Jonathan Swift, thou should'st be living now! It is difficult to resist the comparison with the Academy of Lagado to which Gulliver travels. There he finds characters trying to extract the sunbeams from cucumbers (cf. minds from brains) and to educate students by feeding them propositions written in "cephalic tincture". This seems not too distant from the claim by Zoltan Istvan that in a decade or two "it would be possible to upload the informational content of a Harvard or Yale degree directly to [his children's] brains",[34] so there would be no point in saving for their education. The entire Chapter V of *Gulliver's Travels* is an extraordinary anticipation of the fantasies of Silicon Valley billionaires.

CHAPTER 6

Thatter: knowledge

[Martin Heidegger] had regained for philosophy "a thinking
that expresses gratitude that the 'naked that' had been given at
all"   Hannah Arendt[1]

Knowledge is central to our inquiry into the sense-making animal. Our
approach has not followed the path of traditional epistemology that addresses
questions about the sources and limitation of our knowledge and the criteria
for demarcating knowledge from mere belief. Our primary concern has been
with making knowledge *visible*. This has required, above all, highlighting the
profound difference between sentience, "raw" sense experience that we may
share with many other species, and the kind of sense-making that is mediated
by, or delivers, knowledge. The difference is not just of degree but of kind. The
feeling of warmth is not to be conflated with the knowledge *that* it is warm,
knowledge that will ultimately lead towards the kind of judgement that it is
5°C hotter than it was yesterday. At the heart of the difference is explicitness,
reflected in the word "that" as in "*that* x is the case". Hence the "thatter" of
the title of this chapter. Denying the fundamental nature of this difference –
and squeezing out thatter – lies at the root of a scientism which overlooks or
minimizes the radical break between humanity and animality and (ultimately)
between humanity and the material world. It overlooks the essential character
of the sense-making creatures that we are.

The view of Ernst Mach, one of Quine's most illustrious predecessors as a
naturalizer of knowledge, summarized by Leszek Kołakowski, expresses this
with exemplary clarity: "there is no difference between ordinary experience

accessible to any being endowed with a nervous system and scientifically organized experiment. There is no break in continuity between science … and modes of behaviour characteristic of the entire animal world."[2] Or, to quote Mach himself:

> Scientific thought arises out of popular thought, and so completes the continuous series of biological developments that begins with the first simple manifestations of life … Indeed, the formation of scientific hypotheses is merely a further degree of development of instinctive and primitive thought, and all the transitions between them can be demonstrated.[3]

Mach's "primitive thought", however, is not thought at all but mere sentience, which is "accessible to any being endowed with a nervous system". Consistent with this extreme naturalism is Mach's view that conditioned reflexes were "rudimentary concepts".

This has been hugely influential in psychology where the phenomenon of "stimulus generalization" (discussed in Chapter 4) has been seen to be a behavioural proxy for, or expression of, general terms and the ordering of the contents of the world under concepts, allocating them to general classes. Supposing I have been conditioned to be frightened of a certain kind of spider, this fear may generalize to all spiders, to toy spiders and even pictures of spiders. On this basis, so we are assured, we have the first step in the process of abstracting classes from clusters of objects or events that bear salient similarities. We pass seamlessly, so the story goes, from an organism's perceptual systems that automatically allocate stimuli to classes defined by a common, appropriate mode of response, and then proceed without interruption to the laws that represent the most general characteristics of the material world.

The main reason for resisting this story is that passivity of stimulus generalization is profoundly different from the activity of allocating items to classes, questioning their classification, and re-classifying them. We touched on this in the previous chapter when we glanced at the contrast between mere gawping and systematic observation. It highlights a fundamental difference between automated responses to stimuli and the kind of active, interrogative sense-making (that may or may not lead to immediate or delayed behaviour in response) we have already discussed. The most striking manifestation of this difference is measurement, a mode of scrutiny that has little in common with the differential response of organisms triggered by sense organs. Measurement is the paradigm expression of our inhabiting a world of knowledge (and its sense of bounding ignorance), of certainty (and doubt), and truth (and false-hood – since truth and its opposite co-emerge). It is the realm of "thatter" that occupies a widening distance between sentience or sensation (that may be wired into reflex or programmed responses) and knowledge.

We can best approach the task of elucidating what is distinctive about knowledge, and what goes into "thatter" by considering a cluster of terms: explicitness, propositions, facts and truth. But first we should begin with their common root: intentionality out of which blossoms an entire world, the common world of shared intelligence, mediated by signs, artefacts, insti-tutions and history. It is in this world that sense-making grows in a soil of referents, carved out of what is actually or potentially present, by communal awareness forged out of the trillions of bridges of joined attention that is the cognitive history of humanity.

Intentionality lies at the root of the distance that is implicit in knowledge and in the many modes of separation of the knower and the known. Sentience, at its most basic level, is not about anything other than itself. A primordial sen-sation, such as a tingle or a pain or an itch, or a feeling of warmth, is not "about" anything. Or, rather, it is what it is and any "aboutness" it has is ascribed to it from without – as when I ascribe my itch to an insect bite.

Aboutness is not reciprocated in the way that the pushes and pulls of the mechanics of the material world reciprocated. Most of the things I see do not see me: my visual field does not look back at me in turn. And this is true even at a rather humbler level. As I sit on a seat, there is reciprocity at the mechan-ical level. The downward pressure through my bottom is met by an upward pressure through the chair. But my sense of comfort at sitting in the chair is not complemented by a chair's feeling oppressed by my sitting on it. The chair I am aware of is not aware of me (I think this may have been a point made by Bertrand Russell).

Let us now consider the distance opened up by intentionality, by "awareness of". It is most evident in *telereceptors* that sense what is "out" or "over" there. The dominant telereceptor is vision, which has a continuous field in which contents are arrayed for a subject who is situated at its point of origin; has internal and external limits defined by what is visibly invisible; and it senses items that are explicitly more than it sees.[4] We may think of vision as being on the threshold of the transition from sentience to knowledge. That which is perceived is explicitly separate from the perceiving subject. This fact that has two aspects. The first is the (visible) distance between the body of the perceiver and the object that is perceived. This presupposes that the perceiver who sees the object "over there" or "near to me" is self-aware to the point of identifying herself with her body as an item located in space. Such a mode of bodily awareness may be fully developed only in human beings.[5] It is connected with a second aspect of human vision: the explicit distinction between the object of perception and the experience in virtue of which the object is perceived. This licenses the intuition that the object has other appearances available to different perspectives, to other knowers, and to different kinds of inspection (that may, for example, reveal its interior or its material properties). This mode of distance built into perception lies at the roots of the more complex difference between seeing as an animal sees and what Fred Dretske has called "epistemic seeing"; between a cat seeing a bird in the garden and a human seeing *that* there is a bird in the garden.[6] Likewise, the cat may see the bird in my garden but not that the garden in which the bird is located is someone's garden. Animal seeing does not entrain perceptions in a network of (quasi-logical) entailments.

Seeing is the most "epistemic" of all our senses, a fact that must lie behind the presence of light at the earliest moment of creation in various religious myths – as discussed in Chapter 2. "Let there be light!" is "Let there be *that!*", the co-creation of Stuff and Sense, both populating the void and revealing its contents in a single, beneficent sense-and-stuff-making act. The epistemic character of ordinary seeing is underlined by the contrast between pure reception of light – as when one is dazzled – and the experience of light as revelatory of a visual scene.

The journey from epistemic senses onwards can be traced in many ways, none of which fully captures the distance between sentience and knowledge. It is sufficient for our present purposes to follow one track to make the point and re-visit something we have discussed already. The epistemic object of vision is a) enduring and b) public. These are the outer aspects of its being ascribed intrinsic properties independent of any individual's experience of it. Indeed, it *exists* independently of any particular person's perceiving it: me, you, or anyone at all. It transcends actual experience.

We have scarcely left ground floor sense experience and we already have arrived at mystery and controversy. For David Hume, objects are collections of sensible qualities but the idea that these sensible qualities – which entitle the object to be called a thing – are underpinned by an underlying substance is "a fiction". Our belief that sensible objects continue to exist when nobody perceives them is also a fiction, he claims, although a natural and necessary one.[7] Subsequent glosses on this view – by J. S. Mill that the material of objects is "the permanent possibility of sensation", by certain analytic philosophers that objects are "logical constructions" out of sense experiences, and that for Quine objects are "posits" – only serve to underline the gap between sentience and the ground floor of knowledge, namely knowledge of material objects.

Vision points to the invisible, to that which lies beyond the horizon-bounded space in which it locates objects, visibly separate and connected, beyond the actual into the realm of the possible. When I see an object, it is in the same space as me. When, on the other hand, I suspect the existence of an object outside of my visual field it is not spatially related to me, although I may have a rough idea of its position; and it is on the border between that which is the case and that which may be the case. The penumbra around the perceptual field is the antechamber of another kind of outside: explicit, articulated possibility.

The perceptual field is riddled with, and bounded by, possibility. The characteristics of possibility are central to the nature of knowledge and what distinguishes it from sentience. That possibilities are not located in space and time in the way that tables, chairs, and my body are, follows from their necessary generality. The loose association with places and times that some possibilities have does not contradict this. For example, I may hear a rustling in a thicket and postulate the possibility of a bird with a certain location. The possibility does not, however, share the boundaries of any actual bird that may materialize. After all, the rustling may turn out to be due to the wind. This highlights two key aspects of possibilities; namely that a) they may or may not be realized; and b) they are at some level general. The two aspects are of course connected: a generality falls short of existence which (Platonism and other magic thinking aside) is confined to particulars. My explicit diagnosis of the rustling – based on memory "that" – highlights the different kind of space opened up by knowledge. The articulation of explicit possibility locates it in that different kind of space, as opposed merely (as in the case of animal expectation) to assimilating it to the flow of experience.

Enter at this point the idea of truth – and, of course, its inseparable other, falsehood. Truth, as the saying goes, "supervenes on Being" but something has to make Being true, and beings truth-makers. Evidently, Being cannot supervene on itself, be true in itself, or true of itself: something additional is required to make it be "of" itself. Upper-case Being has to be tasted by a lower-case being, by a conscious subject. Not all consciousness, however, can deliver what we might call full-blown truth. Mere sentience, as has often been pointed out, is incorrigible. This is not because it is infallibly true but because it is below the level at which issues of truth and falsehood arise: it cannot even be wrong because it does not make judgements. It would be inappropriate to speak of an itch as "true" not because it is untrue but because it is neither true nor false. Only when it is remembered as something that happened at a certain time, or interpreted as having a specific cause, does the question of truth or falsehood arise. Itching, unlike the assertion that I had an itch on a certain day, is not a matter of knowledge or a matter for testimony. More generally, I am not (for example) extraordinarily knowledgeable for having a continuous flow of bodily sensations, any more than chronic colicky pains make me an expert on the intestines. Sensations do not supply the "of" that enables Being to be (true) of itself. "Being + sentience" is not sufficient to generate items to which it is appropriate or possible to assign truth values.

Truth is deeply connected with communication, with testimony. It is applicable to something that is actually or potentially articulated (including to one's self – although such private truths, if they are to count as truths, are secondary to public ones) and hence actually or potentially shared. To be shared, it must be articulated, and to be articulated, it must be generalized. My itch may be shared through being registered as an instance of a general type, thus losing its uniqueness, and giving up its location in space and time. Itch *qua* referent is not located on my (or indeed anyone else's) body. Speaking of my itch obviously does not spread it from my body to the bodies of those to whom I disclose it. The itch can of course be reconnected with a spatiotemporal location by means of further articulation, as when I speak of "the itch on my forearm that I had yesterday". The location is not, of course identical with that of the original itch: "my forearm" as a concept is not the same as the forearm attached to my body, any more than "yesterday" is identical with time t_1 at which something happened. The itch, however, can now in a virtual sense outlast itself by being available to be referred to indefinitely, located outside of space and time. "That itch I had yesterday" is an itch with a (virtual) posthumous existence, outliving the scratch that extinguished it. I may speak truthfully about an itch I claim to have had yesterday but no itch could in and of itself be "true" any more than it could be a lie.

We are touring the foothills of knowledge: objects beyond experience; possibilities beyond actuality; an outside of discourse beyond space and time; and the beginning of the realm of truths and falsehoods that supervene on Being. We have entered the space of propositional awareness; of what-is elevated to "that-which-is" or "that which is the case": the realm of "thatter". It is here that we find all three elements of the standard, if problematic, definition of knowledge: true, justified belief. Truth, justification, and belief all belong to the same space, that has much in common with what Sellars (to whom we shall return) called the Space of Reason, which is fundamentally different from the space of mere sensation.

More broadly, "thatter" accommodates, and indeed is woven out of, instances of "what is the case" heralded by a sense, a thought, or an out-loud or written down assertion, of what might be the case, at present, in the past, or in the future. This is the space in which we are deployed in our everyday practical engagement with each other and the material world, where possibilities are ceaselessly articulated. From the slightly topsy-turvy standpoint of this space, actuality seems like the fulfilment of prior possibilities, possibilities that have already been entertained. We do not, however, leave behind the space of sentience or the space and time occupied by our bodies. When I shake hands with you, this greeting has its meaning in the "thaterial" world of symbolic meaning, but it must be executed by flesh occupying the physical world: our hands have to clasp each other.

It is important not to rush the journey from sentience to knowledge and arrive too early at articulate discourse and the higher-level world-pictures that have prompted our inquiry. Before we reach the kinds of sentences that are exchanged in chatter and more measured communication, in gossip and science, we should pause at those propositional attitudes that make up the sea of "thatness" out of which specific propositions crystallize. Man is the believing, fearing, desiring, regretting, doubting, wondering, supposing as well as asserting, thinking, affirming and denying animal. While in some cases (for example "wondering") "that" may be replaced by "wondering if" or "wondering whether", the latter really incorporate an implicit "that". Even idle wondering is haunted by the ghost of an assertion corresponding to a seriously entertained possibility.

There is a distance between (say) wondering and its articulation as something that carries a full-blown truth value just as there is a distance between an anxiety and what we say to someone to whom we are looking for comfort. Even so, there is a free-floating "that" implicitly present in both the wondering and the nail-biting. Our circumscribed propositional attitudes are a half-way house between on the one hand a general "propositional awareness" that characterizes unfolding human consciousness and on the other formal propositions which assert or deny *that* "X is the case". Propositional awareness is the bridge between Being and things that are asserted or denied to *be the case*. It is that in virtue of which truth supervenes on Being. While any sentient being may suffer on account of what is there, only for the propositional (human) animal is what-is transformed into "That x is" and "That not-x is not".

This paragraph may seem to do no work but it is intended to emphasize the distance, often overlooked or compressed, between sentience and knowledge whose most developed form is propositions corresponding to facts. I have not attempted to explain the basis of this transition, even less to explain why man is uniquely "The Knowing Animal".[8] Our present concern is not with genetic epistemology but with highlighting the two-stage journey to "that" if we adopt sentience as a starting point: first, the passage from sensation to the experience of objects that are intuited as existing independently of experience; and secondly, the transition from an intuition of a world of free-standing objects to an epistemic realm of "that".

The latter realm is so prominent in our lives that there is a temptation to assert that it gathers up all that there is. Take this passage from Wittgenstein's *Tractatus Logico-Philosophicus*: "To give the essence of a proposition means to give the essence of all description, and thus the essence of the world".[9] It is as if the world were entirely dissolved into "that", such that "matter" had been superseded by "thatter". This assertion is of a piece with the famous oracular opening of the *Tractatus*:

1 The world is all that is the case.
1.1 The world is the totality of facts, not of things.
[...]
1.13 The facts in logical space are the world.[10]

This is probably not as linguistically idealistic, or at least language-bound, as it may seem. First, Wittgenstein may mean the *human* world rather than (say) the universe of which the human world is a minute and brief part. Secondly – although this is not Wittgenstein's point – it has to be acknowledged that within the human world there are no naked or pure objects. We see objects through the lens of knowledge: we cannot separate sentience from intelligibility; there is no return to the innocence of sensation. Tables, chairs, even trees, rocks and clouds, come to us saturated with meaning: they are not inscrutable lumps of matter. Even useless objects engage our attention as items which intervene between us and our goals or as the background to our goal-oriented activity. And all objects have a potential significance, even naturally occurring ones: trees as possible cover, clouds as the threat of rain, rocks as potential missiles. Even nonsense has a privative sense as a bounded interruption in sense. General meaning is thus wall-to-wall, which may seem to license the notion that Being dissolves entirely into thatter – although this (to reiterate) was not Wittgenstein's position.

There are, however, dangers in gathering up all that there is in "thatter". The obvious objection comes from the self-evident point that "That x is the case" presupposes x, even though the x may not be self-bounding. The dangers are often concealed when "thatter" is identified not with "knowledge" in the broadest and richest sense but with "information" a term so hospitable as to be able to encompass every event in the universe. We have already mentioned, and will return to, John Wheeler's "IT from BIT". For the present, I shall focus on something a bit more mainstream: the view that "All is Information". It is exemplified in this passage from David Chalmers:

> [W]herever there is causal interaction, there is information, and where there is information, there is experience. One can find information states in a rock – even when it expands and contracts, for example – or even in the different states of the electron. So there will be experience associated with a rock or an electron.[11]

This extraordinary claim not only assimilates material events in the material world to conscious experiences but also (more relevant to our present concerns) collapses the distance between experience and knowledge – given that "information" is a large part of what knowledge knows – as well as between consciousness and the material world. It is a version of a panpsychism that (to use Chalmers's words) "makes consciousness less 'special' in some ways, and so more reasonable" because it is "better integrated into the natural order".[12] The obverse of assimilating matter to information is to assimilate thatter to matter. We have a universe that is not only self-intimating at every level but identical with its own self-intimation.

It is a view that pops up in all sorts of surprising places. The determinedly tough-minded, materialist philosopher D. M. Armstrong makes the, perhaps uncontroversial claim, that the world "is a world of states of affairs". More controversially he concludes from this that "it is not made up of things, but of *things-having-properties* and *things-related-to-other things*".[13] He concludes from this that "Reality has a propositional structure".[14] The idea that Reality (with a capital initial letter, so it must be the real thing) is propositional suggests that it constitutively has the form of a proposition. Just how odd this is can be highlighted if we remind ourselves that a proposition is what is expressed by a sentence – or the information content of a sentence. Such information has a structure somehow connected with that of a sentence. We can, it appears, cut out the middle man; namely humanity that divides it up through looking at what-is through a propositional lens. The path to such a strange conclusion – a rather literalistic form of the logical atomism espoused by Russell and Wittgenstein – is easy to see. Armstrong seems to ascribe to the basic stuff of Reality a proto-propositional form. His "*things-having-properties*" and *"things-related-to-other things"* look suspiciously oven-ready to be turned into the kinds of subjects and predicates, or relations between objects, that are in fact only picked out by articulate judgement.

To avoid this result it is necessary only to restate the obvious and to resist identifying the realm of knowledge either with the basic stuff of the world in which humans live (although only humans are knowing animals) or even with nature. We affirm the existence of two distinct realms. The temptation is to label these two realms that of knowledge and that of the known but that carries dangers because there is a sense in which that which is known is to some degree a cognate – but real – object of knowledge. This relationship is rather like that of the recto and verso of a sheet of paper but only in the sense that they are cut out at once: "the fact that x" is scissored out by the sentence that specifies it. This is clear in the case of knowledge of abstract objects such as (say) economic trends, social attitudes, or items that are badged with "-ness" and "-hood". But it is true wherever items are brought together in a state of affairs expressed in a sentence – such as "The chairs were arranged untidily". And indeed, it applies in the case of a single item whose qualities are identified and attached to it as predicates to a subject: something as elementary as "The chair is green" – never mind "The chair is old" where the predicate cannot be contained in any moment-to-moment state of the object.

In short, the natural world does not serve itself up in fact-shaped or fact-sized pieces nor does it have a propositional structure. Consequently, pieces of knowledge could not result simply from the impingement of bits of nature on the sensorium of an organism. Richard Robinson's claim: "States resulting from events are very common in nature; and knowledge is one of them. Knowledge results from apprehension as the blackened and roofless state of a house results from a fire"[15] could not be further from the truth.

It is an appropriate time to examine a particularly striking way of characterizing the distinctive realm of knowledge associated with the twentieth-century American philosopher Wilfrid Sellars, in his famous attack on "The Myth of the Given", a myth that we have already touched upon in a different way in our critique of the notion that there is something called "reality" which corresponds to the self-intimation of Being and the related idea that there is a capacity of (material) Being in virtue of which it would generate the truth about itself without the assistance of a consciousness or a community of minds interacting with it. The myth we are addressing could be characterized as "the myth of the *self*-given".

Sellars's argument was directed against foundationalism – the idea that all our knowledge rests on cognitive states that are basic in the sense of not depending on other cognitive states for their truth:

One of the forms taken by the Myth of the Given is the idea that there is, indeed *must* be, a structure of particular matters of fact such that (a) each fact can not only be noninferentially known to be the case, but presuppose no other knowledge either of particular matter of fact, or of general truths; and (b) ... the noninferential knowledge of facts belonging to this structure constitutes the ultimate court of appeal for all factual claims – particular and general – about the world.[16]

The elements in the "ultimate court of appeal" for factual claims would typically be the offspring of direct experience of, or acquaintance with, their object. Such "foundational" knowledge would presuppose no other knowledge. In the analytical tradition which Sellars was rejecting, they would be characterized as "sense data" or (direct) knowledge of appearances. Against this atomism, Sellars argues that knowledge is all of a piece; or at very least connected with other pieces of knowledge: it is this that justifies their counting as full-fledged cognitive states. Acquiring knowledge noninferentially would involve the exercise of conceptual capacities just as much as does higher-level or more explicitly inferential knowledge and such capacities are based on prior knowledge.

Knowledge cannot, therefore, be acquired incrementally or atomically from discrete encounters with the world through sense experiences. It belongs to what he called the logical space of reasons: "In characterizing an episode or a state as that of *knowing*, we are not giving an empirical description of that episode or state; we are placing it in the logical space of reason, of justifying and being able to justify what one says".[17] In short, knowledge acquires its immediate warrant through a side-ways connectedness with other pieces of knowledge rather than via a ground floor vertical connectedness between a piece of knowledge and the personal sensory experience that both generates and justifies it. This is most clearly evident in the case of scientific knowledge in which, as Quine, (whom we have already quoted) states "face the tribunal of sense experience as a corporate body" even though he envisaged knowledge, and its validity, being tracked ultimately to the impingement of energy on nerve endings.[18]

Knowledge, even when it takes the apparent form of discrete facts, is both networked and constrained in the way that Sellars described – as did many twentieth-century, particularly American, philosophers after him, notably Donald Davidson. The veto forbidding "p and not-p" is usually exercised in a less formal demand of consistency and coherence. If I was in Paris at 12 noon on Tuesday, I can't have been in London at 12 noon; nor could I have been in

London at 12:05; nor could I have directly witnessed two people walking down a street in London at 12 noon, but I could have seen two people walking down the street outside my hotel in Paris. These constraints may seem like a direct transcription from the physical world to the logical space of reasons. However, the physical connectedness of my being in a specific hotel in Paris and my seeing two people walking down the street is not like the connectedness of (the fact) that I was in Paris and (the fact) that I saw the two people in the relevant street. In neither case are the facts located side by side or connected through such a location. The facts about what occupied what space and at what time do not themselves occupy a particular space and a particular time. This may be clarified by another example. The Battle of Hastings took place just north of Hastings and began at 9 am on 14 October 1066 and ended at dusk of the same day. *The fact that* the Battle occurred did not end at dusk on 14 October nor is that fact located just north of Hastings. As a denizen of logical space, as something for which there is empirical justification, evidential proof, as an item that rules out other possibilities, it has no location in space or time.

We now come to Sellars's essential point. Theories are connected by implication with what Quine calls their "checkpoints" in observation. Nothing in nature, however, *implies* anything else: implication arises in the space of inferences. At the heart of the space of reasons is the possibility of conflicts utterly unlike the collisions and constraints of the natural world. The most straightforward expression is the veto on "p and not-p". In the logical space of reasons, two items cannot occupy the same point at the same time: the cat cannot be (p) and not be (not-p) in a specific state or place at time t. This mutual exclusion of two possibilities may seem to map on to the kinds of mutual exclusion seen in physical space-time but the latter applies to material actualities and not possibilities. "Not (p and not-p)" does not describe a forbidden collision.

Beyond this, there is indirect justification arising from more complex trails of consistency, from networks of connected beliefs, or from appeal to the habits of the material world expressed in the laws of nature given propositional form. This space is a space of quarrels unlike those known to nature where, for example, two objects exclude each other from the same space, or consequences such that one event has a causal consequence. There is no "if-then" in the material world; it is no more populated by protases and apodoses than by narratives.

The boundary between the space of reasons and the space of nature may seem semi-permeable, as when we see quasi-necessary connections between events, or types of material events, that are regularly associated or whose fidelity of association is discovered to be the manifestation of a general, if in the last analysis contingent, law, a more fundamental habit of nature. The essential point is upheld however: that knowledge is something that can be, and indeed should be, *justified* – typically as a result of being compatible with other knowledge. In short, knowledge is a *normative* term. Individual experiences would not deliver cognitive norms.

One does not have to agree with Sellars that the conceptual capacities that underlie knowledge rely on language to accept his point that knowledge is not something given in, or built up directly out of, sensory experiences and served up in discrete, independent atoms that do not presuppose other knowledge. "The Myth of the Given" – of an uncontaminated epistemological ground floor – is a reminder of just how derivative is even knowledge based on seemingly basic observations. There are, for instance, reliability conditions that justify an observation counting as knowledge; for example, the "good light" in which we can safely judge that something is of such-and-such a colour. What counts as "good condition" is also knowledge. And there are, of course, no intrinsic scales of observation in what-is that pick out its contents.

The identification of the realm of knowledge, of thatter, with a space of logical reasons would confine it too much. There is the narrow point that knowledge is necessary to serve unreason as well as reason: without knowledge or suspicion based on the exercise of the epistemic faculty, irrationality could not get off the ground.[19] And there is a wider point that knowledge nourishes many kinds of propositional attitudes – wondering, disbelieving, daydreaming, hoping and so on – as well as straight knowing and the action of making assertions. Even so, Sellars captures something very important which it is worth dwelling on before we dig a little further.

The "Myth of the Given" that Sellars criticizes is rooted in a deeper myth that we have already alluded to: the "Myth of the Self-Given". We may characterize it as the notion that the material world is somehow self-intimating – so that what is real for us is Being-in-itself. We addressed this in the previous chapter. Even further fetched is the idea that givenness – "that" – naturally divides into the referents of propositions that we simply harvest or hoover up with our senses. This is reflected in those assertions of Wittgenstein that we have already quoted: "1.1 The world is the totality of facts, not of things ... 1.13 The facts in logical space are the world. 1.2 The world divides into facts." To the contrary, the world – or at least the natural world – is neither a totality of facts, nor facts set out in a (presumably single or continuous or unified) logical space because it is not of itself divided into facts. More specifically, not even thatter is broken up in this way: it is not a bag of frozen ps – bounded perhaps by a bigger (even boundless) bag of not-ps[20] (indeed, not-ps are parasitic on ps; there is, by definition, nothing corresponding to them). When we awaken to a truth – or The Truth – this is more than the switching on of a nexus of propositions inherent in the natural world.

Even so, it is easy to see why we may be seduced into reading propositions or a propositional structure back into the world we express through them. Yes, "knowledge ... is essentially expressible in propositions" as Strawson said – or some knowledge anyway.[21] Yes, we sometimes have p-shaped thoughts; more often make p-shaped assertions; and even more frequently encounter p-shaped written discourse. Because what is committed to print is most public – most conspicuously what we have in common and what we trade in as we engage with each other in trying to articulate our shared world – we tend to think of it as being the essence of "thatter". In truth, however, it is simply the most visible expression of, the public face of, thatter.

The "Space of Reasons" therefore goes beyond the realm of propositions or indeed of knowledge or facts. As for the latter, it is important not to think that they fall neatly into two categories – those that belong to Nature and those that belong to a cultural, interhuman, space that is remote from nature. John Searle, mistakenly in my view, distinguished what he called "brute" physical facts from "social" and "institutional" ones with the former being natural.[22] In truth all facts are in some sense social or institutional. Nature does not carve itself into facts: it does not even pick out items such as "The dog is barking" or "The tree is green". If there is such a thing as brute reality, it is not composed of facts ("that"); facts belong to the thatter-sphere which is not part of brute reality; facts are not alongside trees, bird and stones.

We can therefore accept Sellars's fundamental point and acknowledge that what we know is not built out of cognitively basic elements hoovered up by our senses from the natural world. We must not, however, reduce "thatter" to facts or propositions, and facts and propositions in turn to those frozen entities that we encounter as *written* sentences – as opposed to dynamic and evaporating spoken ones. Yes, it would, of course, be difficult to over-estimate the role that writing has played, over a relatively short span of the history of humanity, in vastly expanding the empire of "thatter". And the written word is the meeting place of so many acts of sense-making. Even so, we must resist retro-fitting into propositional attitudes – thinking, believing, considering, even desiring or hoping – the formed propositions through which we communicate them in everyday conversation or (because we privilege this) formal, written discourse. Or read them back via propositional attitudes into the free-floating propositional awareness that constitutes our moment-to-moment consciousness.[23] The latter is in constant interchange with the pre-propositional realm of sentience, as items enter and leave focused attention, that characterizes so much of human consciousness. The most formalized discourses comes to represent propositional awareness and thus marginalize, even conceal, the less formal aspects of propositional attitudes. Logic – the general theory of propositions – does not embrace the ocean of explicitness that is "thatter". Individual propositions are simply the bubbles that arise out of the brew of expectation, recollection, intention, and so on.[24] The unfolding of natural and human worlds is not a working out of a valid argument passing from premises to a conclusion or an expression of logical necessity. The veto on two objects occupying the same place at the same time or one object occupying two remote places at the same time is not the same as that on two contrary propositions.[25]

The coherence of the material world, in other words, is not the same as the logical consistency demanded of accounts of the world, of reports on knowledge, if they are to be accepted as true. And this is a way back to our more fundamental point: "thatter" with the truth values that it upholds is not a spontaneous glow of self-givenness by Being, irrespective of whether the latter is characterized as "Isness", "Matter" or "Nature". Nature did not acquire its own name: "Nature" would not be part of nature, even if it could have a view on itself. X does not generate "There is an X" or "X"; rather, it is through the propositional awareness of humans that Being becomes the existence of entities eventually picked out by existential quantifiers.

A pebble, a tree, or a chair is neither true nor false, valid or invalid: it simply is. Truth or falsehood arises only in relation to knowledge claims when propositions are asserted about the chair, such that the latter becomes a truth-maker, a guarantor *that* something or other is the case. The chair is neither in agreement with itself or at odds with itself. Only when it is asserted of a chair that it is, for example, located in a particular place can it participate in truth-making; and only when two contrary assertions are made about it can it be the apparent site of a contradiction, although the contradiction lies not in the chair (wherever it is located) but in the realm of thatter where assertions are located. This is the obverse of the fact that only in the Space of Reasons is there something corresponding to justification of belief transmitted through entailment, or the undermining of belief transmitted through inferred contradiction.

For truth (and falsehood) to emerge there must be a relationship that goes beyond the empty relationship of identity captured by a peculiar sentence such as "x is x". Neither material objects nor pure sensations go beyond themselves and establish a true relationship of "aboutness". It is this relationship that holds open the distance that turns what-is into "what is the case", transforms x into "that x is" and makes a parallel reality in which the world is an object of knowledge (and of conjecture and of that which is shown not to be knowledge), what-is is affirmed as being a reality rather than a mere possibility, and finally, there are explicit constraints on what is permissible.

This is a world we *face* from a kind of outside, an epistemic outside that seems to be inside in virtue of being other than all outsides. It is what is given, in the *non*-mythical Given. It is worth briefly reflecting on this inside-outside. Its seemingly basic platform is the place where we began this chapter: the individual accessing what he or she experiences as "surroundings" from a viewpoint defined by the location of telereceptors, most notably vision. This is a reality indexed to "me", "here", "now", whose location is that of the existential centre of the body. But from the earliest days the reality is a shared one, temporally extended and not clearly delimited in space, and, created, curated, and elaborated by the community of minds into which we are inducted in the early years of our development.

The indexation of the world to our body and our present moment is therefore loose and discontinuous, with the immediate world being dappled by the deindexicalized reality of a world we access through knowledge. The most basic element of knowledge, even when applied to here and now and me, and accessed here and now by me, has no location in the literal space around, and the time of, my body, and belongs to everyone and no-one. Knowledge, unlike experience, is ownerless, is intrinsically something held in common.

Such is the thatter that we inherit and domesticate in our own world. It increasingly dominates our consciousness where pictures, words, texts, screens, speak to us from places not directly accessed by our senses. The facts are not in the paper they are written on and the truth is not in the filing cabinet where they are kept and only metaphorically in the mouths where they are recited. The archive is not located in the day or the century, the room or the country, of which it speaks.

The distance between knowledge and the world of direct encounter, between the space of thatter and the space of the material world, is underlined by the nature of the signs – words – in which knowledge is typically deposited. Words are utterly different from causal signs ("clouds mean rain", "footprints mean beasts") or iconic signs (reflections, pictures, shadows, echoes) in two fundamental respects: they do not typically occur naturally; and their signifying power does not depend on their having a natural connection with what they signify. Their phenomenal appearances – colour, size, shape, etc. – are irrelevant, like those of the results of measurement we discussed in the previous chapter. We look through or past the token sign. The word "blue" written in red does not mean anything different from "blue" written in blue or blue written (as it is on this page) in black. Likewise, "tomato" written in blue does not have a different meaning from "tomato" written in red or (indeed) black (it may have a slightly different significance).

The arbitrary or conventional nature of linguistic signs – and of the way they are combined according to grammatical rules – is the strongest possible reminder of the extent to which humans, inhabitants of the realm of "thatter" are not causally wired into the world or merely echoing it, but turned round to *face* it from an outside that is outside the outsides of the material world in which the material body and the objects that surround it are located.[26] The irrelevance of the phenomenal appearance of linguistic signs to what they mean, the discretion we have over how we use them, and the fact that they are mobilized actively to *mean* meaning, is a striking reminder (if one was needed) of the uncoupling of human consciousness from the natural or, more broadly, the material world. It exposes the error of causal theories of knowledge even when they dare not speak their name: "One does not have to adhere to a causal theory of knowledge to accept that trivial contingent truths cannot be known other than by the evidence to which they are causally connected".[27] The idea that "evidence" (in support of knowledge claims) can be the *effect* of the natural world is no less reductionist than that knowledge can be. It assimilates intentionality to causation. Wittgenstein noted this error when it was applied to emotions: "We should distinguish between the object of fear and the cause of a fear. Thus a face which inspires fear or delight (the object of fear or delight) is not on that account its cause but, one might say, its target."[28] And by the time we have got to testimony – as when I say "His face frightened me the other day" – the domination of targeting over causation is evident. And most of our knowledge comes from testimony. The causal relationship is relevant to your hearing the sounds of my testimony and (less straightforwardly) to the fear caused by the face but not to my meaning the factual information you derive from it.

This is no trivial point since the uncoupling evident in knowledge whose intentionality is (to simplify things) in the opposite direction to causation creates the possibility of free action – a story for another place.[29] What is more, the causal theory of knowledge is almost standard among philosophers. Let us stay with Quine whose view (as Barry Stroud summarizes it) is that: "Considered relative to the irritations at our sensory surfaces [the source of our knowledge], the physical objects we believe in are 'posits'; statements of their existence are 'far in excess of any available data', past, present and future."[30] This is, of course, at odds with a truly *causal* theory of knowledge, if "cause" is to be taken in its proper sense; namely, the way it is intended in the very natural science to which Quine looks for his naturalized epistemology.[31] For even at this seemingly most basic level of knowledge of material objects, Quine overlooks the usual expectation of the proportionality between cause and effect. It is hardly reflected in the relationship between objects and the "sensory irritations", especially given that objects are "posits".

Positing is an odd thing for an effect to do; positing its cause, even stranger; and positing a construct (an object) on its cause stranger still. This is not the kind of thing we are used to seeing in the material world, such as when lightning causes thunder. The thunder revealing, even illuminating, the lightning, hardly *posits* it.[32] The causal theory of knowledge tries to gather up beliefs, their truth and their justification, what is known with that in virtue of which it is known, into a single mechanism. My belief that there is a dog in the room is supposed to acquire its status as a piece of knowledge (at the very least both true and justified) from the impact of the dog in the room on my nervous system. The causal link generates the belief, its normative status as being justified, and its standing as a piece of truth, all from the same source – quite some achievement for the causal energy of material events.

Quine and others have taken us up a useful cul de sac. By its very inadequacy, the causal theory of knowledge highlights the distance between "thatter" and what can be lived in the sense of being organically experienced; between Sellars's space of reasons and the space of nature. Overwhelmingly, in the natural world, effects are *nothing like* beliefs, or truths, or the justification for ascribing truth to beliefs. Effects do not point to, or posit, their own causes: they require the assistance of conscious subjects who see effects as signs of causes. Nor is there in the material world any basis for there being a causal chain that does and one that does not justify a belief or make it true. There is nothing in causation as generally understood sufficient to generate truth and falsehood, or propositions with truth values.

There is nothing, also, to count for the fundamental difference between beliefs (or opinions), which are personal, and knowledge (of which there is no personal ownership). While I own my testimony to the effect that there is a dog in the room, and the belief on which it is based, I have no ownership of *the fact that* there is a dog in the room – more generally *that* there is a dog in such-and-such a place at time t. Likewise, the fact that there was a battle at Hastings in 1066 belongs to no-one while my erroneous belief that it took place in 1067 is mine or belongs to the community of people who believe this. No causal chains can capture this difference between personally owned false beliefs and ownerless truths. What makes a belief knowledge is not to be found in the property of the belief or of a person who holds it.

Another manifestation of the non-natural nature of knowledge – that it is not to be understood as a material effect of a material cause – is that it does not translate back into sense experience, though the latter may be used to test knowledge claims. So even if perception were a mere effect of causes (which it is not), it remains the case that the contents of knowledge cannot be cashed without remainder as experience. That facts have a draft greater than any possible experience is not restricted to gigantic facts such as that the universe has such and such a diameter. Nobody could have an experience equal to "All swans are white", never mind "Africa has had a troubled history" or "$E = mc^2$". Even the ordinary facts of our own lives, such as that I have lived for many thousands of days or am 200 miles from London, or the million facts about our own bodies (everything from the size of my spleen, the function of my liver, and the level of my blood potassium) are untranslated and indeed untranslatable without remainder into experience. And while the truth of empirical propositions is tested against experience, the experience is not itself translated into something equal to the referent of the propositions. This is the obverse of the fact that knowledge always exceeds experiences, including the first-, second- and third-hand experiences that justify its standing as knowledge. It transcends experience by being stripped of experience, as is most obviously the case in the processes of measurement discussed in the previous chapter.

The most potent argument for the causal theory of knowledge would seem to be the fact that we have to be situated in a certain place to be in receipt of knowledge. However, while this applies to perception, we typically receive knowledge without being in the vicinity of the states of affairs or events that are its objects. Most knowledge is mediated by the spoken or written testimony of others. An attempt to rescue the causal theory by arguing that the testimony is an intermediate cause does not work. The intermediation is not comparable to paradigmatic causal sequences such as those seen in the natural world. The putative causal chain driving testimony would be anomalous, to put it mildly.

The causal theory of direct or mediated knowledge ultimately implies that the material world ventriloquizes itself, or truths about itself, through the mouths that are causally wired into it. The Truth (and The Untruth) is not located in the objects, events, processes that truths are about and generated as the causal effects of those states of affairs, objects, events and processes. The recent "e-ttenuation" of our reflective, epistemic consciousness dissipated through countless electronic devices with the capabilities they confer on us and the enticements they offer is only the latest stage in our deindexicalization through pages and pictures to a boundless elsewhere, that is the realm of "thatter". The contents of computer screens that reveal and conceal the world are the most recent manifestation of the primordial pre-thatter of the visual field which reveals a reality that it in part conceals.

Thus, and such, is our life in *"that* which is the case". Our life in the sea of thatter, of truths that can be contested, set against one another, united in confirmation, exposed to the test of set-piece experience, connected and separated, and are available to be challenged or developed, over minutes, days, weeks, years, decades and centuries, as sense-making humans pursue both local solutions and ever-widening understanding.

It is important not to end this inquiry into "thatter" without emphasizing the extent to which sense-making is *active*. Sentience requires no work on our part; indeed, it is inescapable. Even where we actively seek out basic experiences – for example travel long distances to sunbathe – the final step involves no effort: it is receptivity. "Thatter", however, is the fruit, often hard-won, of scrutinizing, testing, measuring, puzzling over and puzzling out. The effort may be individual or collective or (typically) that of an individual jumping off from a cognitive plaform constructed by the collective. And sense once made (note the verb) may be made for all time or (more often) made and lost, requiring to be made all over again. The different dimensions of mental effort – mobilizing attention, recollection, reasoning – are some of the most constant accompaniments of our life in the sea of thatter – in the "thaterial" world.

That our gazes reach out, and form the basis for discovery, invention, construction, interpretation – often based on the joining of experience or a platform of pre-joined experience, implicit in concepts and prior knowledge – underlines the extent to which sense-making is not merely mirroring what-is, even less is an effect of outside material events. Our thoughts are not the mere slaves of our impressions, and the interpreted world is not simply the givenness of objects confiding their intrinsic nature for our enlightenment. The aureole of possibilities that surrounds what is outside of us is also in part imposed by us on it.

And there is another important point. In Chapters 3 and 4 we examined attempts to explain the efficacy of our sense-making by closing the distance between the sense-maker (or, narrowly, the mind) and the world (narrowly, Nature) that is made sense of. We can now see that collapsing the distance does not solve the problem: we *need* the distance if knowledge is to count as knowledge. By an irony that we noted in Addendum 2 to Chapter 5, both the purest materialism and panpsychism, notwithstanding their seeming to be opposite extremes, have this problem in common. They both lose the distance implicit in the fact that (say) matter becomes "matter" only in certain privileged pieces of matter – namely human beings; and that the Given is "given" to or for minute instances of itself – namely, we human beings. By reducing mind to matter or spreading mind throughout matter, we fail to account for the necessary distinction between the knower and the known.

In the next two chapters, we shall return to the limitations of knowledge and sense-making – beyond the fact just examined – and argue that it is not, and cannot be, the Pure Givenness of What-is. At the heart of understanding is the sense that that which is understood lies beyond the process of understanding, even beyond the language in which understanding is expressed. There needs to be an at least partially opaque Other for something to be seen. In the final chapter, we will take this argument further and examine critically the very idea of complete understanding.

Addendum
Squeezing out thatter: deflationary, disquotational, disappearance theories of truth

Even where it is not actively resented and denied – along with the intentionality that opens up the space it comes to occupy and expand – thatter is easily overlooked by philosophers. A revealing expression of this is to be found in so-called deflationary, disquotational, or disappearance theories of truth. While these theories have been developed with considerable sophistication, their origin can be traced to, and their essence captured in, a couple of very simple ideas, associated in particular with Frank Ramsey and Alfred Tarski.

Ramsey argued as follows that the idea of truth was vacuous or redundant:"Truth and falsity are ascribed primarily to propositions. The proposition to which they are ascribed may be either explicitly given or described. Suppose first that it is explicitly given; then it is evident that 'It is true that Caesar was murdered' means no more than that Caesar was murdered."[33] To generalize: to assert that "p is true" is to assert no more than that p. The seeming qualification "is true" therefore adds nothing. "Truth" is neither a predicate, a property, or a grammatical feature altering the sense of a proposition of which it is affirmed. Thus is truth deflated, to the point where it looks like disappearing.

A close inspection of the players in the deflationary theory takes us, via Tarski, to the disquotational theory. Tarski illustrated the truth predicate as follows:

"Snow is white" is true if and only if snow is white.

While it is by no means certain that he wanted to deflate truth, his theory of truth was taken to this conclusion by many, among others (and most famously) Quine. Quine focuses on the fact that there are two players in the statement, one in quotation marks "Snow is white" that is embedded in the other:

Quotation marks make all the difference between talking about words and talking about snow. The quotation is the name of a sentence that contains a name, namely "snow", of snow. By calling the sentence true, we call snow white. The truth predicate is a device for disquotation.[34]

Many philosophers have found cutting truth down to size in this way very attractive. It seems, for a start, to bypass the problems associated with other theories of truth. The correspondence theory – persuasive for many reasons, including the fact that it seems to capture how truth "faces" the world – presents the challenge of defining the corresponding partners in the relationship. Even where their fundamentally different nature – for examples utterances on the one hand and bits of the mute world on the other – is denied to pose a problem, there are still difficulties in specifying what it is that true statements state and consequently in picking out the truth-makers that make them true. Coherence theories, such that the truth of one proposition resides in its consistency with other true propositions seems to suggest a "pass the parcel" responsibility for truth warrants, though it does reflect the facts already noted that the Space of Reasons to which knowledge belongs is not populated by atomic individuals with their own separate truth grounds: the truth claims of theories face "the tribunal of experience corporately". Coherence theories seem to allow truth to be affirmed independently of any genuine external reality. And pragmatic theories, as we have seen in Chapter 4, fail dismally to connect truth with the much-touted, tough-minded "cash value", least of all a contribution to biological survival. However, if the disquotational theory avoids all these problem, it does so only by entirely missing the nature of truth and consequently locating it in the wrong place.[35]

Let us go back to the beginning. Deflationary theories conclude, from the fact that there is no difference between saying p and saying p is true, "is true" adds nothing. This, Ramsay's conclusion, would be valid if the correct place to look for the nature of truth would be in the difference between "p" and "p is true". The category of truth (and falsehood) however lies upstream of both sentences. Truth must already be in place for there to be assertions "that p" and assertions "that p is true". All Ramsay's argument establishes is that truth is not a predicate applicable to propositions, sentences, or assertions. If it *were* such, then the truth of (say) a proposition would be an intrinsic or constitutive property of the item in question. We would then have the absurd consequence that propositions, sentences, or assertions would be true (or false) irrespective of anything else in the world. Truth is an irreducibly relational property. That is why the opposite view – that the truth of a proposition resides exclusively in the world it is about – is also incorrect. A state of affairs is neither true nor false, though its existence may make an assertion true. If states of affairs had truth values in themselves, they would be the site of an infinite number of contradictions, as they would be both true (of all propositions that say true things about them) and false (of all the propositions that say false things about them).

Quine's disquotational deflationary theory, notwithstanding its surface differences from the disappearance theory, has this in common with it; namely, that both theories seek the nature, the location, of truth in the difference between two sentences or types of sentences. The difference in the disquotational theory is between "snow is white" and snow is white. The former sentence names or specifies itself and the latter strips off the quotations and names or specifies a piece of the world. This is roughly the difference between a sentence being mentioned – referring to and hence talking about itself – and between a sentence being used – referring to and hence talking about the world. The same criticism applies to both theories: they fail to find truth because they look for it in the difference between assertions that, being assertions, are downstream of the establishment of truth (and falsehood). Truth is already in place in "p" "snow is white" and so it won't be found in the difference between "p" and "p is true" or between "snow is white" and snow is white.

Truth is, at the very least, a *relationship* that requires two relata: a proposition (typically asserted through a sentence) and a piece of the world. It is not a property of the relata such as sentences as we have seen; but neither is it a property of the world. Tarski, for example, would not question this. But we need then to examine the relata. A proposition is not in itself either true or false. Nor is a piece of the world such as a chair in a room either true or false. It may become a truth-maker of the assertion *that* there is a chair in the relevant room but it is innocent of its role: being the truth-maker of an assertion is not a monadic or constitutive property of a piece of the world such as an object or a state of affairs. The relationship is located in the space between thatter and what it is *that* is. Deflationary theories of truth are a symptom of the endeavour to collapse the gap between matter and thatter.

To summarize, we may think of truth as "thatter" or explicitness that may be captured in different ways, the most powerful, precise, and elaborated being language, typically when it is used to make declarative statements. To seek the stuff of truth in the difference between one set of sentences (p) and another (p is true) and to declare the notion of truth redundant because no difference can be found (Ramsey) or to reduce it to the difference between sentences about sentences and sentences about the world (Tarski/Quine) is to seek it in the wrong place. Making truth an internal relationship within language is certain to result in losing the distance between Being and truth; or to collapse the distance opened up when articulate, conscious (human) beings encounter Being as *that* which is. Truth supervenes on Being and Being does not supervene on itself in order to make itself into truths.

Deflationary theories of truth make it easier for the advocates of a naturalism that aspires to do without intentionality – which fits so badly into the physicalist world-picture – to wire our humanity into the material world. It is exemplified by this claim from Quine: "knowledge, mind and meaning are part of the same world that they have to do with, and ... they are to be studied in the same empirical spirit that animates natural science".[36] They are all products of "neural intake".

Such naturalism – which has often had the ambition of finding "ought" in "is" by translating values into the biological imperatives and moving validity from the space of reasons to that of nature by a similar pragmatic wheeze – strays even further off course when it tries to find "is" in is. Finding an "is" in is presents a more profound challenge to naturalism than the venerable problem of deriving an "ought" from "is".[37]

CHAPTER 7

Senselessness at the heart of sense

Kick at the rock, Sam Johnson, break your bones
But cloudy, cloudy is the stuff of stones.   Richard Wilbur[1]

Some knower must remain behind the lens for anything to be
known.   Thomas Nagel[2]

We have arrived at the image of ourselves as sense-making animals *facing* the world, individual representatives of a community of minds. This was an affirmative note since it underlined the extent to which we are liberated, through thatter, particularly in the form of knowledge, from our material surroundings and indeed from the biological mire that supports sentience. Our flesh of course is a necessary condition of our being sense-making animals; and the needs of the flesh give sense-making its primary, although not its sole, purpose, contributing overwhelmingly to its content, in virtue of supplying the needs that are its first and last agenda. Those needs are, of course, transformed over history and the viewpoint from which that agenda is pursued and its knowledge is acquired and organised is not socketed in an ecological niche as is the case with other animals. Looking on a world that for the most part does not look back at us, is the ultimate basis for our ability to *bring about* events, to utilize material happenings as handles that can be used to shape what happens in accordance with our goals, and to be the authors of genuinely free actions. The present chapter is less optimistic and prepares the way for a critical examination, in the final chapter, of the seemingly uncontroversial idea of absolute cognitive progress and the perhaps more obviously questionable hope of our getting ever closer to a complete understanding of the world (including ourselves as part of it.)

The idea of the subject facing a world of objects is of a *relationship*. The quorum for the cognitive tango is two – something that is reflected in the connection-across-separation that is our mode of relating to and engaging with the world and is most clearly acknowledged in the correspondence theory of knowledge and truth. Unless we subscribe to idealism, the two relata will be in some important sense external to one another;[3] there will therefore be an irreducible otherness in what is known – the first relatum. Less obviously, there will be an otherness within the knower – the second relatum. Less obviously still, there will be an otherness within knowledge itself. Without these modes of other-than-knowledge at its heart, knowledge would lack specificity; without their opacity, it would lack being; without the distance they mark, it would lack transcendence. In support of these claims let us examine the two relata in turn.

First, the world that is faced. If we begin with a literal facing whose paradigm is visual perception, it is evident that opacity is necessary for something to be seen. An entirely transparent world would be invisible. We would look not at it but through it and consequently see nothing at all. Without the opacity of things, there are no things "there". There would be no (visible) difference between observing a busy scene and staring into empty space. Similar principles apply to other senses, such as touch. We touch only surfaces and when we break through surfaces it is to other surfaces. A breaking through that exposed the entire object as tangible surface with nothing beneath it would result in an intangible object. The sense of touch is delivered by the resistance of that which is not currently being touched. To generalize, the world faced by the subject, therefore, must have a residual opacity or, more generally, hiddenness. Without the (as yet) unrevealed, there would be nothing "out there".

There are two immediate objections to this conclusion and they are connected: a) the hiddenness is only temporary and can be amended; and b) what is true of perception is not true of the knowledge and concept-based understanding with which we are most centrally concerned.

To take the first point, consider that which must be hidden from sight in an object such as a cup, necessary to block the light so that it is visible. I can (in part) correct the invisibility experienced from one direction by examining it from another angle: walking round the other side of it, turning it round or upside down. And I can correct the intangibility of the depths that make it tangible by breaking it and palpating its fragments. This, however, does not result in complete visibility liberated from invisibility, or total tangibility without residual intangibility. In the case of touch, the fragments would still have hidden depths beneath the palpable surface if it were to be palpable. And in the case of vision, even if the gaze had been comprehensive, there would still be an inside of the material of the cup, hidden from view. More tellingly, the hiddenness would not be abolished at any given time but only varied as the gaze or the touch moved from place to place. There would be no all-at-once revelation: as I touch the under-surface of the cup, I lose touch with the rest of its surface. And this is true a fortiori of a landscape we are looking at and the ground we stand on or, more generally, the perceived world in which we pass our hours. We could express this by saying that without opacity, without evident limits, experience would not be experience *of* – experience of something that exceeds the experience.[4] It is the warrant of the otherness, and hence the reality, of the experience.

Let us now look at the second objection to the claim of irremovable, residual opacity – that our concern is not with sense-experience but with sense-making; not with perception but with a mode of comprehension that encompasses and transcends it. My speaking of the "cup" makes it a referent. As a referent, it does not have angles from which it can be, or is necessarily, viewed only partially. Indeed, as a referent, it is not the object of any specific sense: it is no more looked at than it is touched. Does this mean that the seemingly necessary otherness of the object is overcome and sense-making can proceed to ever more complete transparency? It does not; because the gains are offset by losses. Let us develop this point.

Everyday objects such as cups as they figure in everyday discourse are no longer objects of vision or of touch but instances of general types. They have been stripped of qualities such as colour and weight, not to speak of location, being within or beyond reach and use. But the journey does not stop there: the passage from actual cups to "cup" is only the first step in the ascent towards the kind of higher-level comprehensibility that is our primary concern. Allocation of an entity to a general category sets it on the way to becoming instances of, or portions of, something yet more general; for example, matter or mass-energy (if we are en route to the latest physics) or "things", "substance", or "stuff" (if we are thinking metaphysically or mobilizing a folk ontology). Opacity, and the associated otherness, of the world that faces us thus returns in a different guise.

The obvious next step towards cognitive transparency – reducing things to concatenations of the values of variables – will achieve too much, taking away the very face of the world. To put it this way is simply to reiterate the view from which we began; namely that the primordial sense of some thing's being real is shot through with the intuition that has a cognitively unbiddable residue

– what philosophers used to designate by the term "obstance". For hard-bitten realists, reality is incompletely soluble in the mind, irrespective of whether we are talking about perceptions or thoughts. Pukka objects not only exist when they are not perceived or unthought of but they can never become experiences or thoughts without a remainder of the unperceived or the unthinkable. There always has to be something beyond the solvent of cognition. Some basic stuff such as matter seems to be the ultimate guarantor that experience and knowledge are "of", or "about" that which is other than themselves.

This much may be obvious but there is another tension within the aspiration to complete sense when the project is driven by the gaze of natural science. Consider the most advanced, or at least the most widely applicable, approach to sense-making: the mathematization of the stuff of the world, as described by Quine with his characteristic wit:

> Numbers and other mathematical objects are wanted in physics anyway, so one may as well enjoy their convenience as coordinates for physical objects; and then, having come thus far, one can economize a little by dispensing with physical objects ... As physicalists, we have welcomed bodies with open arms ... On the other hand the mathematical objects attained the ontological scene only begrudgingly for services rendered ... It is ironical then that we at length find ourselves constrained to this anti-physical sort of reductionism from the side of physics itself ... Physical objects, next, evaporated into space-time regions; but this was the outcome of physics itself. Finally, the regions went over into pure sets; still, the set theory itself was there for no other reasons than the need for mathematics as an adjunct to physical theory.[5]

The consequence of rendering the stuff of what-is transparent in this way may vastly enhance our capacity to manipulate it (for reasons that are not entirely clear) but not necessarily to advance its comprehensibility. Everyone knows that quantum mechanics – the current *ne plus ultra* of our account of the physical world – does not translate into anything that makes other than mathematical sense. As has often been said, anyone who thinks they understand quantum mechanics clearly does not. More alarming is this suggestion by the American physicist, Robert Geroch:

> [I]t seems to be the case that physics, at least in its fundamental aspects, always moves in this one direction: fewer things making

sense ... In quantum mechanics ... such notions as "the position of a particle" or "the speed of a particle" do not make sense. It may not be a bad rule of thumb to judge the importance of a new set of ideas in physics by the criterion of how many of the notions and relations that one feels to be necessary one is forced to give up.[6]

The price of transparency seems therefore to be loss rather than a gain of intelligibility – as well as a loss of substance, the evaporation of a world that is being *faced*.

Something rather similar happens when we consider the evolution of the scientific account of the insentient powers that are thought to be expressed in the unfolding of the world – in the succession of events, and the apparent necessities connecting them. The first step is the abolition of agency from the natural world (an aspect of the displacement of *Mythos* by *Logos*): God, Providence, Fate, Fortune and Necessity are superseded by energies and forces that lack intentions, meanings and purposes; mindless causes that imbue matter with normless regulation. The first law of motion – $F = ma$ – is light on sense, although it has gigantic scope. This, and other laws, pave the way to a unification of those energies and forces with which we are familiar because we can perceive them directly – light, heat, inertial, gravitational – into energies and forces with which we are unfamiliar: electromagnetic, intranuclear. Alternatively, familiar energies and forces are transformed out of all recognition as when gravity becomes curvature of space-time. The ascent to greater generality and power may take us even further adrift – shedding not only a Divine Mind underwriting the sense of the world but ultimately every aspect of ordinary sense. We see the limits to sense most blatantly in those nodes where laws intersect; namely, the constants of nature which are scotomata in the would-be all-seeing gaze. Nothing could be more contingent than the speed of light or the ratio of the mass of a proton to that of an electron.

They illustrate how arriving at the fundamental level is to run into a brick wall of brute what is. Indeed, that which is susceptible to further explanation seems to fall short of fundamentality. As if this were not bad enough, there is an additional conflict within explanation. Any explanation that seems to encompass the totality of things needs to leave particulars behind: explanatory terms, of necessity, leave out individual features. The tension between ascent to general explanation and truth and, necessarily particular, actuality is reflected in the notion of matter which seems to be at once inscrutable, because it is instantiated only in particular bodies, and at the same time is absolutely basic and general. The relationship between matter as stuff that is bumped into and "matter" as a concept that appears in scientific discourse is vexed, and has been a happy hunting ground for those who wish to engage in the debate about realism and anti-realism of science.

We have moved – risen or fallen according to taste – a long way from world-pictures in which what happens makes sense because it is willed by a Mind making it happen; or even because it is a consequence of the way things are sewn together as we see them in everyday life. Geroch's observation about quantum mechanics seems more widely applicable: as the human mind advances into the universe, mind seems to retreat from it. The contribution of the theory of evolution to the disinfecting of the natural world of agency, intention, even consciousness, is only a small part of a much more general trend. The bigger picture is of the advancing mind encountering its Other at every turn, as it gives up qualities for quantities and even intelligibility in favour of generality of application. In extending its gaze, the collective consciousness extends the sense of blankness. We have to live with the trade-off in our world-picture between that which is intuitively satisfying and that which delivers extraordinary predictive power and hugely enhances our capacity to control nature. This is scarcely an unexpected outcome, given that scientific advance has been predicated on an ability and willingness to set aside our common-sense intuitions. But there comes a point at which the divorce between how the world looks and feels and our scientific understanding of it comes to feel like a deep cognitive wound.

Thus, the first partner in the relationship of the subject facing the world from the (comparatively safe) distance of knowledge: the known object. What of the other member of the duo – the knowing subject? The story here is, if anything, even less promising.

To face the world, it is necessary to have a (literal) face, that is part of a body equipped with senses, to give it location, to lay fleshy claim to space that will make a conscious being a viewpoint. The embodied subject is something of a cognitive mess, being an ontological chimera that the literal-minded translate into a mind distinct from, and caught up in, a body. For many, the mess can be tidied up by neural accounts of the mind in which it is able faithfully to represent the world in virtue of being causally wired into it. Neural activity, it is claimed, is both a set of events clearly located in space and time, and a knowing consciousness, an openness to the world that belongs to the space of sense-making. In Chapter 4 and elsewhere, we have criticized the very idea that causal interaction between the world and the brain will generate an image of the world in the brain. But even if such an account were true, its picture of the mind as being woven out of the mindless physico-chemical operations of the brain, with the brain being innocent of what the person is up to and the person innocent of what her brain is doing, would highlight the fact that the human body, the condition of the knowing subject, is for the great part inhuman.[7]

The relationship between my body (a thing that is) and me (a person that "am") – which we have touched on in Chapter 5 – has many dimensions which are worth a brief visit.[8] There is a sense in which I am my body, inasmuch that it cannot be separated from me. When I am standing up, this is not distinct from my body being in the upright position. My body does not "stand in" for me. This identity is even clearer when I am cowering in anticipation of a blow. And much of the time we are (or am) parts of our body, as when we smile, or grip something, or dance.[9]

Nothing however is entirely straightforward. To take a trivial example, I can put on a smile in order to deceive someone, thus *using* my face – as if it were a kind of tool – as a signalling system. My whole body engaged in pushing a car can become an instrument which I utilize strategically to maximize my pushing power. And I can exploit my weight instrumentally, as when I sit on my opponent's head in a fight (something I have not done recently) or on an overfilled suitcase I am trying to close (something I do all too frequently). The boundary between *being* my body or parts of it and *using* it is highly labile even during a single action. And one part of my body can use another – as when I use the left hand to steady the right or one part of a hand to support something the fingers are working on, or my left hand stabilizes the notebook on which my right hand is writing.

It will be noted that use is woven with possession: "my" hand, etc. Use and agency are two dimensions of a kind of distance from identity-with-this-body. They intersect with my awareness of "my" appearance. I look at and judge my face in the mirror through eyes that are not exactly my own but belong to an imaginary observer and I may manipulate it to make or ward off a certain impression. Woven in with body-as-possession, body-as-tool, and body-as-object-of-judgement seen through my own or others' eyes, or my own eyes assuming the attitude of another, is the body-as-object-of-knowledge. Once we enter the realm of knowledge we are in very tangled terrain indeed.

The most direct experience of my body as an object of knowledge is when I note that my skin is cold to touch, even though I don't feel cold, or I am surprised that it is damp despite my being unaware of sweating. I can discover the colour of my skin, even be surprised at it, and other features that I do not sense directly. Beneath the skin, the knowledge relation becomes even more tangled. Evidently, we cannot have direct knowledge of that which we cannot even sense and much of my body, not being sensed, is inapparent to me most of the time. The greater part of my fleshly being (for example my spleen, my bone marrow, my appendix, are typical denizens) never figures in my consciousness unless something goes wrong. Raymond Tallis's body is largely *terra incognita* to Raymond Tallis. Mindlessness begins at home. My brain is enclosed in a skull that is insentient bone that has grown and moulded itself mindlessly. My grey matter is unaware that it is grey, my cortex does not know that it looks like a walnut. My body is for the most part "my-less" and "me-less" as well as mindless.

The darkness alienating me from my flesh may be illuminated by the expertise of others, expertise I may myself share. Foremost among this body of knowledge is the vast *corpus* of scientific facts about the human body in particular and living tissues in general. Seen through the lens of this knowledge, my body becomes anyone's body, even though that "anyone" is also inescapably me. There are basic macroscopic facts such as my height, weight, and temperature and how these relate to desirable or recommended norms. There are facts about the way my organs work together and separately. There are facts about the dozens of physiological and biochemical parameters regulated by homeostatic mechanisms. There are facts about blood, lymph, other secretions, interstitial tissues, and so on. All of these bear directly on our well-being, our capacity for action, and our chances of survival, although most of us are unaware of most of them, and none of us can be aware of all of them. As organisms, we are the site of innumerable interlocking mechanisms. When we drill down to the level of cells and of their microscopic interactions we enter a labyrinth of pathways described in thousands of flow diagrams representing a bewildering dialectic between "the soup" and "the scaffolding", the minute drops of chemical brew regulated by cytoskeleton on the border of structure and function.[10]

In the multi-layered darkness of my body grow the seeds of a multitude of shocks and surprises. Some are joyful, like the mysterious pleasure of orgasm; many are neutral, such as the feeling of satiety or of simply carnally being there; and many of course are unpleasant in the extreme. The latter may be straightforward, such as the swelling that follows its own course after we have turned over an ankle; more obscure as when a ruptured artery results in loss of speech and the capacity to make cognitive sense of the world; and yet more occult as in the case of impaired metabolism of purines resulting in deposition of uric acid crystals in a joint with agonizing results. In the darkness, too, may be prepared the ultimate shock that will bring all shocks to an end.

Thus, the incarnate subject: *someone* tied to *something* that breathes, aches, feels warm, stands up, is pleasured, urinates, and does all those things that are necessary to keep it capable of doing all the things it needs or merely wants to do, as it faces the world. Given the vexed and largely unconscious relationship that this partner to the cognitive relationship has to itself, or to the body that makes it possible, it may seem astonishing that the subject is not irremediably cognitively curdled. How can this salivating, pulsing, aching, sweating, mass of flesh, scintillating with showers of sensations from within as well as without, heir to a thousand ills and wells, wake up to the world sufficiently to arrive at the general theory of relativity that caused Einstein to marvel at the miracle of the comprehensibility of the world and set this book on its path of inquiry? To try to understand this, let us return to vision.

When I see the world clearly, with unimpaired vision, my body is out of the way. My eyes are invisible, my head is in the background, and the remainder of my carnal being is simply implicit as the physical and physiological support for my head. Such telereception enables me in a modest, intermittent, and conditional way, to transcend the flesh of which I am composed – and all the immediate physical self-presence it has that would otherwise occlude the world-as-scene – retaining it only as a cognitive partner. The intentionality of perception (dominated by vision) opens a crack in Being, such that part of it – a subject – faces it as a world populated by beings, transformed into "my surroundings", and ultimately into the theatre of my activity and my ultimate destiny. This also opens the distance between the incarnate or embodied subject and the flesh of which it is made. The relations of possession (the body or parts of it as "my such-and-such"), explicit agency (my body or parts of it as tools), judgement ("my appearance", "my performance") and so on that I have discussed, are dimensions of that distance.

But that is not all. Between me and my body, and between me and that part of what-is that becomes my world, innumerable third parties intervene. The primordial manifestation of their presence is their reciprocating and reciprocated gaze. It is your gaze (before me in reality or in the idea of it) that helps to make the body that I am into a body that I *have* and that which I see, into something that belongs to all seers and consequently to objective, or at least intersubjective, reality. It fastens my seeing to a viewpoint that is itself located in a place in shared reality; and my mind in a community of minds. It is out of the latter, and not the sweating, pulsing, etc., flesh, that my world becomes less egocentrically defined as "the world", a place of participation. Our individual understanding of the world, thus made aware of its individuality, its partiality, is equipped to begin its ascent through the lower slopes of general understanding towards a gaze implicit in the great cognitive achievements of science. An objective world, as the asymptote of inter-subjective reality, looms into view and grows beyond the bounds of the body and the sphere of its sensibility. It is with this assistance (whose medium is the semiosphere in which knowledge is shared through linguistic and many other kinds of signs) that we progress from sense experience, via that which is not present to our senses but made present through the testimony of individual or anonymous others, to world-pictures. While individually we never escape our bodies, collectively we can transcend them; and individually we can access collective transcendence.

Thus the basis of the possibility of escaping from the windowless parish of an embodied subject. This seems an appropriate juncture for a sideways (and critical) re-examination of the claim, associated with Mach and Quine, that there is a continuum from irritation of nerve endings to the highest reaches of science. Here, it will be recalled, is Mach: "there is no difference between ordinary experience accessible to any being endowed with a nervous system and scientifically organized experiment. There is no break in continuity between science ... and modes of behaviour characteristic of the entire animal world."[11] We can now see at least two major breaks in the path "from stimulus to science", long before we get to the decisive break constituted by measurement, as discussed in Chapter 5. The first is the full-blown intentionality of a telereceptor such as vision, which locates its perceptual object at an explicit distance from itself. The second is the reflexive location of the perceiving subject in its field of perception, explicitly shared with others. The sense that "it" is out there, which has as its correlative the sense that I am here, is transformed into the sense I, too, am "out there". This mini-Copernican revolution comes from the experience of being in another's perceptual field and consequently being an "over there" object to another's "over-here" subject. We are displaced from the implicit centre of the places in which we find ourselves. We are over-there as much as over-here.[12] When I tell you that I am here, I know that the "here" in question is "there" to you.

This deindexicalization of the ego is a crucial step in the transcendence of the body en route from *umwelt* to *Weltanschauung*, sense experience to world-pictures. There is a democratization of the space in which we find our place as an "anywhere", so that we can feel ourselves to be at the edge, on the outside, or at an address that belongs to a system of addresses. We shrink as our knowledge grows and the frame of reference in which we locate ourselves as objects of knowledge expands, growing from chair to room to street to village to town to country to planet to galaxy. The growth that shrinks us – at least when we see ourselves as objects of knowledge – is driven most potently by the deindexicalized space of discourse. The world of facts, which we enter via the spoken or written testimony of others, is liberated from here and now and from there and then. Facts belong to no-one and are anchored nowhere. The face with which we face the world is a collective face; or an individual representation of a collective gaze.

There is a yet more fundamental discontinuity necessary for the transition from the organism wired into material nature courtesy of its nervous system and a knowing subject facing the world. It becomes evident by default in Quine overlooking it:

> To account for knowledge of an external thing or event in itself, the naturalistic epistemologist looks rather to the external thing or event itself and *the causal chain of stimulation from it to one's brain*. In a paradigm case, light rays are reflected from the object to one's retina, activating a patch of nerve endings each of which initiates a neural impulse to one or another center of the brain.[13]   (emphasis added)

Quine conflates the process by which the light from the object gets into the eye and stimulates the brain with that by which the gaze looks out and sees the object. By fusing the two, he takes away the ground-floor discontinuity that uncouples the perceiving subject from the perceived world and so opens the path to the knowledge available to the subject as a participant in a community of minds. He seems, however, to acknowledge the need for a discontinuity in order for a transmission of energy to count as a stimulus: "an economical strategy in defining the stimulus is to intercept the causal chains just at the subject's surface. Nothing is lost, for it is only from that point inward that the chains contribute to the subject's knowledge of the external world."[14] It is not clear why the surface of the organism should be so privileged, given the causal continuity from object to brain. Or, indeed, the brain. As we observed with functionalism, naturalist epistemology offers nothing to supply the viewpoint, the reference point, that divides input from output, the embodied subject from the world he or she faces. It fails in this regard because of an almost wilful tendency to overlook the intentionality that turns incoming light into outward looking vision and creates the space of knowledge.

It is in the space of knowledge that the subject is distanced from the body that breathes, aches, feels warm or cold, and imports its own darkness and opacity into the cognitive realm. To see how things might be if the body were left on its own to manage its portfolio of knowledge, we have only to look at what results when carnality reasserts itself through dysfunction as in toxic confusional states. The body doing its own thing – as when my parts of my brain are engulfed by spontaneous discharges and I lose consciousness and make involuntary movements in an epileptic fit – is closed off from the shared world.

Thus, the good and bad news about the second relatum: the knower who is not an organism but an embodied subject. The cognitive history of the person is distinct from a register of the processes of the human organism, which (as we have discussed above) are for the most part hidden from us. While it is possible to trace the steps by which the primate organism *H. sapiens* became the platform of personhood, the story is complex and this is not the place to attempt it.[15]

But we are still not yet out of the wood, although the knowing subject is in part liberated from the flesh that is its necessary condition. We began with the observation that "thatter" and "facing the world" imply an *external* relationship between two relata – the object and the subject must be radically other. The understanding of the object must sooner or later bump into a brick wall – which we might call "matter" or "stuff" or "substance" – if its objectivity is to be authenticated. Without such an opaque underpinning, we are in danger of dissolving the world into something internal to the mind, a view rejected – and hopefully discredited – in Chapter 3. And the subject, too, seems to be denied the possibility of being utterly transparent, given that it must be inseparable from a body which must have intrinsic, non-transparent properties if it is to support the life that enables it to be conscious and hence to be capable of knowledge and for it to lay claim to a viewpoint, localized in space and time, from which to experience the world. The carnality of its being seems to threaten to cloud it as a lens on reality other than itself. However, through intersubjectivity, particularly that mediated through language, it seems able to wipe its spectacles, break its attachment to time and place, and, at least partially, get out of its own way.

The gap between an, in some residual respects senseless, subject and an, in some respects senseless, object remains but this may not seem fatal to any endeavour to drill down to unpeeled *reality*, given that "reality" is a relational notion: it is real for someone. What is more, even the brick wall of cognitive opacity, is made of "stuff", "matter", or "substance" which are *terms* that carry a halo of meaning, occupying a location in a semantic field, which enables them to be incorporated into a world-picture that aims to be complete. As Keskinen, glossing Quine, has put it:

> The notion of reality "apart from human categories", as separate from
> the parochial point of view of one or another theory, is from Quine's

perspective meaningless ... The notion of reality is always part of a theory, and the real objects in the real world are always objects of some theory ... theoretical posits.[16]

We must conclude, therefore, that the very idea of a world-picture without a separation between the image and that which is depicted in it, and without an irreducible remainder of opacity in both relata, is a contradiction. It is one that is close to the delusion that the truths that supervene on Being can somehow rejoin it, in the guise of an intrinsic, unmediated givenness of Reality, the self-intimation of what-is in an entirely transparent language. Such a world-picture would simply be an iteration – and *per impossibile* an iteration without replication of, or addition to, it – of what is imaged. The categories of truth and reality would be swallowed up into the relationship things have to themselves in virtue of being themselves; which is no relationship at all. If "being themselves" seems to be a relationship, it is so only when the question of *re*identification arises. A pebble is the pebble it is – is "that pebble" – when the question of its identity arises, when it is picked out, and this could hardly be extended to the totality of things, even less to that totality picking *itself* out.

In the vicinity of the intuition that is driving us to such strange places is the idea that there is, or could be, or indeed ought to be, a language, a mode of representation that is not only without ambiguity but which is, as it were, the native tongue of things-in-themselves – a *characteristica universalis* that was not only universally understood but potentially understood by the universe.

There are evident problems with this idea – which we shall discuss in Chapter 8 – but we encounter serious difficulties long before arriving at what seems to be a *reductio ad absurdum* of the notion of rendering the (human and natural) world we live in cognitively transparent. It concerns an apparent darkness at the heart of mental contents, alarmingly in the very place where the subject seems to escape the cloudiness coming from the knowing subject's being embodied. It has attracted much philosophical discussion in recent decades under the heading of "externalism about mental contents". It is the concern that we may not know what our desires and beliefs and above all our thoughts are actually about. This is a particularly intimate form of ignorance. It is connected with the very fact that liberates us from the parish of our individual carnal being: namely that the cognitive face we turn to the world is a collective face and speaks with a language that belongs not to ourselves but to a boundless community of speakers.

Externalism asserts that whether mental contents have a certain property is not determined solely internally but depends at least in part on their environment or context. Consequently, they may not be what we, who have them in mind, think they are. For the present I want to focus on those mental items that are most closely related to language: namely, thoughts. Nothing would seem to be more cognitively transparent than the thoughts I am thinking to myself. I may not know what my body is up to but at least I should know what my mind is up to – at least to the extent of knowing what I think – believe, hope, etc. – and, more particularly, knowing what I am thinking *about*.

Alas, this does not seem to be the case. Counter-intuitively, I am not, in the end, an infallible judge of the content of my own thoughts.[17] At a very basic level I may be thinking about something that I believe exists when in fact it does not. Consequently, I may be mistaken that the object of my thoughts corresponds to a referent located in the real world. I may also mis-identify the item I am thinking about. I have a clear image of a man doing something I saw him doing yesterday and think that I am thinking about Roger when in fact it is William that I am thinking about.

But it is more intimate mistakes that are more relevant to our present concerns. *Semantic externalism* is "the thesis that the meaning and reference of some of the words we use is not solely determined by the ideas we associate with them or by our internal physical state".[18] The contents of our thoughts depend in part on communal linguistic practice: I think using Everyman's words. To use the favourite example introduced by Hilary Putnam, consider a situation where the earth has a remote twin. Water on earth is H_2O. On twin earth there is a twin-water, identical with H_2O in every respect except that it is composed of a different chemical compound XYZ. When the inhabitant of twin earth thinks or believes that "Water quenches thirst" his belief is not about water but about XYZ. In other words, the content of his thought or belief is dependent on external facts.[19] I am mistaken as to what I think I am thinking to myself.

Semantic externalism has been challenged on many grounds. My own view is that its apparent significance is at least in part based on a muddling of levels at which judgement is being made. Such a muddle could make the case for externalism with respect to accurate perception. I correctly see an object in front of me as a chair. I happen also to subscribe to the view that chairs are made of atoms, not knowing that the idea of discrete atoms has been replaced by the wave functions of quantum mechanics. This does not discount my seeing a chair as seeing a chair because correctly seeing a chair is independent of (say) seeing a chair made of atoms on the basis of (incorrectly) seeing that it is made of discreet atomic particles. It might be argued that semantic externalism is not about the correctness or otherwise of our thoughts but about how terms get their meaning and that the term "water" gets its meaning independent of what one believes of the concept water. Even so it still seems to undermine the assumption that we know what we are thinking about. It does not seem to deliver the reassurance that, from an objective point of view, we are unassailable authorities on what we are thinking about.

What remains relevant to our discussion of semantic externalism, and more broadly of externalism with respect to mental contents, is the very possibility that there can be a divorce between what (say) I am thinking about and what I think I am thinking about. To say of someone that he does not know what he is talking about is bad enough; but it is more disturbing to discover that there is the permanent possibility of our not knowing what we are thinking about; that the thoughts in which we present our sense-making to ourselves may be characterized by a divergence between psychological content and linguistic content, or between the intentional objects of on the one hand psychological and on the other linguistic contents. There seems to be a darkness in the most intimate mode of sense-making. This is additional to the fact (which we shall discuss in the next chapter) that our idiolect – the personal vocabulary used and understood in a way unique to ourselves – does not map directly on to the language in which collective sense-making is expressed.

While it is possible to be mistaken as to the object of our thought, and hence as to what we believe or hope or wish to be the case, for the most part we do know what it is we believe. It is, however, sufficiently disturbing that it is possible that our thoughts may not only deceive us about the nature of the world but they may be deceived as to their own contents. There is, however, a further greater challenge to the notion that we make cognitive progress. We have seen how the cognitively curdled state of the incarnate subject is at least in part redeemed by the collective transcendence of the community of minds. However, understanding and the intelligibility of the world is not ultimately a matter of the collective, any more than it is experienced by the archives and databases where it is stored. In the end, it is individual minds, individual subjects, who are the bearers of the comprehended world. While our world-picture is rescued by the community of minds from our messy individual bodies, it has to be known by or in or to our individually messy minds.[20] The messiness of our individual minds is the other side of our uniqueness; of our irreplaceability; of the fact that we are never to be cashed without remainder into finite clusters of general classes which we instantiate.

Thus, the inevitable resistance of "what is there" to full comprehension, in virtue of its necessarily being "other" to our inquiring, knowing minds, and the latter being situated in, and to some extent, coloured by our status as embodied subjects. Even where there is no such colouring, the necessary mutual otherness of mind and the world it endeavours to comprehend, so that the former is *about*, *of* the latter, would ensure an incommensurateness between them; between thought and its objects. This necessary distance is evident even in the most powerful acts of understanding of what there is: natural science. The reduction of the world to values of variables and those values to patterns, to mathematical structures, empties what-is of its "stuffness" as well as draining it of phenomenal qualities. This emptied vision of reality is an inevitable consequence of imagining that it is revealed at the end of the process by which we are gradually cognitively liberated from experience, which is local and perspectival, to a viewpoint that is the totality of things seen from the totality of all possible viewpoints. In short, featurelessness.

We don't have to subscribe to the largely nonsensical ideas of Jacques Lacan to acknowledge the profound truth of his famous assertion that "The real is what resists symbolisation absolutely".[21] That which resists – in the sense of being other than – symbolization might seem to be almost a matter of definition: reality is that of which things are said, not what is said.[22] More profoundly, reality, thought of as pure-in-itself, must lie beyond the reach of the interactive relationships that are evident in, because they underpin, perception, occasion discourse, and are the substrate of action, indeed all that enters sense-making. There can be no self-portrait of reality; no unmediated ontology. It has always to be mediated. Ontology without epistemology is possible only at the level of abstract argument.[23] It is not available as the undistorted, unmediated, givenness of Stuff, of what-is. It can be given only through the lens of a recipient other than the Given; or makes that-which-is The (mythical or non-mythical) Given.

There is, therefore, a darkness at the heart of the known. It is not merely interstitial, in the sense of lying in the interstices of any explanatory schema, but is infra-cognitive, eluding the ordering of things. This is a sense in which order, even that which is most faithful to what-is, is imposed as well as found. Whether we call it "matter" or "energy" or "Being" or "beings" it is there at the start and at the end of the cognitive journey. We end with bare existence, the necessary bearer of properties, with the faceless fact that there is Something (to be faced) rather than Nothing. When we engage with that Something we do so through individual things that, as we ascend cognitively, are generalized to the point where they are featureless, often represented through purely mathematical structures. Thus, the inexpungable darkness at the heart of things and what we might call "the law of the conservation of mystery". We must not conclude from this that the world is overall without meaning – if only because the sense of the lack of overall meaning could not be found in a truly meaningless world.

The explicitly relational nature of cognition, and of "reality", the involvement of two partners both of whom must have a degree of opacity, raises questions about the idea of absolute, or even real, progress of intelligibility towards a final goal. It is to these questions that our inquiry will be directed in the final stage of our reflection on the sense-making animal.

CHAPTER 8

Towards a complete comprehension of the world?

> We should not look down on the standpoint of theory as make-believe, for we can never do better than occupy the standpoint of one theory or another.   W. V. O. Quine[1]

We began with Einstein's awestruck observation that the comprehensibility of the world is "an eternal mystery". The reach of our understanding seems to be incomprehensible, especially in the light of what we know about ourselves. Attempts to eliminate the mystery by closing the gap between the comprehending mind and the world it comprehends proved unsatisfactory. Locating the world inside the mind (Chapter 3) and making the mind part of the material world (Chapter 4) were equally unconvincing. Indeed, the latter approach, which treated us as a piece of nature, and consequently an object of scientific knowledge, made even everyday knowledge, never mind higher-level understanding of the world, entirely incomprehensible. Our scientific image of the world and of our place in it does not seem to be able to accommodate the very faculties that we must have to form such an image.

In subsequent chapters, we identified reasons why we might expect the comprehensibility of the world, however impressive, to remain only partial, although it still exceeds what we might reasonably expect. The knowing subject proved to be a necessary condition of, as well as a constraint on, objective knowledge. Disinfecting cognition of the contamination of the subject (Chapter 5) would be close to being self-contradictory. Knowledge requires to be known by someone – an embodied someone: it is impossible to envisage what-is as having a subjectless view on itself. That someone, however, would always have access to the body of knowledge arrived at, and held in trust by, a vast community of minds. What is more, sense-making, and more specifically, knowing-that – "thatter" – *requires* a distance between mind and the world it comprehends (Chapter 6). Given that knowledge is a relationship between two independent relata – the knower and the known – the conformity of the latter to the former is deeply problematic. Indeed, the standing of the object of knowledge as an object – distinct from what is known – implies that it should have a residual, irreducible opacity; that there should be something senseless at its heart compounding the opacity of the embodied subject (Chapter 7). When it came to letting his *piéce de résistance* in on the secrets of his Creation, God seemed to have said "Let there be half-light". He sent his best beloved on a long, still unfinished, journey of enlightenment.

Unfinished – but unfinishable? Our knowledge is incomplete and our sense-making a work in progress. Must this be the case forever? If so, the very idea of cognitive progress is problematic, even illusory. Surely every little step – and of these there appears to be no shortage – contributes to overall advance. The judgement of absolute progress, however, presupposes a bench-mark of complete understanding against which it can be measured. While I can acknowledge that A is bigger than B, even if I cannot envisage a maximally large object, such comparisons cannot be made in the case of overall under-standing. Can we make sense of the very idea of rounding off the sense of the world, such that inquiry is concluded and there is no more sense to be made? This seems doubtful, given the story so far. But there is more to be said about this, if only to highlight the extraordinary nature of the sense that – despite everything – we have collectively made of ourselves and the world in which we live out our brief lives. What follows picks up the story we left incompletely told in Chapter 1.

There are several compelling models of apparent cognitive progress in indi-vidual lives and in the history of humanity. I most certainly knew and under-stood more when I was 30 than when I was a toddler. I made more sense of a much bigger world: the longer I was at large, the larger the large got. And it was possible for me actively to pursue the goal of cognitive advance by seeking out sources of information, undergoing training, struggling to master various disciplines, and so on.

There is a tempting analogy between personal development (which includes development into a person) and the cognitive growth of the human race. Successive epochs are associated with an ever-expanding body of knowl-edge and, possibly, bandwidth of understanding. Such growth, what is more, is driven by a willed sense of our ignorance, by cultivated doubt, by active uncertainty, by the feeling, based on previous experience, that our objectivity has serious limits. The latter is in part fuelled by what objective knowledge tells us about our insignificant place in the universe. Increasingly powerful techniques of inquiry, enhanced by qualitative and quantitative methodologies, proliferating concepts, and the thousand ingenious instruments to enhance the power and precision of direct and indirect perception, accelerate the rate of cognitive growth. Horizons expand and the skies are no longer the limit.

This Whiggish history of inexorable advance might be challenged by the worry that modes of understanding, modes of consciousness, have been lost even as others have been gained. Perhaps the insights and intuitions of early philosophers and poets and novelists have not been surpassed; perhaps they seem to know and understand less only because we do not really know what it was they knew and the nature of their understanding. Natural science – particularly physics and biology – however, seems to provide incontrovertible evidence of some kind of objective and possibly absolute progress, building on, rather than being captive to, its own history. The convergence of ever more precise scientific theories, that have increasing generality, and tested incessantly in their practical applications, in the gadgetry that surrounds us, seems to provide irrefutable evidence of advance towards ever more complete and ever more robust truths regarding what is, was, and shall be the case.

Even science looks vulnerable, however. The history of the most spectacularly successful disciplines is a story of successive theories being vanquished by other theories, either because the latter encompass more of the data or, more focally, because critical observations predicted by the new theory are not accommodated by the one it has superseded. The permanence of its revolutions is, of course, the source of the strength of science. But the process does not seem likely to be coming to an end; with so much unfinished business, stability would amount to impasse. Every phase of science therefore looks like part of its history, a step in an unfinished and unfinishable journey. What is thought now already looks, from an imagined future standpoint, simply what "they" (that's us) thought "then" (our now). As has often been pointed out, the most powerful theories currently on offer – general relativity and quantum mechanics – are not only incomplete, being unable to explain certain phenomena, but also conflict with one another. We consequently have no idea of what a Theory of Everything would look like, even if it were confined to being a Theory of Everything Physical and the world of physicists were identical with the physical world and the latter with Everything.

Given this, we are in no position to claim that our present theories are closer to complete understanding of the natural world than those of previous centuries. We have always been wrong in the past (that is implicit in the very idea of continuing progress in science), so why should we imagine that the present is a cognitive vantage point on the universe, on the All (including ourselves), or is en route to such a viewpoint?

Structural realists have argued that something *is* conserved, as theories are replaced by other theories: namely structures that are (ultimately) mathematical. In fact, this is too modest. Many of the discoveries, techniques and applications of science still hold up, even when the theoretical framework changes fundamentally. The underlying point, however, is upheld: previous theories, if not actually misconceived, are clearly incomplete. The structure that is conserved across successive scientific revolutions is remote from anything that looks or feels like complete understanding. And much is lost en route to individual theories, before their reduction to structures they have in common with their predecessors and successors.[2]

A quick glance at what is shed en route to any high-level scientific theory should put paid to the notion of natural science being a path to a complete understanding of the world. Its theories are quantitative, typically taking the form of equations, correlating the sizes of abstractions – parameters – with the sizes of other abstractions. The scope of a theory such as $F = ma$ – Newton's second law of motion – is vast; but its content is not proportionate to this scope. Indeed, science gains scope at the price of specific content: it spreads wide because it spreads thin. The key inputs to these theories are measurements. We discussed the passage from experiences to measurements in earlier chapters. Measurement drains objects of their qualitative characteristics and, of course, of their human significance. While measurements require experience, they are ultimately empty of experience; of sense-making infused with sense experience. The extraordinary precision and scope of (say) $E = mc^2$ distracts from the fact that it relegates most of the world to an invisible background. The sharpness of its sharp edges is the consequence of the winnowing away of the fluff of particularity – the variety, multiplicity and dynamism of the world. We can seem to see everything because we overlook almost everything, forgetting that we may lose (important aspects of) the measure of things because we measure them. Knowledge at the highest level of natural science seems to be a form of sense-making void of many important aspects of understanding. The constants of nature, which we discussed in the previous chapter, are a scotoma or floater in our intellectual gaze. We shall return to these issues presently but let us examine the more basic constraints on the advance of understanding.

We have discussed the (necessary) contamination by the subject in even the most abstract knowledge, arising out of the fact that knowledge has to be experienced by someone. We can never know "reality" independently of the means by which we know it, so that what-is, or more precisely the sum total of things other than the knower, directly intimates itself. Knowledge from no perspective – without the visible or invisible constraints of bodily being, of sense experience, of culture, and of history – is in danger of becoming blankness or darkness as the variousness of people, places and things converges to theoretical, mind portable, generality. This applies not only to individual subjects but to the collective subject who defines what is available to be known – and shapes the received ideas of the time. Knowledge falls within schemata, defined by concepts. Kant identified some very broad categories of understanding such as "causation" or "unity versus multiplicity". Our concern here is with the constraint of schemata that apply at a less fundamental level than Kant envisaged. Without the accidents of culture and history, there would be a featureless terrain. It is only within a highly formatted, prescribed cognitive field that the effortful advance of our understanding can take place. Each generation picks up the story where it has been left by the previous generation. Inquiry is visibly or invisibly framed by assumptions that give the concepts that guide or prompt inquiry, and the techniques that assist them, their intuitive validity, which allows them to provide a jumping-off point of "the taken for granted".

The most visible, if not necessarily the most limiting, constraints are those that come from the history, the customs and practice, of the specialty within which the pursuit of knowledge takes place. There are two opposing tendencies: the convergence of principles and explanatory paradigms from different disciplines (particularly evident in natural sciences); and the splitting off of disciplines and sub-disciplines with their own languages, techniques and areas of interest. The tendency to division is driven in part by the increasing numbers of individuals involved in advancing knowledge – or at least having to seem to do so – and by the multiplication of the institutions supporting cognitive advance within the sciences and the humanities.

Fission can occur in the most surprising places. While we might expect a division of labour in intrinsically discursive empirical fields such as the study of literature or history and the special sciences, it is perhaps less to be expected in philosophy or mathematics. Even so, expertise in partial differential equations, topology, algebra, geometry, algebraic geometry, logic(s), probability theory, numerical analysis, is scattered over many (often non-communicating) minds. Beyond these more explicit constraints are the elective limits of scholars, paradoxically most evident in the humanities, where it is entirely acceptable to devote one's entire life to a minor poet or a particular dialect and to know remarkably little about adjacent fields of inquiry. Even so-called "polymaths" are merely individuals who are slightly less "oligomathic" than the run of schol-ars – just as those who are deemed to be "well-read" are merely a little less ill-read than their fellows – though we imagine that we have got a sufficient inkling, even a measure – of what we have not read "personally".[3]

Ahmed Alkhateeb has pointed out that there were 1.2 million papers pub-lished in the biomedical sciences alone in 2016, although "the average scientist reads only about 250 papers a year":

> Scientists are deriving hypotheses from a smaller and smaller fraction of our collective knowledge and consequently, more and more, asking the wrong questions, or asking ones that have already been answered. Also, human creativity seems to depend increasingly on the stochas-ticity of previous experiences – particular life events that allow a researcher to notice something others do not. Although chance has always been a factor in scientific discovery, it is currently playing a much larger role than it should.[4]

Alkhateeb believes he has a solution to this problem when it comes to facili-tating scientific advance. The point, however, remains: we individually know little of what is known. We are less aware of this than we should be because what we do "know of" are often summaries of summaries of summaries. Or results that are the end of a multitude of intellectual journeys of which we know little or nothing. By such means we also imagine we can encompass histories – of the novel, of science, of England – at a glance. We are too easily satisfied with inklings.

Behind this is a larger truth: that, while we develop ideas collectively, they must still be known individually. We often overlook this because our collec-tive knowledge and understanding is "out there", being collected, or at least simultaneously present, on paper, magnetic media and the internet. This is deceptive, of course, because we cannot outsource knowing to insentient paper, hard discs, or the electronic bearers of data that have boundless capac-ity – although the careless use of the word "information" conceals this. Only a minute fraction of what humanity has come to know or understand is cap-tured in any individual human mind – in whom alone knowledge is known and understanding is understood.

How knowledge actually lives in a token mind – as opposed to that illusory collective "humanity" or "the human mind" – is not entirely reassuring. Even the cognoscenti make inattentive, frequently inhospitable hosts. The con-sciousness of a busy (and who is not busy?) and distracted (and who is not distracted?) individual is a poor receptacle for a large idea. Understanding ideas is at best intermittent and, in being understood, they are often diminished, shrink-wrapped by our narrow and intermittent hearkening. The general theory of relativity lives a wretched life in the Wednesdays even of a physicist. Its magnificence glimmers only intermittently – or not at all if it is reduced from a Himalayan view of the world of motion to a set of equations that can be used to make calculations. As for the rest of us, who are not physicists, though we live in a world in part created by Einstein, the theory presents itself as opaque chains of symbols, clumsily and inaccurately translated into words we can understand just about or not at all.

If we add to this standing disability, fluctuations of awareness and interest, misting and demisting of consciousness, tiredness, confusion, and boredom, dozens of rival preoccupations, quotidian concerns that appropriate our thoughts, we can see what a precarious existence the major cognitive advances of any time have in the life of those very few who are aware of them. Even the torch-bearers of the cognitive advances of the age tend the flame intermittently. The higher level of sense for the most part sleeps in us and the knowledge known to the race is unknown to the greater part of humanity, even those who benefit from it.

This may sound rather pessimistic but we have hardly begun to take the measure of the chaos of the token mind where, ultimately, collective cognitive advance has to be experienced. Yes, we are structured or at least stitched together by memory and responsibility and the standing conditions of our lives. Within this informal trellis, however, we are a scattering of occasions. Things of the mind are always in competition with more compelling attractions and repulsions. And our moments hold only a minute portion of our cognitive sum. What we are at any given time reflects little of what we have passed through; our active knowledge reflects little of our passive knowledge; and our passive knowledge, available on prompting, is dwarfed by what has been returned by forgetfulness to the huge realm of those things of which we are ignorant. There is no moment at which we can access the sum of what we have known or understood.

Ignorance, as we have noted particularly in Chapter 7, begins close to home. Understanding ourselves is necessarily incomplete, and falls short of humanity's self-knowledge for a variety of reasons. Two are entirely obvious. Firstly, to build on a point just made, understanding must be a matter of moments and there is no moment that can capture the entirety of the understanding self to which it belongs. No second can capture an hour, even less a day, a week, a year, or decades. Secondly, we are irreducibly singular and there are no individual differences that can be guaranteed not to make a difference. I have no idea how the general theory of relativity is present in the lives of my fellow men. This may be thought of as irrelevant, given that it belongs to a public body of knowledge and is not a matter of a private succession of experiences. Even so, how knowledge is actually known touches intimately on the question of the cognitive advance of humanity.

We have already noted how our subjectivity is invaded from below by the sub-personal characteristics of embodiment. Here, it is the invasion from above by the collective consciousness out of which the language of self-understanding grows that is highlighted. We do not understand ourselves entirely from within. First, we judge ourselves from an imaginary standpoint of an understanding superior to the part of ourselves we are passing judgement on. Secondly, the language we use to characterize ourselves is external to us; self-ascription is mediated through the voice of the General Other whose authority can be devastating as when we are driven to suicide by guilt or shame. We shall return to language presently.

How little we are aware of our ignorance is a tribute to our capacity for self-deception, as we sometimes aim to deceive others, regarding the extent of our mental reach. We can refer knowingly to things we do not know, nod allusively to many things we do not truly understand.[5] The shallow trickle of internal soliloquy can imagine it has sufficient draft to contain ideas and concepts and theories that are in fact little more than recited sentences, phrases echoed with ditto-head subservience in our internal soliloquy. We can entertain many thoughts without truly having, or being, had by them: this would include all thoughts containing the word "universe". Even on those rare occasions when we busy ourselves with the things of the mind, they are reduced to cognitive splashes and shards. The most examined life is mostly not in the business of examining; and the examination is often just a flow of words, shells uninhabited by that to which they refer, as it would appear if it were truly imagined. We all have ideas above our station because our station cannot ascend to even the most commonplace ideas.

The flow, the inner momentum of thought, drives us on and past, even where it is not deflected or interrupted by outer events. We are like Leopold Bloom in *Ulysses*, endlessly nattering to ourselves, in a barely controlled monologue – scarcely less random than the rain of events – that we hardly listen to, or into, not pausing to inhabit what we are articulating, or which effortlessly, articulates itself, a jabbering that at times threatens to become mental tinnitus. This incessant low-grade activity (poised between happening and agency, between activity and passivity) is not entirely verbal of course.[6] Images may be swept into and out of the flow of consciousness, particularly since the latter draws heavily on the uniquely human episodic and semantic memory.[7] It seems that, without the scaffolding of a coherent external world collectively constructed inside a physical universe that is stable and predictable, we would be in a state of delirium. And some of that delirium still remains in the most supported moments of engagement with larger ideas. Plato's dialogues present a flattering image of individuals fully, undistractedly engaged in philosophical dialogue. The joke that "a lecturer is someone who talks in *other people's* sleep" acknowledges that there is the slenderest of tightropes of articulation connecting one inner chaos on the podium with rows of such chaoses in the auditorium. These are the unflattering truths about our token minds, that reflect so little of what the notional collective mind knows, though such minds are the only place where knowledge is actually known and understanding understood. They are minute compared with the collective consciousness and the boundless archive where our cognitive achievements are stored. They are pinprick drops in a waterfall.

This is one of the reasons why our individual minds often cannot follow where the collective mind indicates. It is most obvious in the case of those very large and very small numbers which are found everywhere science looks. Highlighting this is to focus on one of the consequences of what we might call "the fall of the mind" from a supernatural entity to something scattered through humanity; of *Logos* from an eternal soul, made in the image of God and able to mirror His creation, to manifestations of living, local, parochial human beings. Our sense-making is realized inside a biography, of an unfolding self-consciousness that is not a timeless category reflecting the universe as a whole, offering the opportunity to the universe to tell the truth about itself. This dialogic, social mind, indexed to historical and intersubjective contexts, cannot aspire to encompass all that is known, to achieve a full understanding of what is now understood.[8]

Our minds, then, are not The Human Mind. Even less are they Cartesian timeless substances curated by God to ensure their access to truth and transparent to themselves. Of course, Descartes' mind left certainty as soon as it left itself; or, indeed, went beyond the self-evident truth that it was thinking. I cannot be mistaken over the fact that I am thinking because such a mistake would be composed of thinking. How much, however, the *cogito* argument – "I think therefore I am" – delivers is highly controversial. Once we get beyond the existential tautology – "I am thinking therefore I am thinking" – there is not much on offer. The most intimate barrier comes not so much from uncertainty about what I am thinking about – although the "I" is somewhat indeterminate – as what I am thinking with or, more precisely, what I am thinking *in*: language.

In the last chapter we touched on semantic externalism – the thesis that "the meaning and reference of some of the words we use is not solely determined by the ideas we associate with them or by our internal physical state". We alluded to the dream of an entirely transparent, rational language that would not be subject to the accidents of cultural and intellectual history.

The semiotic utopia of a *characteristica universalis* was most famously articulated by Leibniz although the notion of an entirely transparent language has haunted thought since Plato's *Cratylus.* The allegory of the Tower of Babel may indirectly express the worry that "discourse is the violence we do to things".[9] Leibniz avoided that violence by privileging abstraction. His ideal language would encompass mathematical, scientific and metaphysical concepts. A less ambitious version of this was Gottlob Frege's *Begriffsschrift* or "Concept Script" that was influential in implanting in twentieth-century analytic philosophers the dream of an entirely transparent mode of philosophical discourse conducted in the terminology of formal logic. Using such a language, we would know exactly what we are talking about: our words would not get in the way of the thoughts they express. By not employing terms and grammars that have developed through the accidents of history, we would avoid the risk of finding that we have taken on board conceptions and assumptions that we are not aware of, or that our interlocuters have done the same. Consequently, we would not waste our time quarrelling over implications and connotations lurking in the untidy lexical "crannyware" that fills potential hiatuses in the fabric of everyday discourse and the idiolect out of which we weave it.

Unfortunately, disinfecting discourse of baggage might result in emptying it altogether – rather analogous to removing the knowing subject from knowledge. Nothing particular, or even substantive, can be said in the *characteristica universalis* as is evidenced in the models that Leibniz referenced – notably mathematics. The *characteristica universalis* would be suitable only for the Theory of Everything – or highest level mathematico-physical discourse – which seems like the Theory of Nothing-in-Particular and hence perilously close to the Theory of Nothing-at-All. The fact that the century-long endeavour to get philosophy to speak in a kind of *characteristica universalis* – namely formal logic – has delivered so little itself speaks volumes (just how little it has delivered is concealed by the fact that it has become a branch of philosophy of its own, happily getting on with its own thing).[10]

The idea of such a language is not far from the notion of the language that God might speak.[11] The secular equivalent would be the native language of the givenness of things. It is perhaps too frivolous to characterize it as the language that pebbles, or a field, or a landscape might choose to speak if they were inclined to talk about themselves. It is probably not necessary to add that if a stone could name itself it would not call itself a "stone"; that is to say, it would not locate itself in the network of concepts, categories, and classes we place over the world, even if *per impossibile* it were able to allocate itself to a general type.[12] If the whole universe uttered itself, the pandiculation – and *res ipsa loquitur* – would be insufferable as well as incomprehensible (cf. the question "If God truly spake, could any bear to hear?").[13]

An idea (touched on in Chapter 3) that has attracted some attention and even in some quarters commanded belief is that the universe *is* identical with information; that, to use John Wheeler's formulation, "It [arises] from Bit".[14] If this were true, and the idea of information retained anything of what it means in daily life, this would suggests an intrinsic language of the universe, in which Being would be identical with a givenness that would articulate itself.

It is worth dwelling on this briefly because inadvertently it shows the absurdity of the very idea of a shadowless language that discloses, without distortion, the givenness of things. Such a language presupposes that givenness, even things in themselves, are intrinsically linguistic or at least composed of information and that the latter does not require for its standing as information recipients who are distinguished from information itself. Wheeler's "It from bit" – which derives its rationale from observer dependency in quantum mechanics – gives ontological priority to information:

> *It from bit.* Otherwise put, every *it* – every particle, every field of force, even the space-time continuum itself – derives its function, its meaning, its very existence entirely – even if in some contexts indirectly – from the apparatus-elicited answers to yes-or-no questions, binary choices, bits. It from bit symbolizes that every item of the physical world has at bottom … an immaterial source and explanation; that which we call reality arises in the last analysis from the posing of yes-no questions; and the registering of equipment-evoked responses; in short, that all things physical are information-theoretic in origin and this is a *participatory universe.*[15]

Bits are "individual, detector-elicited electron hits". As Julian Barbour expresses it, for Wheeler "anything physical derives its very existence from discrete detector-elicited information-theoretic answers to yes-or-no quantum binary choices: *bits*".[16] Information "is the ontological basement and is more basic than quantum fields or energy".[17] It is the ground of being, or ultimate reality.

There are obvious problems. If every "it" derives not only its function or meaning but its very existence from apparatus-elicited answers to yes-or-no questions, to binary choices, we are left having to explain the existence of the (macroscopic) apparatus, of material elevated to the status of being apparatus, of questions being posed, of the posers of the questions (characters such as Wheeler and his colleagues) and choices being made. In short, if Wheeler were right, very sophisticated behaviour on the part of very recent (and minute) parts of the universe (quantum physicists), would appear to be necessary for a universe to come into being. The existence of everything, in short, depends on the existence of certain items (and associated activities) that seem only recently to have emerged from everything, the kind of items for whom what happens counts as information.

"It from Bit" derives some of its respectability from an interpretation of quantum mechanics according to which the universe is a) digital – bitty, granular – rather than analogue or smooth; and b) indeterminate until measured. Claims to respectability are, however, groundless. Firstly, the notion of a field or a wave function presents the world as a continuum that becomes granular only in response to questions that bump up against the limits of certainty; and, secondly, uncertainty is in the eye of the beholder and without beholders there is neither certainty nor uncertainty nor resolution of the latter into the former.

There is an irony in the invocation of hard-headed physics to support idealism, as reflected in Wheeler's claim that "No phenomenon is a real phenomenon until it is an observed phenomenon".[18] This may at first seem like a truism, given that a phenomenon is etymologically "that which appears" and there can be no appearing without a sentient being to whom appearing appears. However, the use of the word "real" suggests that it is identical with what-is, with something that exists independently of sentient subjects.

The echoes of Kant in Wheeler's idea of the *participatory universe* – that the observer has a key role in bringing law-governed nature into being – were touched on in Chapter 3. They are only distant echoes because what Wheeler calls a "phenomenon" is in fact the outcome of a measurement, a highly mediated experience, that generates a somewhat dephenomenalized number or a "0" *v.* "1" answer. Wheeler's claim also raises questions about the entity in virtue of which there are observers. Presumably observers themselves are not real until they have been observed – but by what? At any rate, it is a striking expression of what may seem to be counter-intuitive – namely that hard-boiled materialism can lead, via extreme scientism, to idealism.

Here is not the place to argue with this ontologizing of the procedures of fundamental science. Wheeler's ideas earn their place in this chapter on the grounds of their heroism: they take to the limit the idea of the intrinsic language of reality, the pure accent of the givenness of things in themselves. For Wheeler, reality, observation and discourse (embedded in the idea of information) are all one. What the rocks and trees and mountains and planets utter is a *sotto voce* 4-dimensional utterance of the 0s and 1s that they themselves are. It is clear that neither existence (things [19]), meaning, or reference could be constructed in this way. If the condition of cognitive completeness were that our sense-making – knowledge, thought, speech – should be expressed in the language of things in themselves, then it will be an impossible goal.

As we have seen, the wider the application of the sense that is made, the less it seems to grasp reality. The aseptic discourse of theories and laws and equations lacks nutritious content. The seeming precision of, for example, $E = mc^2$ – true to many decimal places – conceals the fact that its vision is blurred: particulars, qualities, here and now, are sacrificed to generality, an entire world utterly out of focus; the world is seen from an aeroplane, a space-ship, a distant galaxy, from increasing remoteness until it vanishes. It is a world that is flattened by distance, without the depth that comes from the odour of significance. But in using ordinary discourse we are hostage to the constraints, unchosen implicature, the tints and accidents, of a language that has grown without a guiding purpose or directing mind.

It is an exaggeration to think that ordinary language "speaks us" (to borrow Heidegger's phrase[20]). While being "spoken by" this language we may be liberated to some degree from the parish of ourself, we are still hostage to the unrecorded jumble of influences that determined how language takes hold of the world. And there is a price even for this modest transcendence. We are distanced from ourselves such that the abstract thoughts that we have, and are had by, may seem alien, stale, and empty even as they are uttered. They lack existential weight. And what they shake off, even mislay, may be precisely that which is central to our own existence.

The limits to our understanding do not, of course, begin only when we think of the universe as a whole. Our token minds are rooted in token selves and those selves are invested in other selves. Trying to understand those other selves is fraught with difficulty. The romantic-pessimistic notion that we are monads, each entirely sealed off from the other, is a distraction from less absolute quotidian limitations. For much of the time, we know "very well", or "damn well" what X or Y is up to, what he or she means by it, and how it is experienced by others. Being justifiably despised by another person for bad behaviour torches off the layered distances that seem to insulate and conceal one person from another. Successful deception is built on an at least instrumental understanding of the way the other person sees or imagines the world. And we know, too, how to be kind and caring and to help in a way that is truly helpful. While we can journey towards romantic pessimism and play with the idea of ourselves as windowless monads, therefore, we do not quite arrive there. All but the most solipsistic among us are aware of what will make another person happy or sad, annoyed or pleased, notwithstanding that there are always surprises, not always gratifying, even in the most communicative and longstanding relationship.

Even so, there are scotomata at the heart of our understanding even of those closest to us, never mind the hordes with whom we interact as members of other hordes, or who stream past us in parallel crowds or who are simply known to us by a name (sometimes attached to a smidgeon of reputation or a cluster of attributes). We have little inkling of how they cohere inwardly, how *they* experience *us* from moment to moment, and what it is like to be them. The hearts of others sometimes seem more opaque even than the material world, if only because it matters so much more to know them and because there is so much more of moment to know.

There is a poignant reflection on this in the case of Einstein himself. At the time of his greatest intellectual triumphs, when he sensed most acutely that he was getting close to the Pythagorean dream of a mathematical understanding of the universe, he was in the midst of distressing family conflicts. He could make no sense of his older son's marital choices or his younger son's severe mental distress.[21] There could be no more tragic illustration of a fundamental disconnection within sense-making between objective knowledge – the classic path by which we mark cognitive advance – and lived meaning. We can share knowledge but not experience, even when we are exposed to the same events. My experience of what happened is registered in the context of a different viewpoint steeped in a different history.

Limitations arise even closer to home. Consider the extent to which we are surprised by our own thoughts – as when, as so often we finding ourselves inexplicably thinking of, remembering, or humming something. And then there is the question, touched on in Chapter 5 of the extent to which we are and are not our bodies, and our limited insight into the biological means by which we are able to continue in being. But more intimately still, there is the unsurprising, taken-for-granted utterly familiar ongoing self. We cannot get an overview of, even less gather up from 10,000 lost days, sufficient of ourselves to see, interpret and understand what we are or even truly to imagine what it must be like to meet, share a room with, or live with ourself. And there are experiences we do not fully understand in which meaning seems to converge on one intense, laser-lit spot. The paroxysm of meaning that is the unbearable hunger when desire fixes on a contingent other, and the joy of music that conveys strange and delicious significance without definite reference – these are episodic headline examples of a more continuous reality of an internal opacity we usually fail to notice because we are looking out rather than in.

There is a wriggle. My awareness of my lack of insight into either what I am, or what I am like for others, surely suggests another kind of, possibly higher-level, insight. To know what one does not know is the venerable Socratic wisdom, however ill-defined it must be. A desperate remedy, perhaps – analogous to the Pascalian claim that, since we are capable of recognizing that we are minute accidents in a vast universe, we must be more than minute accidents in a vast universe. Our unique sense of insignificance makes us special – even significant: the knowledge that makes us small is a testament to our greatness.

Thus, the fightback against the encroaching sense of our cognitive limitations that seem unaltered by advances in knowledge and our power to explain things. And there are other strategies for propping up our self-esteem. One is to argue that the limitations I have just identified may seem not to count since they are not limitations on objective knowledge and it is this that counts. We could press this argument further by suggesting that an unlimited or completely objective understanding of another's subjectivity, or of our own subjectivity considered from an objective viewpoint, is a contradiction. What would it be like to have an inside-outside view of another or an outside-inside view of ourself? What's more, instead of seeing them as evidence of a limit on understanding that begins close to home and extends outwards into an unbroken cognitive darkness, we can point out that the limit of our understanding applies to something merely local. If I can understand what regulates the movements of 200 billion galaxies, does it count if I don't know why you are so upset today?

Not so fast. The failure to understand something that matters so much is the other side of the failure of huge facts to matter at all. The limitations of the token mind whose blood supply is the token self, the embodied subject, exposes the extent to which our knowledge exceeds our capacity to imagine it and our general understanding falls short of something that we can live and make full-blooded sense of. It further highlights the disconnection between the collective cognitive advance of humanity (if we allow that there is such a thing) and its realization in the individual human beings in whom alone it is actualized.

It exposes something else of that collective advance. As we progress, we leave much behind that cannot, or should not, be discarded. As we have noted, science, in its majestic ascent to awe-inspiring generality, via measurements generating or testing purely quantitative laws, loses not only the indexicals of human existence ("here" and "now" and so on), and meaning and significance, but also qualities. Abstract patterns replace the garden of the world, and marginalize everything that differentiates one particular from another, beyond size and location (which are anyway borrowed from coordinates imported from without). Reality loses its ontological weight, being made of numerical ghosts. Matter, evaporating to a smoke of mathematical symbols, loses its connection with mattering. Long before we reach the acknowledged affronts of general relativity and quantum mechanics, we have entered a world that cannot be truly thought in the sense of being imagined, conceived, a cognitive atmosphere in which our imagination cannot breathe. We face a fundamental intellectual failure: the divergence, or at least non-convergence of scientific and existential sense. This is most poignantly expressed in the fact that existential sense tells me that I, and those whom I love are irreplaceable, infinitely valuable, and at the centre of what-is, whilst science, in its most advanced development, tells us that none of this has any truth. The trajectory of our journey of understanding at its most advanced – in fundamental science – was succinctly captured in the passage from physicist Robert Geroch quoted in the previous chapter, when he argued that we might judge the importance of new ideas on physics by the criterion of how many notions one might be obliged to discard.[22]

The ascent to generality seems to be simultaneously explaining and "de-explaining" and *Logos* veers towards *"Patho-Logos"*. The more powerful the explanation, the less it seems like an explanation, an affront not merely to common sense, but to everything in us that is tutored and reinforced by our senses and the physical and social intercourse of everyday life. And the reward for such self-denial is not entirely satisfactory. As Austrian physicist Anton Zeilinger put it: "[C]enturies of the search for causes ... leads us to a final wall. Suddenly, there is something, namely the individual quantum event, that we can no longer explain in detail".[23] Thus, the end-point of the appeal to postulated, hitherto hidden, entities, causes, forces and fields.

In an endeavour to correct de-explanation, reductionist explanations are reversed in the form of counter-reductionist explanations that invoke ideas such as "emergence" and "supervenience" mobilizing the all-purpose appeal to "complexity". For this writer, "emergence" is a hand-waving move, reminiscent of Tommy Cooper the magician and comedian who used the phrase "just like that!" when he pulled a rabbit out of the hat or tried to make the audience believe he had done so. The appeal to supervenience is an attempt to heal the self-inflicted wound of "infravenient" descriptions that often take the smallest units of being – such as atoms – as the most real, and most basic, elements of reality. When atoms dissolve into entangled mathematical structures, macroscopic building and the medium-sized blocks that populate our everyday world become inexplicable.

As we set ourselves aside in pursuit of explanation, those selves and the cognitive journey they have collectively taken, look to be part of what needs to be explained. Understanding is faced with the challenge of understanding itself, and knowledge with trying to find out how knowledge is possible. At any rate, we encounter what we might call the "ouroboros" paradox or enigma, expressed particularly clearly by Russell: "Naïve realism leads to physics, and physics, if true, shows that naïve realism is false".[24] This could be updated by noting that quantum mechanics, which denies or problematizes the existence of localized, macroscopic objects, interacting causally, depends on observations made by localized, macroscopic objects, interacting causally.[25] The physics which depends on people and things as normally understood is used to develop a world picture in which people and things are put into question.

This gives us another angle on the fact that advance towards complete sense-making is compromised by our being part of that which we are trying to understand; that science, and metaphysics, must be carried out from within their objects of inquiry. The objects of our knowledge and understanding, however, must necessarily be separate from the knower, the one who understands, the more so as their scope widens and they aim to become foundational. There cannot therefore be any return to our starting point, enabling us to apply our cognitive gains to the platform from which the journey took its rise. This is evident at even a fairly basic level. The coherence in a set of equations does not map on to the all-at-once of a visual field or a sense of unified "now". At a more basic level still, propositional reality cannot be reinserted into the unfolding *umwelt* of our moment-to-moment existence. At the most basic level of all, words can seem insoluble in experienced reality: they both exceed what is there, what is happening, in virtue of encompassing a whole class of instances, and fall short of it, being unable to capture the thisness of what-is.

The latter is an issue that has exercised poets, for whom "the exact curve of the thing" seems to elude the template of language. Hugo von Hofmannsthal captured both aspects of this unsatisfactory relationship between Word and Being. In his wonderful poem "Of the Outer Life",[26] he reflects on how the fragmentary nature of experience can be redeemed by words; how the heap of fragments connected only by "and" that is an ordinary evening with its innumerable objects and to-ings and fro-ings, its small change of beings and becomings, is redeemed when the word "evening" is uttered. The scattering that threatens to reduce reality to disconnected dross is reversed in the gathering up implicit in the word "evening".

In his semi-autobiographical *The Lord Chandos Letter*, however, Hofmannsthal tells the opposite story. His protagonist, Lord Chandos, a young writer, sends a letter to his friend the philosopher Francis Bacon explaining why he has not delivered on his promise: it is a crisis in his relationship to language. He no longer believes in the capacity of words to capture things – a revelation that came to him when he reflected on the unimaginable suffering of the rats for which he had laid down poison:

> I have lost my ability to think or speak of anything coherently. [...] My mind compelled me to [see] all things occurring in [ordinary] conversation from an uncanny closeness ... I no longer succeeded in comprehending them with the simplicity of the eye of habit. For me everything disintegrates into parts; no longer would anything let itself be encompassed by one idea.[27]

Thus, man the sense-making animal encounters in the most direct way the limits to the sense he can make of the world in which he finds himself.

Those limits are many and various, as we have seen, but they seem most obdurate when the sense-maker tries to include himself in the sense that is made – a task whose full complexity is spelled out by Nagel:

> [A] self-transcendent conception should ideally explain the following four things: (1) what the world is like; (2) what we are like; (3) why the world appears to beings like us in certain respects how it is and in certain respects as it isn't; (4) how beings like us can arrive at such and such a conception.[28]

A challenging agenda. It incorporates the impossible task of finding a kind of light that endeavours to illuminate, and indeed see, itself as part of the seen. And it is one that is provoked not, or not only, by the fact that we are finite parts of an infinite or boundless reality but that we are also aware of this and, in this respect at least, seem to enclose or even surmount our condition. We are consequently able to entertain the dream of doing so in other respects.

Any sense of our helplessness may be mitigated by seeing that the laws of nature do not underpin any actual happening: they do not reach so low. Law-abiding nature is yet more helpless. The laws require the existence of basic stuff they have not brought into being to act as their substrate. This is the most fundamental of the "initial conditions" which they presuppose. At the same time this represents a limit to our understanding. And its other side is the melancholy truth that our most advanced form of understanding yields a picture of the world drained of all that makes up the life of the one who would understand it; drained of sensibility and even sense experience. Meaning, significance, sense that makes sense are lost. Equations and general statements fail to flower into a world-revealing, horizon-bursting revelation. Progress in objective understanding does not amount to progress towards a complete wakefulness.

Such is the price of the liberation of *Logos* from *Mythos*. It should be a signal to return to the preoccupations described in Chapter 2 that might seem to have been consigned to the history of thought. We need to rejoin that history; though precisely at what point we should rejoin it is not at all clear. What is clear is that we should do so in a spirit of wonder, even humility. And the most pressing challenge for secular thought is to reunite strands of understanding that have come apart; to unite the meaning of the glimpse of order we have when we comprehend the most general laws of nature with that which we see in the face of one with whom we are in love and the pleasure of a successful inquiry that takes us to a new landscape of possibility. We may have to accept that there may be no return to the union of the meanings of life and of the way to live with the laws of nature as seen for example in pre-Christian Stoic philosophy or pre-Galilean science.

One thing at least is clear: that certain paths lead to barren land. The attempt to merge the aims and ends of life biologically construed with the basis of our knowledge and understanding – exemplified in evolutionary epistemology and other manifestations of the naturalism that is ubiquitous in contemporary thought – is an instructive failure, not the least for a breath-taking superficiality that misses the profundity of the meta-cognitive challenge of making sense of the fact that we make sense of so much. We need to look elsewhere for a mode of understanding that will encompass the astonishing mind-portability of the laws and principles uncovered by natural science on the one hand and on the other our ineluctable everyday common sense; the pursuit of objective knowledge and the most general explanation with a narrative that incorporates the meanings we live by, inside, or against in our daily existence; the local explanations with the grand all-encompassing vision; the great facts that enclose us with the small facts that preoccupy and define us. The journey to such a destination must involve an awakening from the parochial wakefulness of the quotidian taken-for-granted.

This is scarcely a modest ambition and fraught with contradictions. The ascent to generality, as we have had occasion repeatedly to observe, means the loss of locality. Actual events, the items that populate our days, elude the laws that have the widest application, as they have a singular residue that resists digestion. At the same time to understand anything fully, it seems to be necessary to have a full understanding of everything, because all particulars have a direct or indirect explanatory connection with all other particulars.

We should be prepared to arrive at strange places. In this respect, contemporary physics, while it should not be taken to be the last word on what is out there and what we are, should be an inspiration. After all, the most powerful theory in contemporary physics – quantum field theory – can license the idea that our localized viewpoints have irrupted into a universe which is a single unified wave.[29] If, however, "thatter" is an irruption into Being, it is difficult to see how it – or the knowing subject – could have been the product of processes (physical, biological) taking place in Being, including those described by quantum or any other kind of physics.

The admirable Hegelian aspiration to arrive individually or collectively at the merging of knowing with the totality of Being in an Absolute Subject seems not only grandiose but unachievable in principle, given that minds are necessarily multiple (our main reason in Chapter 3 for rejecting Kant's transcendental idealism) and mattering inescapably parochial.[30] At the very least, there would be a loss of the very reality, the material world, that is made sense of as we token minds ascend to the conditions of a general mind fused with – well, generality. It would moreover result in the collapse of the necessary gap between the knower and the known, without which there is no "thatter". Even so, like contemporary physics, its ambition and fearlessness should inspire us.

The vision of the Absolute Subject does not, moreover, engage with the most obvious limits to understanding which can be designated by the unanswerability of certain questions that seem legitimate even if our asking cannot match their depth: Why is there anything at all? Why is it unstable rather than static? Why does it unfold in a law-like way? Why do its laws seem to take the form they do? Why (to return to an earlier question) do the constants associated with those laws have the values they have? And how is it that there are conscious beings and among them some consciously making sense of the world and of themselves in it? These are, of course, necessary conditions of there being a world in which we can live, live together, and ask these questions. But this invocation of the anthropic principle simply moves the question on, though it highlights the accidents behind the capacity for knowledge – accidents of origin which seem to taint our knowledge. While it does not necessarily throw into question the knowledge we have, by implying that other accidents might have led to other knowledge, other realities, it does imply that knowledge cannot *pace* panpsychists be elevated to a metaphysical feature of the sum total of what is, taking its place alongside space, time, matter, energy, forces, fields, and so on – unless of course we are prepared to accept a full-blown idealism, when space, time, matter, energy, forces, fields are swallowed into the knowing mind.

If we accepted the possibility of a state of complete understanding, another question would face us. Would it be a terminus? How would it continue in time? The intuition that where there is a question, there must be the possibility of an answer – because the question seems to open a space to accommodate it – seems problematic in the case of a question that encompasses everything. But this slides into another, perhaps more disheartening, problem. We think of sense-making, understanding, as *dynamic* – a *passage* typically from a question to an answer. This passage seems unlikely where the question is the totality of things, including our own lives, warped into a question mark. Would it be something that was iterated in token instances of the same type? This hardly seems likely or even desirable. Sense-making, and the sense that sense is being made, is driven by a gap in sense. Explanation is characteristically the elimination of a temporary cognitive hiccup or even outrage. Understanding is a mode of becoming – hence its participial form: understand*ing*.

Even knowledge seems to be known only in coming to be known – or known again in recollection. Knowledge – such as my knowing *that* such-and-such has taken place – does not cut much presence as a state, stored in waiting for the call that may never come. In short, sense as stasis does not, well, make sense any more than a consciousness that has come to a halt. Even so, it is stasis that is sought. A false stasis often tempts us: completed thoughts are too readily satisfied with themselves, with their local arrivals. The full stop that is supposed to mark something completed in thought, should really unpack itself to an encircling horizon.

For the broadest living daylight, it is necessary to return to the flesh and blood knower and the Relative Subject. Scaling up the puzzle of the sense-making animal tends to freeze the passage from question to answer, so that clue and solution are gathered up into, for example, equations, which lacks for example a beginning and an end. $E = mc^2$ could just as well be $mc^2 = E$. There is a tendency within our explanation of the physical world to converge on something static, such as an algebraic matrix. This stasis – which is not due simply to the fact that a Theory of Everything encompasses a totality that cannot, by definition be added to – is at odds with the intrinsic dynamism of meaning.

If the completion of sense-making is impossible, even self-contradictory, and the very idea of absolute cognitive progress lacks criteria beyond the compromised ones relating to the advance of the welfare and ambitions of humanity, every age must be equidistant from the goal of rounding off the sense of the world. When sense-making comes to an end, therefore, it is not because we have arrived at complete comprehension of our condition and the world in which we pass our lives. It is because our sense-making has been terminated by bodily extinction.

For secular thought, the Word that is made flesh is fated to interruption before it can complete its own sentence. Lacking the hope of resurrection and the full illumination of an after-life, we unbelievers must live with the knowledge that our extraordinary capacity for comprehending the world is an incomplete mitigation of our helplessness, and of the darkness that surrounds our light, of the ignorance that bounds our knowledge and of the senselessness that delimits the sense we make of things.

Coda

It is necessary to combine recognition of our contingency, our finitude, and our containment in the world with an ambition of transcendence, however limited may be our success in achieving it.   Thomas Nagel[1]

One might say that the history of thought could be summarized in these words: *It is absurd by what it seeks, great by what it finds.*   Paul Valéry[2]

It is time to conclude our inquiry into the sense-making animal, our endeavour to understand or (if that is too ambitious) to see a little more clearly the fact that we are able at least in part to comprehend the universe and that we seem to progress to ever higher or more complete levels of comprehension. This becomes all the more extraordinary as cognitive advance enlarges the scale of its own object. We have always been pin-pricks in a world that out-sizes us many-fold but the billions of light years that now routinely populate our conversations have reduced us proportionately. It is even more remarkable, given that we cannot get ourselves out of the way as the necessary subjects of knowledge and, as Nagel puts it, "our ambitions of transcendence" have to be combined "with recognition of our contingency, our finitude, and our containment in the world". The very idea of total understanding is inescapably absurd but the history of thought it has prompted is "great by what it finds".

We have always been smaller than what we know: if we are great in virtue of our knowledge, we are minute in the light of that knowledge. This is evident, at the level of perception, in our visual field, where we are located at the centre of a space given all at once that may exceed many-thousand-fold the volume occupied by our bodies. The widening, encircling horizon shrinks us to a mustard grain. Vision is the metaphor of knowledge – and for good reasons. Knowledge is mediated awareness: I can access that object over there without being in direct contact with it. This asymmetry liberates us from the equality of action and reaction that is evident in touch, where I am pressed by that which I palpate. The inequality of the seer and the seen empowers the seers even at the cost of their feeling dwarfed by the vastness of the visual field. That I can be aware of more than I am, or could fill, or even could engage with, is the acceptable price of a mode of awareness that exposes us to things to which it is not itself directly exposed.

A visual field being an incomplete revelation – objects are too distant, are puzzling, are half-hidden – awakens the possibility of further sense to be made. I can see that there are things I cannot see. Like more advanced forms of knowledge, sight comes with insight (the word is not accidental) into its own limitations. Vision is, as we have said, the most "epistemic" of the senses.

All of which goes some way to explaining the prevalence of vision and light as metaphors of cognitive advance and intelligibility (touched on in the Appendix to Chapter 2). "Illumination", "outlook", "enlightenment", "glimmers" of understanding and "flashes" of insight, critical "reflection" – these are just a few of the terms revealing our sense of the close relationship between vision and cognition. Traditional mythological understanding of *Logos* is rich in metaphors of light. As the first intimation of transcendence, prefiguring "that-ter", "Light" according to Sir Thomas Browne "is the shadow of God".[3] The distinctive feature of eternity is *lux aeterna*. God incarnate as Jesus Christ is "The light of the world".[4] Conversely, failure of understanding, or a limit to knowledge, is captured by metaphors of darkness.[5] Limits to *Logos* – ignorance and death – are also imaged in darkness, with death being endless night. Temporary vehicles of *Logos*, we arc through the light, before we dip down into the dark.

Notwithstanding its dependence on the flesh of which it is made and in which it is embedded, therefore, vision is the primordial, ubiquitous source of transcendence, the means of our escape from the confines of our body, our passage from subjectivity and selfhood to objective knowledge. It lights up a world to be made sense of, enabling hesitation between what is presented and what is understood, the gap in which inquiry becomes possible. The mystery of the sense-making, as opposed to the merely sentient, creature begins here.[6]

There is an obvious rival candidate in the other major telereceptor – hearing – which also brings with it the sense of "more sense to come". However, hearing is patchy and intermittent and does not create the basis for a continuous field, for a world in which other items are located. The importance of hearing in the extension of sense-making, beyond episodes of "Wazzat?", as sounds are traced to their sources, is a relatively recent development – with the movement of language to centre-stage in human experience of a world they have jointly created within the natural world. Even then, vision does not concede hegemony to hearing, and additionally reasserts itself through written symbols[7] and ever more ubiquitous images.

The present inquiry has been a continuation of a lifelong humanist project to see humankind more clearly, not through the darkened glass of religion or of the equally darkened glass of a reductive naturalism. Both approaches disparage humanity. Religious doctrine sees us as fallen creatures and as infinitely less than the God Who created us. Seen through the lens of naturalistic secular thought, we are unrisen creatures, defined by the putative biological processes and needs that forged the species of primates to which we belong.

The vision of us as "risen" will seem self-flattering. Worse, it might seem cruelly sentimental given how human beings have treated each other in the past, and continue to treat each other in the present. If we are "risen" our cognitive ascent has not been matched by ethical advance. A species that commits bloodshed, torture, enslavement, and unjust incarceration on the scale we continue to see, that espouses a political order that moralises making the world safe for the rich and intolerable for the poor, where public, workplace, and domestic life is often characterized by bullying, is not to be judged, even less defined, solely by its extraordinary cognitive achievements. The spectacular collective development of our understanding – which has involved cooperation on a scale and of a form not before seen in or imagined by any other sentient creatures – has produced technology that often serves brutal or degrading ends. From the large-scale horrors of weapons and communications systems that make savagery more efficient, to the small-scale shallowness, petty-mindedness or smuttiness of the internet, the fruits of our shared genius have frequently been subordinated to ends unworthy of us.

Against this, however, we should acknowledge that technology has on balance been put to good uses, that the behaviour of humans seems overall to be improving[8] and that our cognitive advance has contributed largely to a global increase in average life, health, and comfort expectancy. We take the civic order of the world – even where admittedly, it means, even in advanced democratic societies, that the odds are stacked against many who live in them – too much for granted.

In his essay on James Joyce's *Ulysses* T. S. Eliot spoke of "the futility and anarchy of contemporary life"[9] expressing a view that has been standard among critics of modernity for over a century. We could, however, talk with equal justification of the over-charged meanings and intricate, tightly controlled order of modern and postmodern life. The seething mass of shared and opposed senses of daily existence is nothing short of a miracle, irrespective of whether it enables people to flourish or fail, to enjoy their lives or simply suffer their existence. (The question of how well-qualified *anyone* is to make such observations will be set aside).[10]

And yes, we often use the gift of life and free time, made possible by technology rooted in science, to pursue narrow appetites and obsessions, to expand our portfolio of pointless possessions, and to be preoccupied by trivia energized by jealousies, prejudices, and hatreds founded on reactions fuelled by primitive takes on our small parts of the world. But ... but ....

Yes, there is no clear point of arrival for humanity's cognitive advance and our individual participation in the collective sense is limited in our often narrow daily round, and cut short as our lives reach their term. Our personal trajectory – the very fact it is explicit and bespoke in some aspects of the direction it takes – depends on the impersonal mechanisms of our largely mindless bodies, and our end will typically result from processes that in all probability are not meant. We are more likely to die of a material cause than for a meaningful one; or *of* an efficient rather than *for* a final cause.

And yet ... the mystery of the sense-making animal goes deeper than our moral failings, our shallowness and our cognitive limitations. For that which makes us capable of failing morally and living shallowly is not seen elsewhere in the animal kingdom. In the opening sentence of his magnum opus, Derek Parfit declares that "We are the animal that can both understand and respond to reasons".[11] This is true so far as it goes; but reasons are not there in advance, waiting to be harvested and acted upon. Our cognitive distinction, therefore, lies not in merely understanding and responding to reasons but in observing, extracting, imagining, inventing, in short, sensing that there are or might be reasons in the world in which we find and locate ourselves or that there ought or must be. This is the primordial intuition that has, in some difficult to characterize sense, opened the way to the universe dimly awakening to its own nature in the human mind.

I will end with an image that in part prompted this book. If you approach the Greek island of Patmos, said to be the home of St John of the Apocalypse, the first thing you will see is a cluster of wind turbines. They are rarely still. Their somersaulting vanes are turning the mindless energy of the wind into usable electricity that will illuminate and warm the houses of the islanders and power the countless gadgets they employ to make their lives more comfortable and to connect their means with their ends. This technological miracle is a late consequence of the transformation of the many dialects of the air – whistling canyons, threshing trees, calling birds – into articulate speech.

The turbines are *Logos* at work on the island where St John's namesake[12] preached his doctrine of the Four Last Things. Between the wind blowing across the island and the world in which the wind has been transformed into power subordinated to human purposes there necessarily intervened the Word, the transformation of the air, in the lexical turbine of the human throat, into meanings shared and transformed, driving the journey of humanity to its present distance from the natural world.

The itinerary of the *Logos* has been extraordinarily complex, with many false leads, moments of inspiration and delusions, illuminations and occlusions, discord and concord, dissent and consensus, quarrels, bloodshed, and acts of extraordinary goodness and evil. The most consequential step has been the gradual separation of *Logos* from the *Mythos* of the kind St John transmitted. While this is traditionally seen to have been emancipating and as having liberated the pursuit of sense from a disabling respect for the constraints of authoritarian traditions of understanding, it has also separated sense-making from something absolutely profound, something that we, aware of our mortality, cannot do without: an idea as deep as the fact that we have finite lives, and that the sense we make of them is provisional and incomplete; an idea as profound as the mystery of our human being and the unimaginable fact that it is an *augenblick* in eternity; that this profound sense "That I am!" – which was the remote prompt of this present inquiry – lights something that is true only for a short time.[13] The idea is, of course, that of God – for which there is no adequate secular replacement.

We cannot embrace *Mythos* to order. We do, however, need to reawaken the sense of the depths for which it once stood and its acknowledgement of the mystery of the sense-making animal, evident in every nook and cranny of our shared world of ideas and *praxis*. The world we endeavour to make sense of is unimaginably greater than we are and, even within the candle-lit parish of our days, has a complexity that should constantly astound us. The future of *Logos* – of the interwoven senses we make of the natural and human world and the sense they make of us – will be central to the evolving future of humanity and may even be a determinant of whether, or for how long, we have a future. The sense-making animal will continue to see horizons not as encircling limits but as a promise of an open, a beyond where the presently unimaginable will be imagined, conceived, and brought into the fold of coherent sense.

For the present, we have to settle for the elusive joy of the realization *That I am, That it is, That "that" is.* This is where I began fifty or more years ago – and where I must end, albeit in the knowledge that the world I shall in due course leave has much unfinished – and in the light of the foregoing inquiry probably unfinishable – business of understanding.

Notes

PREFACE

1. Recently I came across an extraordinary passage in a memoir by a fellow doctor, the neurosurgeon Henry Marsh: "I ran fully clothed into the sea and stood with the waves lapping about my knees, soaking my school uniform. As I stood there, I was suddenly struck by an overwhelming awareness of myself and of my own consciousness. It was like looking into a bottomless well, or seeing myself between a pair of parallel mirrors, and I was terrified" (*Admissions: A Life in Brain Surgery*, 130). This struck me as the other side of the "that" revelation.
2. "Thus in all men, as soon as their reason has become ripe for speculation, there has always existed and will continue to exist some kind of metaphysics" (Kant, *Critique of Pure Reason*, 56).
3. His reference to "that sense of arbitrariness which the objective self feels at being someone in particular" (215) rings a carillon of bells with me.
4. Santayana, "Introduction" to *The Works of Spinoza*, vii.
5. Beckett, *Worstward Ho*.

OVERTURE

1. Einstein, "Physics and Reality", 351.
2. I owe this phrase to Karl Friston's "The Mathematics of Mind-Time".
3. The inconceivable size of the universe is engagingly discussed by Michael Strauss in "Our Universe is too vast for even the most imaginative sci-fi". In passing, he cites astronomer Neil deGrasse Tyson's observation that "The Universe is under no obligation to make sense to you". You bet. According to Martin Rees, we can see out to 13 billion light years – or 78 billion trillion miles ("Conversation with Martin Rees").
4. Quine, *From Stimulus to Science*, 16. Quine famously asserted that "philosophy of science is philosophy enough" in "Mr. Strawson on Logical Theory", 446.

5. As Einstein said: "The whole of science is nothing more than a refinement of everyday thinking" ("Physics and Reality", 349). He was echoing the physicist and philosopher Ernst Mach (to be discussed in Chapter 4). Mach's empiricism had a huge influence on Einstein's early thinking. Einstein later distanced himself from the anti-realism according to which Mach regarded "atoms", "electrons" and other entities as mere constructs defined by the experiences they most parsimoniously made sense of. The anti-realism of the Copenhagen interpretation of quantum mechanics rather disgusted him. As David Bodanis notes, Einstein insisted "that all underlying reality was clear, exact and understandable" (*Einstein's Greatest Mistake*, 332).

CHAPTER 1

1. Kant, *Critique of Pure Reason*, B 75.
2. *Ibid.*, 92.
3. Quine, *From Stimulus to Science*, 16.
4. This may have been the intuition behind Kant's assigning the "categories of the understanding" such a fundamental place in our knowledge. He seems, however, to locate them at too fundamental level – something that becomes apparent, when he lists them. They look to be a rather raggle-taggle army drawn from an inchoate philosophical logic: Quantity (Totality, Plurality, Unity); Quality (Reality, Negation, Limitation); Relation (Inherence and Subsistence, Causal Dependency, Community or Reciprocity); Modality (Possibility, Actuality, Necessity).
5. I am grateful to Tom McClelland for this point.
6. Fodor, "Semantics, Wisconsin Style", 232.
7. The character of man as "the problematizing animal" is manifest not only in the serious business of endeavouring to advance understanding but in the delight we take in puzzles and problems, in solving riddles set not by nature but by our fellows; in competition as well as in cooperation in problem-solving.
8. Such separation of personal interests from the direction of inquiry, and the results of inquiry from their practical application, is at odds with the views of certain sociologists of science. Strong sociology of science argues that physics and chemistry and the other natural sciences, just as much as theology, literary criticism, or politics, are activities whose outputs are dictated by the institutions within which they take place. They are cultural products determined by the power relations between people. Theories that become the dominant orthodoxy are those that are propounded by the dominant groups. This, of course, would account for a certain conservatism in scientific paradigms but not the extraordinary progress reflected in the predictive, explanatory, and practical power of the applications of science. Most importantly, it has nothing to say about the dissemination of useful sense from the individual scientist, institution, or discipline to the anyone, anywhere, or "anywhen" where it proves to have unique power to predict and manipulate the natural world which, being antecedent to humanity, is not impressed by public relations.
9. Ernest Gellner, quoted in Merquior, *Foucault*, 150.
10. Gibson, *The Ecological Approach to Visual Perception*, 127.
11. This is discussed with exemplary clarity in Thomas Suddendorf, *The Gap: The Science of What Separates us from Other Animals*.
12. For a discussion of the world reduced in physical science to "a system of magnitudes", see Tallis, *Of Time and Lamentation*, especially §3.5 "Mathematics and Reality".

13. The idea of natural necessity or necessity within nature deserves a more careful and detailed treatment than it receives in this book. At its heart, it qualifies something – an event or a conclusion – as unavoidable but that heart has many chambers.

    Physical events may be deemed necessary because they are the inevitable consequences of the preceding events, the inevitability being dictated by the laws of nature. As such, they may seem to have a post hoc rationality. They are what a reasonable, fully informed, person would expect. Given that the laws of nature cannot be bucked, their necessity seems to engulf agents, both as a limit to their freedom, and in the form of the necessities required to sustain their life.

    In another chamber, we find logical necessity. Logical necessity not only shares the inescapability of material necessity but it, too, is reasonable – it "makes sense" and in a more direct sense. The tautology "If A, then A" does not owe its reasonableness to the laws of nature. "If the ball is dropped, it will fall downwards" – where downwards is defined as the direction in which gravity operates – has an impure necessity (even leaving aside the circumstances that must be specified to ensure that the laws of gravity can manifest themselves).

    Thus, the braiding of necessity and reason. Inevitability of a material outcome or logical output, transformed into that which a reasonable person would expect, becomes itself reasonable and ineluctable. It is ripe to be transformed into Fate, even the wisdom of the Gods. There is no tragedy that remains indefensible. In the famous passage from Anaximander, even the fact that everything dies is seen as "justice": "But where things have their origin, there they must also pass away according to necessity; for they must pay the penalty and be judged for their injustice, according to the ordinance of time" (as quoted in "The Anaximander Fragment", in Heidegger, *Early Greek Thinking*, 32–3). Actuality, inevitability and rightness are as one. The best of all possible worlds is the only possible world.

14. For one discussion of the confused – or multifaceted – notion of a cause, see Tallis, *Of Time and Lamentation*, 510–27.

15. Suddendorf, *The Gap*, 158. Suddendorf has an apt quote (272) from Carl Sagan: "The library connects us with the insights and the knowledge, painfully extracted from Nature, of the greatest minds that ever were, with the best teachers, drawn from the entire planet and all of history, to instruct us without tiring, and to inspire us to make our own contribution to the collective knowledge of the human species".

CHAPTER 2

1. I have been heavily dependent on many secondary and tertiary sources. The latter include: Craig (ed.), *The Routledge Encyclopaedia of Philosophy*, Vol. 5; Hastings & Mason (eds), *The Oxford Companion to Christian Thought* and Harvey, *A Companion to the New Testament*. The essay on "Logos" in volume 8 of Hastings, Seible & Gray (eds), *Encyclopaedia of Religion and Ethics* has been particularly valuable. My copy is one of many gifts from the ever-generous Robert Jackson (*vide infra*).

2. According to the standard account, He rose from the primal waters and saw the world through to its completion, and thence to its return to "watery chaos" at the end of time. In cooperation with the sun-god Ra he drove the sun through its cycle: the descent into darkness in the west and the resurrection into light in the east. Atum was also the bearer, the home, the realization of the conscious Word or *Logos*, the essence of life.

The later creation myth of Memphis – copied from an earlier text – identified Ptah as the god in whom all the divine forces were encoded. The gods were named and, in virtue of being named, given form and identity, by Ptah's tongue. Ptah was the Word, the *Logos*. Like the God of Judaeo-Christian religions, Ptah created by means of uttering thoughts. In the Word was the beginning, a matter to which we shall return.

3. The extent to which Egyptian thought directly influenced the early Greek philosophers is hotly debated. Jonathan Barnes has asserted that, notwithstanding echoes, and some evidence of intellectual contact, "it is difficult to find a single clear case of influence" (*Early Greek Philosophy*, 6).

4. Nietzsche, *Philosophy in the Tragic Age of the Greeks*, 32.

5. There is controversy over how much *Logos* did mean in Heraclitus' writing. Barnes translates it variously as "account", as "explanation" and as "the human faculty which enables us to offer explanations or reasons for things" (*Early Greek Philosophy*, xxiii). Barnes justifies his deflationary interpretation of the philosopher's fragments with a witty metaphor: "Heraclitus attracts exegetes as an empty jampot wasps; and each new wasp discerns traces of his own favourite flavour" (*The Presocratic Philosophers*, 57).

6. Quoted in Burnet, *Early Greek Philosophy*, 148.

7. F. M. Cornford has claimed that Heraclitus was arguing against the materialism of the Ionian philosophers for whom the world was identical with what was visible (*From Religion to Philosophy*, 184ff.)

8. Cornford, *From Religion to Philosophy*, 51.

9. The Demiurge makes his debut in Plato's *Timaeus* although he retains his importance in various guises in Neoplatonic and Gnostic thought. *Logos* also appears in the *Meno* as that which underwrites beliefs to make them qualify as true knowledge. Likewise in *Theaetetus* knowledge is true judgement with *Logos*. For a brief account of the importance to Plato of *Logos* as a marker of knowledge, as opposed to mere belief, see Welbourne, *Knowledge*, 34–5.

10. Harvey, *A Companion to the New Testament*, 191–2. In what follows, I am especially indebted to Hillar, "Philo of Alexandria". It is extraordinary to think that we Europeans and those influenced by European thought are the intellectual children of a man of whom few of us have heard. Central to the Jewish tradition from which Philo drew part of his inspiration was the notion of "*Memra*" – the creative or directive word or speech of God, manifesting his power in a world of matter. Its meaning encompassed speech addressed to a patriarch or prophet – a piece of the mind of God – and that in virtue of which the world was created – "For he spake and it was done". *Memra*, however, was not the word made flesh and "in recent times the differences between the Christian and Philonic conception [of the Logos] have been widely admitted" ("Philo" in Cross & Livingstone, *The Oxford Dictionary of Christian Thought*, 1279).

11. Hillar, "Philo of Alexandria", 15.

12. Hillar also lists: the utterance(s) of God; the Divine Mind; God's transcendent power; the body holding together all the parts of the world; the immanent reason of the universe, reflected in the reasoning capacity of the human mind; the harmony between the parts of the universe; the first-born and chief of the angels, the revealer of God; soul-nourishing manna; intermediary power, messenger and mediator between God and the world; and even (though tentatively) God Himself. The breadth of the list is testament to the capaciousness, richness – and vagueness – of the concept.

13. *Ibid.*, 17.

14. Craig (ed.), *Routledge Encyclopedia of Philosophy*, vol 5, 818.

15. Diarmaid MacCulloch expresses this more domesticated version beautifully: "The Logos was seen finally and completely in Jesus Christ, a being other than the Father, but derived from him with all the fullness and intimacy of a flame which lights one torch from another: torchlight from torchlight, in a phrase which was embedded in the fourth century in the doctrinal statement which is now called the Nicene Creed" (*A History of Christianity*, 143). The metaphor of the fire being lit from another fire originates from Justin Martyr (100–165 CE).

16. In his book *On First Principles*, the early Christian writer Origen explained the link between the necessity for a mediator between the intrinsic intelligibility of the world and the reason for God's descent to earth in the form of Christ. As MacCulloch puts it: "[H]e grappled with the old Platonic problem of how a passionless, indivisible, changeless supreme God communicates with this transitory world. For Origen as for Justin, the bridge was Logos, and like Justin, Origen could be quite bold in terming the Logos 'a second God', even tending towards making this Logos-figure subordinate to or on a lower level than the supreme God whose creature he is. This doctrine was known as subordinationism" (*History of Christianity*, 153). "Subordinationism" – that made Christ ontologically inferior to God the Father – was a heresy that greatly exercised early Christians and had huge implications for the history of their religion.

17. The extraordinary second-century Hellenic thinker Plotinus, however, warrants some mention. For him, *Logos* was an organizing principle or force which mediated between the divine intellect and forms in, or impressed on, matter. The term, however, was also a circumlocution: God's name could not be uttered; and so divine action should be ascribed to intermediate agencies, including God's Wisdom (*Sophia*) and his Word (*Logos*). The Good is the intelligible unity and *Logos* is the expression or representation of a higher reality in a lower one.

    Plotinus' view that each level of reality is represented at a lower level and that the *Logos* is the connexion between levels of reality seems to anticipate the later philosophy of science in which lower-level laws are localized expressions of higher-level ones. Equally, his claim that reality becomes less real with every descent from unity to greater multiplicity certainly reflects the common contemporary view that the more general the laws, the more fundamental they are, and the more fundamental they are, the more real the things of which they speak and the closer they are to truth. This is consistent with the perhaps not entirely serious claim that the Theory of Everything – unifying all things in a handful of abstractions – would reveal "the mind of God", and thus be the *Logos* coming to know itself.

    For Plotinus, the multiplicity of objects that can be directly experienced by the senses corresponds to the ground floor. There is no subsequent representation in *Logos* upon a still lower level. The deliverance of the senses is empty of intelligence: the physical is the level of being at which there is no form. The greatest multiplicity corresponds to the lowest level of reality. Ultimate Reality is One. We hear perhaps a distant echo of Heraclitus 700 or more years before: "Listening not to me but to the *Logos* it is wise to agree that all things are one" (Diels-Kranz 22B50; McKirahan, *Philosophy before Socrates*).

18. Paul Valéry had the ambition of writing an *Intellectual Comedy* to complement Dante's *Divine Comedy* and Balzac's secular *Human Comedy* of a world driven by material aspirations. The intellectual comedy would transcend or at least synthesize the divine/religious understanding of the world with the secular/human take. Unsurprisingly, it never got written, although it remained a regulative idea that motivated him. And perhaps this writer, too.

19. MacCulloch, *History of Christianity*, 19.
20. There are many strands in the history of *Logos* that I have bypassed. Avicenna's belief that the human mind in its greatest attainment is open to reason and the latter is a divine principle permeating all that there is, so that it is intelligible, and Leibniz's advocacy of the principle of sufficient reason, are just a couple of threads from a very complex and rich fabric of vision, insight and argument.
21. The source of the assertion ascribed to Galileo that the Bible taught us how to go to heaven not how the heavens go, is unclear. It is often claimed that he was quoting a priest Cesare Baronio. It is difficult not to suspect that Galileo thought the latter more interesting.
22. For an entirely sceptical view of this claim, the reader might like to consult Tallis, *Of Time and Lamentation*.
23. It is worth remembering why this might be welcomed as well as mourned. I have said nothing about the conflict between theological beliefs or of the power politics of the inter-actions between believers and unbelievers and the institutions that support both parties. From superior head-shaking and tut-tutting to domestic tyranny and petty prejudice and to mass murder, the record of the treatment of dissent and the consequences of disagreement is not edifying. The thirteenth-century genocide of the Cathars – "purists" who believed in the inherent evil of the physical world and hence denied the Incarnation of *Logos*, the word made flesh in the person of Christ – initiated by Pope Innocent (!) III was just one example of the horror inflicted on their fellow Christians by those who also embraced the religion of the God of Peace and Love.

    And it is a bitter irony that Philo of Alexandria's synthesis of Greek and Hebrew notions of *Logos* would have led to the relentless persecution over the next 2,000 years of those who followed Philo's own Jewish faith. The ubiquitous antisemitism given transcendental justification by the crucifixion of the God of Love and Peace, and by the refusal of Jews to accept the divine nature of Christ, eased the path to Auschwitz.
24. Of course, the very idea of God is a block to sense-making: the Uncaused Cause is the Unexplained Explanation. And any properties that God has – including his ability to create a definite world at a definite time – must go beyond any necessary existence delivered by the ontological argument – even if "That which is perfect must necessarily exist" delivers anything. Necessity granted to an existent cannot be extended to any predicates, which must always be one out of a range. The arguments that prove that God is, do not deliver any What that God might be – even less accommodate His specific interventions in the world and human affairs.
25. Our attitude of superiority towards myths is exemplified in the opening paragraph of the Introduction to Hope-Moncrieff's *Classic Myths and Legends*: "In the childhood of our world the myth-making faculty seems so much a matter of course that the Greek word *mythos*, primarily meaning a word or speech, took on its special sense as a work of fancy." Equally patronizing is the assumption – central to psychoanalysis – that myths are an unconscious expression of unresolved, unconscious inner conflicts and desires.
26. For a critique, see Tallis, *Of Time and Lamentation*.
27. Augustine, *City of God*, Bk XII, Chp 20, final sentence.
28. Gospel According to St John 8:12: "Then spake Jesus again unto them: 'I am the light of the world; he that followeth me shall not walk in darkness, but shall have the light of life'". And this is echoed in *The Festal Menaion*: "Where indeed should Thy light have shone save upon those that sit in darkness? Glory to Thee" (343).
29. Robert Grosseteste, *De Luce*. Full disclosure: I have spent some thirty years dreaming of, planning, writing, and not completing a vast poetic work – *De Luce* – that would capture

the profundity of this thought. My alma mater Oxford University – of which Grosseteste was the first Chancellor – has as its motto, *Dominus Illuminatio Mea*, the opening words of Psalm 27.

30. I owe what follows to a characteristically generous communication from Robert Jackson. Jackson suggested that perhaps I should call my proposed book (*vide supra*) *De Sono* rather than *De Luce*. *Logos*, he points out, which has as its primary meaning "word" probably comes from its nature as a collection of sounds rather than from the more indirect connection represented by the notion of a word as denoting a collection of visible objects.

31. Valéry, "On Poe's 'Eureka'" in Volume 8 of *The Collected Works of Paul Valéry*, 171.

32. Speech as "hot air" is a familiar – all too familiar – trope.

33. The wind, of course, could also be seen as the principle of Chaos as well as of order. Arresting the advance of chaos, and indeed winnowing order out of Chaos is the essential role of technology.

CHAPTER 3

1. Plotinus, *Enneads* 1.6, "On Beauty" Para. 9. It is part of his argument to the effect that we could not experience things unless we were like them. Only beautiful souls can experience beauty, and one has to have something of the Divine in oneself to be able to see the Divinity in God.

2. Redding, "Hegel".

3. The passage is from Sebastian Gardner's excellent *Kant and the Critique of Pure Reason*, 1–2. I am very grateful to Professor Gardner for a rich and detailed response to some of my criticisms of Kant. In particular, he cautions against talk of "individual minds" and "minds-in-general", preferring "subjects of knowledge". I am not sure that this entirely dispels the problem that I have set out below. He addresses my concern that Kant exploits what we might call "a constructive ambiguity" between "mind-in-general" and token minds. The contrast, he argues, is false because the faculties of mind are not individuated in tokens such as Mr Smith and Mrs Jones. The correct analogy is with "an understanding of the Italian language" which has "particular realizations that are not of the same order as the individuals that realize them. And they do not depend for their existence on the latter; remove all human beings and there is still an understanding of Italian ... even if nobody has it" (personal communication).

   Gardner's analogy does not seem to reach to the depths at which space and time are constructed. What is more, "realizations" require minds. Even so, I have a residual uneasiness that I may not have taken sufficient account of Gardner's response to my critique of Kant.

4. Kant, *Critique*, 92. The idea that the mind is entirely passive in receiving "impressions" (a term that reinforces this connotation of passivity) should not be allowed to pass without comment. It assumes that at a certain level the (material) world is self-intimating through interactions with the sense-endings; that Being makes itself Presence courtesy of interaction with, for example, a nervous system. We shall return to this in Chapter 4.

5. Kant, *Critique*, 68 (A23/B37–8).

6. *Ibid.*, 82.

7. *Ibid.* This striking claim is reiterated in Kant's *Prolegomena to Any Future Metaphysic*: "[W]e must not seek the universal laws of nature from nature by means of experience, but, conversely, must seek nature, as regards its universal conformity to the law, solely in the conditions of the possibility of experience that lie in our sensibility and understanding".

(AA 04:34) quoted in Pollok, "The Understanding Prescribes Laws of Nature", 514. In short, the laws are not given in, or to, experience but imposed by the necessary conditions of the possibility of experience. If there were any doubt about how we should take this, Kant asserts that understanding has the function "of prescribing laws to nature, and even making nature possible" (*Critique* B159). This prompted G. E. Moore "to read Kant as holding that the psychological activity of the subject literally constitutes the non-psychological domain" (Gomes, "Kant, the Philosophy of Mind and Twentieth-Century Analytic Philosophy", 17).

8. Kant, *Critique*, 41.

9. Kant was not unaware of this. Ironically, it was one of the key drivers to his *Critique* as is revealed in his famous letter to his friend Marcus Herz in 1772, at the start of his 10-year struggle to formulate his definitive position. He puzzled how "a representation that refers to an object without being in any way affected by it can be possible" (quoted in Gardner, *Kant and the Critique of Pure Reason*, 29). If the individual object, set in a particular place and a particular time, is not in some sense the source or occasion of the experience that locates it in a particular place and a particular time, then it is difficult to distinguish an hallucination from a veridical experience. For experiences truly to be of objects, the latter must affect us and affect us because of our spatio-temporal location. Kant himself was entirely open about the fact that (as Gardner – a sympathetic commentator – puts it): "The nature of the connection between the fact of the existence of things in themselves, and the fact of our being supplied with the material for constituting appearances, is something of which we have no idea" (Gardner, *Kant and the Critique of Pure Reason*, 289).

    Our natural inclination is to say that the thing-in-itself affects the mind, that it causes our experiences of it. If the representation of things were not caused by those things, then they would seem to be unanchored, even illusions. This view seems to be held by Kant himself, as glossed by Gardner: "the transcendental object [i.e. the noumenon] is the underlying ground or cause of inner and outer appearances" (*ibid.*, 153).

10. In this respect, it is analogous to the alternative universes in the "multiverse" interpretation of quantum mechanics. There is no way of accessing these alternative worlds as they are causally disconnected from any reality we could experience or know. Like the noumenal realm, they seem to have been generated by the need to continue beyond the point where intelligibility gives out. Their character is determined solely by the reasons for which they have been requisitioned. They are face-savers defined by the faces they save. To put this another way, the (experienced) world would be no different if the noumenal realm did not exist. (I owe this last point to Roger Jennings, personal communication.) At any rate, the featurelessness of the noumenal realm is jealously protected by Kantians, as if this were a positive feature, instead of a problematic one, given that it seems to remove the capacity of this ground to ground anything in particular.

11. Tom McClelland (personal communication).

12. In a lucid and intelligent brief summary of the *Critique*, Nathan Bjorge points out that I have experiences at particular times, which presupposes that (if they are not hallucinations) they have been triggered by encounters at particular times ("The Self as Noumenon").

    If we propose that there is a division in the noumenal realm between those noumena of which objects are appearances and those which correspond to (transcendental) subjects, then we have a further problem of understanding how the items in these divisions interact. It looks as though we have the mind-body problem in a new guise. Schopenhauer – in his *The World as Will and Idea* – saw the self as a point of access to the noumenal realm: I directly experience a thing-in-itself in virtue of being a thing-in-itself. This is unlikely to have been a development of which Kant would have approved. As Gardner (*Kant and the*

Critique, 298) points out, he opposed the idea that "we know ourselves as we are in ourselves". At any rate, the idea of a transparent self that has immediate veridical knowledge of itself is highly suspect, as has been widely discussed in contemporary philosophy (we shall touch on it in Chapter 5).

In fairness to Kant, we ought to mention that the empiricist alternative does not fare any better. The notion of objects as logical constructions or (to use Quine's phrase) "posits" out of sense data or sense experiences makes it difficult to understand the role (if any) that objects have in prompting and justifying the experiences that are had of them. Objects seem to appear twice: once downstream from experiences as fictions or at least theoretical constructed out of them; and a second time upstream of experiences as causing (veridical) experiences.

13. Strawson, *Bounds of Sense*, 92–3.
14. Gardner, *Kant and the Critique*, 302.
15. Does this, perhaps, put the cart before the horse? There must surely need to be a self in place before ownership of perceptions can be ascribed to it and it can then gather itself up as a coherent sequence of experiences belonging to the same subject or story. The self in question is not, however, a substantive self – so Kant is not committing the cardinal sin of putting the Descartes before the horse – but "a form of consciousness by which we are aware of ourselves as the (single) subject of all our (conscious) mental states" (Gomes, "Kant, the Philosophy of Mind and Twentieth-Century Analytic Philosophy", 7.)
16. Quassim Cassam, turning Kant on his head, argues that "the subject of self-conscious experience must be conceived of as a physical object" and that "to be self-conscious one must be conscious of one's self as a corporeal object among corporeal objects" (*Self and World*, 112). This view is further developed in Tallis, *I Am*, especially, 113–29.
17. As Tom McClelland has suggested to me (personal communication).
18. "Thus the understanding is something more than a power of formulating rules through comparison of experiences; it is itself the lawgiver of nature" (*Critique*, 148 (A126)).
19. There is an important and interesting ambiguity here. Does Kant mean the laws as they have been hitherto discovered, which will be superseded as science progresses, or "laws of nature" as the ultimate goal, the asymptote or regulative idea, of science, laws not conditioned by the limiting context of a particular stage in the history of inquiry or the history of culture? It would seem that Kant erases the difference between provisional laws – such as those related to phlogiston – and more general and powerful laws closer to the asymptote tagged by the moniker "the theory of everything". They are both products of the "synthetic activity of the mind". And he also segues past the standing of the very idea of "laws of nature". Are they items inherent in nature itself? This connects with the old question as to whether nature was an expression of Newton's laws of motion before Newton discovered them.
20. Kant, *Critique*, A114.
21. *Ibid.*, A125.
22. There is another difficulty for Kant arising out of the co-emergence of the unity of the object and the unity of the self, or the unity of the world and the unity of the subject; namely that multiplicity is as important as unity. We have considerable discretion in how we divide the world. We can attend to the room, the chair in the room, the seat of the chair, the tear in the seat. As we adjust the acuity of our attention, so parts acquire the status of wholes or vice versa. What is more, the synthesis of parts into wholes has extra-mental constraints: the tear in the seat is an aspect of the fabric of the seat but we cannot see the tear as part of a city.

23. Gardner, *Kant and the Critique*, 160.
24. The discussion in the preceding paragraphs has been informed by a helpful paper by Siyaves Azeri, "Transcendental Self and Empirical Self".
25. There is another fundamental problem that is worth noting: that Kant seems himself to transcend the boundaries he places on the possibility of knowledge. Whereas, it is acceptable for the categories of the understanding to make visible the forms of sensible intuition, there does not seem to be any mental faculty that makes visible the categories of the understanding and their role in organizing experience. They should be as beyond reach as the noumenal realm. It has been suggested to me (Tom McClelland, personal communication) that we can know the categories through their synthetic activity. This would presuppose that we can know a process through its products but such "backward transparency" does not seem to be the way of the world. The analogy with the idea of knowing God through His works has little to commend it to one of a secular disposition.

    It seems, therefore, that Kant trespasses beyond his own self-imposed limits by claiming to know that there are real and permanent constraints on the understanding and that these are imposed by the mind. His rejection of the metaphysics of predecessors such as Leibniz seems to illustrate something that F. H. Bradley said: that a philosopher who "is ready to prove that metaphysical knowledge is wholly impossible ... is a brother metaphysician with a rival theory of first principles ... To say the reality is such that our knowledge cannot reach it, is to claim to know reality; to urge that our knowledge is of a kind that must fail to transcend appearance, itself implies that transcendence" (*Appearance and Reality*, 1).
26. The problem with (e.g., Lockean) atomism as a prompt to the development of Kantian modes of unification of the world is lucidly set out by Mark Sacks in *Objectivity and Insight*.
27. Heidegger, *Being and Time*, 249.
28. For a more detailed discussion, see Tallis, *A Conversation with Martin Heidegger*. Jan Patocka has highlighted this point from a different angle. It is "on the basis of their corporeity" that "humans are not only the beings of distance but also the beings of proximity, rooted beings, not only innerworldly beings but beings in the world" (*Body, Community, Language, World*, 178). Patocka criticizes Heidegger not for denying corporeity, "or denying that we are also objectively among objects" but because "he does not ... recognise it as the foundation of our life, which it is" (176). Interestingly, Patocka notes another problem with Heidegger's thought, namely that there is "too much that is anthropological" and "an excessive emphasis on what is close to humanity" (168) and a relative neglect of "the primordial, natural world, the world which is not constructed by our mind, by our explicit cognitive activity, the world as it is given" (167). The same could be said of Kant, except that for the latter this was central to his entire system.
29. The "observer" who seems to be placed at the centre of relativity theory and quantum mechanics is in fact a set of numbers or a mathematical structure (see Tallis, *Of Time and Lamentation*, especially "The Erasure of the Observer"). This makes it plausible to interpret the notion that the ultimate reality is "information", as a refashioning of transcendental idealism. Interestingly, macroscopic objects – necessary for the experiments upon which quantum field theory is based – elude quantum subject dependency. The ghost that haunts subatomic spaces deserts objects such as pebbles, trees and tables.
30. Nagel, *View from Nowhere*, 9. Nagel's observation is a distant echo of Alfred North Whitehead's reference to "the muddle of importing the mere procedures of thought into the facts of nature" (*The Concept of Nature*, 20).
31. I have not discussed the idea of "pre-established harmony" according to which – despite the lack of causal relationship between them – mind and body, mind and world are in harmony

(so that mind gives a veridical account of the world) because they are programmed at the Creation to be coordinated. This seems less like an explanation than an abdication of the duty to explain.

32. Describing all conscious content as "inner" does not capture the fact that some elements seem "more inner" than others. My gut sensations (that have minimal intentionality) and my thoughts and memories (that have intentional objects that lack a clear location in any outside – in the sense of extra-corporeal space) seem more inner than vision – a revelation of the seen world whose inwardness is effaced by the outwardness of what seeing sees.

    The fact that much of my body is outside – even that part of it which is hidden from me because it is inside (for example, my spleen) – reveals how complex is the boundary between inside and outside. There could be no more intimate inside than my body in my clothes but my socked feet or my gloved hands can be relocated outside by being employed as tools. The inside/outside contrast in the shared world – the world of the match in the matchbox – does not map onto subject (inside)/outside (object) contrast.

33. The sequence of events is also internalized, being organized according to the "inner sense" that is time. The contrast between the "outer sense" of space – that locates things out there and side-by-side – and the "inner sense" of time would be problematic if it were taken literally. It would suggest a) space is "outside" time; b) that temporal sequences are even more intimately internal than spatial arrays.

34. Quoted in Gardner, *Kant and the Critique*, 185.

35. We should not be entirely satisfied with Heidegger's notion of our being "thrown" into the world. As Patocka noted (see note 27) Heidegger's world is "anthropomorphic", which does not encompass "the primordial dark night of existents", including "brute existents" such as "a hunk of lava on the moon" (168). Morgan makes an interesting comparison between Kant and Heidegger: "If Kant is looking for the conditions of the possibility [of] objective empirical knowledge, Heidegger is looking for the conditions of possibility for the fact that reality shows up at all" (*The Kantian Catastrophe?*, 86).

36. Gardner, *Kant and the Critique*, 90.

37. Kant, *Critique*, B 106.

38. Most commentators seem to assume plurality in the noumenal realm. Consider Strawson: "The cooperation of sensibility and understanding is essential to experience, as is also the excitement of those faculties by things as they are in themselves" (*The Bounds of Sense*, 72).

39. Kant, *Critique*, 125 (A92/B125).

40. There is an excellent discussion of the impact of *After Finitude* on recent philosophical thought in Morgan, *The Kantian Catastrophe?*

41. This argument has an interesting echo in Owen Barfield's *Saving the Appearances*. If we believe that secondary qualities – colours, sounds, etc. – depend for their existence on conscious minds, then the world before minds emerged must be fundamentally different from the way we conceive of it. It would be a world without phenomena. Our world is a system of collective representations – representations (if they are not delusions) that are shared.

42. This is helpfully discussed by Lucy Allais in "A Conversation with Lucy Allais" in Morgan, *The Kantian Catastrophe?*

43. Russell, *My Philosophical Development*, quoted in Morgan, *The Kantian Catastrophe?*, 22.

44. *Ibid.*, 22.

45. See Tallis, "Time, Reciprocal Containment, and the Ouroboros", *Philosophy Now* Oct/Nov 2017, 54–5.

46. Quoted in Morgan, *The Kantian Catastrophe?*, 13. Béatrice Han-Pile makes a similar point, glossing Foucault when she refers to the: "circle whereby Man is both the epistemic condition of the possibility of knowledge on the one hand, and a causally determined object within the epistemic field thus opened on the other. Without Man nothing can be known, but as soon as there is knowledge Man appears to itself as empirically pre-existing his very opening of the epistemic field in a sort of paradoxical pre-history" (*ibid.*, 130).

CHAPTER 4

1. I have discussed this in many places, for example "Biologising Consciousness" in *The Explicit Animal*.
2. That is why a valid critique of the notion that consciousness awoke in the material world as a response to evolutionary pressures would not support arguments in support of "intelligent design". Consciousness would seem to be a daft rather than an intelligent design feature – particularly in view of the huge metabolic cost of maintaining consciousness, that the naturalist viewpoint sees as a function of a complex nervous system.
3. Daniel Dennett has consistently argued that consciousness has so little contribution to make to our human lives that the intuition or belief that it is central to what we are is an illusion (see, e.g., *From Bacteria to Bach and Back*). This is nonsense but his emphasis on "competence without comprehension" is relevant to our present discussion, not the least because he draws precisely the wrong conclusion from this. The fact he emphasises that many competencies do not require conscious deliberation should lead him to conclude not that deliberation is of marginal relevance to human life – it is manifestly central to our lives – but that his own evolutionary account of consciousness (and a fortiori of complex human self-consciousness) misses our nature by a country mile.

    Dennett's "competence without comprehension" – essentially mere mechanism – has a distant echo in Karl Friston's assertion that "nature can drum up reasons without exactly having them for herself" ("The Mathematics of Mind-Time", 2). It is, of course, we who drum them up for nature just as we can drum up reasons for the puddles on the road or the thunder following the lightning. The puddles have a "reason" or a "cause" but they are not brought about by a reason nor are they aware of their cause or the reason for their existence.
4. Samuel Butler is often credited with this evocative phrase. I have not, however, been able to track it down. A Google search takes me to the Darwin scholar and literary critic Gillian Beer and the report – "The Soul Archaeology of Darwin" by Alex M. McLeese – of her lecture "Darwin and the Consciousness of Others". She describes the idea that Darwin "was the man who banished mind from the universe" as a "popular idea".
5. Nagel, *View from Nowhere*, 78–9.
6. The suggestion that possession of that piece of knowledge – and the capacity to learn and retain it – served the purpose of putting me ahead of others via the promotion of life chances through the passing of examinations and thus furthered the motives of my selfish genes by selecting the best and brightest (defined as those who are able to store and retain facts) for the kind of flourishing that will promote the well-being of mankind is as tendentious as it sounds. For the rule that "the geek shall inherit the earth" to become a pathway by which the human race should be increasingly precisely adapted to its environment, the environment in question shall long have ceased to be characterizable in biological terms.
7. See, for example, Dawkins, *The Extended Phenotype*.

8. Dawkins attempts (*ibid.*, 109–10) to address this awkwardness by finding an analogy to the difference between the gene and its phenotypical expression in the difference between the unit of information in the brain – the replicator – and its consequences in the outside world – its "meme products" or phenotypical expression. That is simply to reduce the analogue of the contrast between replicator and vehicle (or gene and organism) to the contrast between brain and culture. It also overlooks the fact that even simple elements like tunes – never mind the more complex examples he cites (such as prejudices or styles of clothes) – are not confined to cells as individual genes are or even to discrete parts of the brain. What is more, a meme such as "a style of clothing" is required to be both a unit of intracerebral information – it replicates by propagating from brain to brain – and a unit of extra-cerebral (or cultural) information, and in each case defined by the words that specify it. This is just another way of demonstrating that the genotype/phenotype distinction cannot be mapped on to memes and their "expression".

By a peculiar irony, Dawkins' memetics is a fundamental betrayal of his gene-eyed evolutionary theory – to the extent of including something which could be construed as Lamarckian. Lamarck is welcomed back into the fold as the agent of cultural evolution, in which the experiences of the phenotype are passed on from one generation to the next – as, of course, they are. If we are going to insist that cultural development is "evolution" in a sense that retains something from biology, then it is clearly Lamarckian rather than Darwinian.

9. See, for example, Dennett, *The Intentional Stance*.
10. Macdonald & Papineau, "Introduction: Prospects and Problems for Teleosemantics", 1. There is nothing especially novel about the naturalization of mental functions such as knowing, judging and sense-making. David Hume asserted that "Nature by an absolute and uncontrollable necessity has determined us to judge, as well as to breathe and feel" (*Treatise on Human Understanding* I, iv, 1, 183).
11. A recent use of this metaphor by Ruth Millikan, a leading figure in teleosemantics, has an unintended irony: "Clearly our original conscious goals are not the same as whatever our genes aim for" ("Useless Content", 104). Yes, our conscious goals are different from anything that genes may entertain, but the extent of the difference will not be appreciated so long as it is not acknowledged that it is entirely inappropriate to ascribe "aims" of any sort to genes which are, after all, just molecules.
12. I am gliding over a vast literature replete with sophisticated arguments, including those that place coherence at the heart of the idea of truth. Some of the most developed coherence accounts of truth are committed in varying degrees to linguistic idealism. They acknowledge (correctly) that how we divide the world into truths is relative to the language or, more broadly, the sign systems in which truths are expressed. For this reason, there are no stand-alone or atomic truths: they come as a package. My assertion, for example, about economic trends may be true or false at the level of correspondence but the correspondence grows in a soil that has emerged from a mode of understanding that gathers up events and objects and patterns of behaviour into a unity named "economic trends". In short, truths are true or false as part of systems of truth shaped by modes of understanding and of discourse. In the end, however, assertions still presuppose a distance between an expression and whatever it is that it asserts to be the case. The connection between the inhabitants of either end of that distance is inescapably one of correspondence.

The centrality of coherence even to naturalistic accounts of truth is reflected in Quine's recognition that there are "bodies of knowledge" (such as are gathered up in theories) which stand or fall as a whole. Empirical claims "face the tribunal of experience corporately" ("Two Dogmas of Empiricism", 344). "The totality of our knowledge or beliefs … is a man-made fabric which impinges on experience only along the edges" (Quine, quoted in a brief biographical note by O'Connor & Robertson).

13. Millikan, "Useless Contents", in MacDonald & Papineau, 100–14.

14. *Ibid.*, 101.

15. *Ibid.*, 105. There is an interesting analogy between the faith that functions designed to meet basic biological needs – using biological mechanisms widely spread through the animal kingdom – will spontaneously mutate into the kinds of intelligence we humans deploy and the much-publicized fear that robots designed to carry out practical tasks will spontaneously evolve into creatures that might out-perform our intelligence. Soon, so the story goes, robots will be so superior to us as to treat us like household pets, after they have stolen our jobs, en route to exterminating us. In the background, I suspect, is the notion of the "spandrel" – a feature that arises only as a necessary but incidental consequence of other features, a phenotypical trait that is not in itself adaptive but is the by-produce of evolution for other traits. It is not directly selected for but may have a happenstance use. This view, associated particularly with Steven Jay Gould has been bitterly attacked by many evolutionary theorists.

16. A similar, even more impressive, story could be told about quantum theory. We are surrounded by its practical applications, many of which are key to our current safety and comfort. But quantum mechanics was developed for several decades (from Max Planck in 1900 to Paul Dirac in 1930) before any applications could be conceived of and several decades more before the first serious quantum-based technologies (transistors and the like) were manufactured.

17. Macdonald & Papineau, "Introduction", 4.

18. *Ibid.*, 19.

19. *Ibid.*, 4.

20. Gray, *Straw Dogs*, 4.

21. *Ibid.*, 26.

22. There is an analogous situation with meme theory (*vide supra*). Judging by its mode of spread, meme theory is itself a meme. It must therefore owe any success it has not to its truth but to its infectiousness. The self-refutation built into evolutionary "explanations" of knowledge and truth is noted by Nagel: "[If], per impossibile, we came to believe that our capacity for objective theory were the product of natural selection, that would warrant serious skepticism about its results beyond a very limited and familiar range" (*View From Nowhere*, 79).

23. It is arguable that non-human animals do not even have a fully developed sense of causation. See Tallis, "The Cause-Seeking Animal" in *The Knowing Animal*. In what respect or to what degree non-human primates have a sense of objects existing permanently independent of their perceptions of them is contentious.

24. Quine's close affiliation with the forms of behaviourism already discussed is evident from the following passages: "Individuals whose similarity groupings [i.e. primitive classification] conduce largely to true expectations have a good chance of finding food and avoiding predators, and so a good chance of living to reproduce their kind" ("The Nature of Natural Knowledge", 70); "The states of belief, where real, are … states of nerves" ("Reply to Hilary Putnam", 429).

25. In fact there is little that is scientific about Quine's aspirational "scientific" reconstruction of our passage from stimulus to science. He relies on the traditional tools of philosophy: intuition, educated guesswork, and selective mobilization of facts deemed relevant.

26. Quine, *From Stimulus to Science*, 16. Barry Stroud's definition of naturalized epistemology is helpful: "… the scientific study of perception, learning, thought, language-acquisition, and the transmission and development of human knowledge – everything we can find out scientifically about how we come to know what we know" ("The Significance of Naturalized Epistemology", 455). Quine is aware of the paradoxes of such an ambition. As he put it elsewhere, epistemology raises "scientific questions about a species of primates, and they are open to investigation by natural sciences, *the very science whose investigation is being investigated*" (emphasis added) ("The Nature of Natural Knowledge", 68). Strangely, he seems to embrace as a virtue the vicious circularity of looking to advanced knowledge to cast light on how there is knowledge at all – providing a scientific account of how we can progress from sense experience or neural intake to scientific understanding – and, more than that, to validate knowledge sufficiently to head off the sceptical challenge.

27. Quine, *From Stimulus to Science*, 17.

28. *Ibid.*, 21.

29. Quine, "Naturalism; Or Living Within One's Means", 251.

30. For a discussion of the case for, and the significance of, the distinctive holism of human belief in contrast to the behavioural dispositions of animals see "Does Rover Believe Anything?" in Tallis, *Epimethean Imaginings*, 25–53.

31. This opens on to vast territory. Some of it is explored in Tallis, *Of Time and Lamentation*, §8.3.2.4, 388–92.

32. Objects and the matter of which they are made have always been a problem for strict empiricists endeavouring to build up a world out of sense impressions, sense data, or irritation of nerve endings. Hume regarded material objects as fictions, and it was a standard position among analytical philosophers of the first half of the twentieth century, inspired by Bertrand Russell, to see such items as "logical constructions". It remains a matter of controversy as to whether Quine himself was realist or anti-realist about "objects". There is an excellent discussion in Keskinen, "Quine on Objects: Realism or Anti-Realism?".

33. Quine, *From Stimulus to Science*, 25.

34. *Ibid.*, 70.

35. *Ibid.*, 29.

36. "Like the animal's simple induction over innate similarities, [science] is still a biological device for anticipating experience" (Quine, "The Nature of Natural Knowledge", 72).

37. Lack, "The Behaviour of the Robin".

38. What is implicit in genuine tool use is discussed in Tallis, *The Hand*. The uniquely human hinterland is enormous. It is part of the yet more extensive hinterland that lies behind even the most commonplace voluntary activity. See, for example, Tallis, *Of Time and Lamentation*, Chapter 12 "Time and Human Freedom".

39. Quine, *From Stimulus to Science*, 40. It is interesting that Quine allows that classes and sets are real but properties are not. That he thinks colour red is less real than the set of all red things can only be ascribed to his partiality for mathematical logic which can handle sets but not properties such as red.

40. The discussion that follows has been assisted by Robert Sinclair's excellent "Quine's Naturalized Epistemology and the Third Dogma of Empiricism". While I have found Sinclair's article helpful, it will be evident I am not persuaded by his defence of Quine.

41. Quine quoted in Sinclair, "Quine's Naturalized Epistemology", 461.

42. Mach, *The Analysis of Sensations and the Relation of the Physical to the Psychical*. This is quoted in Pojman, "Ernst Mach". Some of what follows is indebted to this excellent article.

43. Quoted in Blackmore, *Ernst Mach: His Work, Life and Influence*, 193–4.

44. Mach, *Knowledge and Error: Sketches on the Psychology of Enquiry*, 171. There is the opposite view in philosophy that survival is enhanced by what Mark Sacks has described as "epistemic shortfall" – a world picture that is pre- or sub-scientific (*Objectivity and Insight*, 17). He cites Locke and Russell to the effect that if we could see everything – how things appear in the microscope, individual photons, the world as it is viewed in fundamental physics – we would see nothing. What we actually see is only that which it is useful for us to see. As Sacks puts it, "We have no need to be certain that our perception delivers the world as it is, only that it delivers the world-view that is appropriate for beings like ourselves" (18).

    And to this small extent, naturalized epistemology seems valid: that what we take to be reality is what is "good enough" for our survival. Where naturalized theory of knowledge fails is at the level at which the epistemological question should be posed: How do we have knowledge of "reality" at all; how does what-is become "reality" in us? And it fails even more signally further down the track, when we pose the question of how we come to challenge that reality, to put it in inverted commas, and actively doubt, and attempt to reform our sense of it, so that we see our everyday knowledge (or some aspects of it) as merely "good enough" for survival; in short, when we stand back from our knowledge to adopt a critical stance on it. And when we address the question that is the concern of this book; namely, how we got to be so smart. And, come to that, why did we, given that, if we could see the world only as it looks to our best account of reality, namely science, we would not function effectively in daily life? That we can make use of only a small amount of what we think to have discovered to be reality is not to be answered in terms mobilized by naturalizers.

45. Mach, *Knowledge and Error*, 361.

46. A prominent development of Mach's understanding of science is Popper's evolutionary epistemology – treated in many places in his oeuvre but especially in *Objective Knowledge: An Evolutionary Approach*. Popper applies the idea of natural selection to the battle between scientific ideas. Humans, instead of exposing their bodies to the vicissitudes of the natural world, expose their theories which are subject to the discipline of the survival of the fittest. Problem-solving and error elimination is driven by "selective pressures". While superficially attractive, the direct conflict between ideas, posited explicitly in a disciplinary community, the crucial role of key measurements, hardly seems like the direct conflict between phenotypes which will eventually result in preferential replication of a particular genotype, or the indirect conflict arising out of competition for resources. And in the history of humanity, conflicts between world pictures have as often led to body-on-body bloodshed as to polite and reasoned dissent. Science, however, represents an extraordinary (unnatural) triumph over this.

47. Tom McClelland (personal communication) has questioned this conclusion. He argues that a) our senses might discover things as they are in themselves; and b) if even sense-making is constrained by our needs, this may require us to be sensitive to objects and properties that are wholly independent of those needs. Regarding the first point, the standard naturalistic account of sense experience is that of a material interaction between energy arising from the extra-corporeal reality and the nervous system. What are most directly available are neural effects which seem unlikely to amount to a pure disclosure of what is out there "in itself". The interaction between A and B does not seem likely to deliver an undistorted portrait of A in B. As for the second point, there is much evidence of the filtering and transformation of experience before it enters consciousness and guides needs-related behaviour. In the light of this, it is hardly surprising that many neuroscientists regard the "outside world" as a construct, even an "illusion".

Quine's own position remains deeply ambivalent, given that he regards material objects epistemologically as "posits" we introduce via linguistic reference in our theories of the material world, irrespective of their ontological standing. Quine (quoted in Keskinen, "Quine on Objects") describes himself as having "an unswerving belief in external things – people, nerve endings, sticks and stones". It is often thought that Quine is a realist when he is talking about ontology and it is only when he is talking about epistemology do objects become posits. To be confident of the existence of entities (real objects) that lie permanently beyond the reach of experience is (to say the least) a difficult position for an empiricist. Even so, he believes that to ask "what reality is really like apart from our categorization [as separate from the parochial point of view of another theory] is meaningless" (*ibid.*, 137).

48. This brief note over-flies a vast literature on the anthropic principle and the complex discussion of the different shades and nuances of weak and strong anthropic principles. I wanted only to make a single point.

49. Carter, "Large Number Coincidences and the Anthropic Principle in Cosmology", 294.

50. *Ibid.*, 82.

51. Still the sense that the universe is a "put-up job", put up for us keeps returning. Here is another engaging example: "The Milky Way" says [Caleb] Scharf "is smack-dab in the sweet spot of massive super-massive black hole activity. It is possible that this is not mere coincidence" (quoted in Radford, "Gravity's Engines").

52. Quine is not fazed by any suggestion that thoughts – and their objects – do not readily map on to physical processes in the brain: "Thinking is a bodily activity in good standing, however inadequate our physiological understanding of it" (*From Stimulus to Science*, 93). The bodily activities he refers to are muscular actions typically associated with speech – the standard behaviourist reduction of thought to "sub-vocal speech". The founding father of behaviourism – J. B. Watson – had a similar understanding of the nature of thought.

53. Russell, *The Analysis of Matter*. I am indebted to Philip Goff's "Bertrand Russell and the Problem of Consciousness".

54. As Adam Frank has put it, "our best theory for how matter behaves still tells us very little about what matter is." ("Minding Matter"). And this penetrating observation in the same article bears repeating: "The closer you look, the more it appears that the materialist (or 'physicalist') position is not the safe harbour of metaphysical sobriety that many desire". (*ibid.*, 2).

The identification of matter with what it *does* leads to a "dispositional essentialism" in which stuff is reduced to its law-like interactions with other stuff. The result is a kind of buck-passing that Russell (quoted by Philip Goff in "Panpsychism") brilliantly characterized as follows: "There are many possible ways of turning some things hitherto regarded as 'real' into mere laws concerning the other things. Obviously, there must be a limit to this process, or else all the things in the world will merely be each other's washing" (Russell, *The Analysis of Matter*, 325).

55. Rosenberg, "Eliminativism without Tears".

56. The role of neural activity in gathering distributed, even diffused mental stuff to a localized viewpoint – one that perceives, knows, remembers, thinks, etc., and serves the needs of an individual – remains entirely obscure. In short, panpsychism and identifying consciousness with neural activity emerge as two equally expensive ways of failing to solve or bypass the traditional mind-body problem.

57. It is very difficult to espouse the mind-brain identity theory consistently – even in the case of basic sensations which should be less tricky customers than, say, thoughts. Quine for example speaks of "the pain that x [neural activity] produces is a dull ache", as an example

of the identity theory (*From Stimulus to Science*, 86.) But while the identity seems to hold for the pain and the dull ache, it does not seem to hold for x: if the neural activity produces the pain it cannot be identical with it. If A produces B, A must be distinct from B.

58. Goff, "Panpsychism is crazy, but it's also most probably true". Galen Strawson emphasises that it is important to differentiate between panpsychism that says there is only experiential being and panpsychism that says that physical stuff has experiential being in addition to non-experiential being ("Real Naturalism", 151).

59. One approach to the combination problem is to deflate the conscious subject to a succession of experiences. This hardly begins to address the problem. Firstly, the kind of consciousness putatively enjoyed by an election would hardly scale up to a tingle. And, secondly, we are more than a mere delirium of experiences. This latter point is made persuasively by Janko Nesic in "Panpsychism and the Deflation of the Subject".

60. Discussed in Goff, "Panpsychism". No-one should dismiss panpsychism before paying this article the careful attention it deserves.

61. *Ibid.*, 16.

CHAPTER 5

1. The crucial role of the humble gesture of pointing for the sharing of experience and the establishment and maintenance of the trillion-stranded community of human minds is discussed in Tallis, *Michelangelo's Finger: An Exploration of Everyday Transcendence*. Another elementary manifestation of mind-sharing is the "checking" that infants do: looking at the parent's face to see whether they, too, are seeing what they see.

2. See Russell, "Knowledge by Acquaintance and Knowledge by Description" in *Mysticism and Logic and Other Essays*.

3. Kant's division of the activity or spontaneity of the mind on the one hand from its passivity or receptivity on the other – which corresponds roughly to schema and content – does not capture the many grades of activity that can be observed between (say) gawping and active disciplined inquiry, between staring into space and space exploration. This is another way in which Kant's transcendental idealism fails to reflect our gradual, laborious acquisition of knowledge of the natural world – humanity's hard-won cognitive advance.

   Tom McClelland (personal communication) has emphasized the active nature of our perceptual interaction with the world, and suggested that a sharper contrast is between the informal and unstructured nature of ordinary perception which has no aspiration to yield firm knowledge and the acquisition of intelligence through scientific inquiry.

4. Quoted in Slowik, "The Fate of Mathematical Place", 24.

5. Galileo, *The Assayer* from Burtt, *The Metaphysical Foundations of Modern Science*, 85.

6. Schrödinger, "Mind and Matter" in *What is Life and Other Essays*, 119.

7. Stace, "Man Against Darkness", 2.

8. For a discussion of the case for and against realist interpretations of science, see Tallis, *Of Time and Lamentation*, especially §3.6 "Mathematics and Reality".

9. Nagel, *The View from Nowhere*, 5.

10. *Ibid.*, 4.

11. Yeats, "The Circus Animals' Desertion".

12. Locke, *Essays* II, xxiii, para. 12.

13. Ladyman & Ross, *Everything Must Go: Metaphysics Naturalized*, 2.

14. Quine, "Two Dogmas of Empiricism", 344.

15. Von Uexkull, *Theoretical Biology*.
16. Austin, *Sense and Sensibilia*, 70.
17. Nagel's investigation into the problem of combining "the perspective of a particular person inside the world with an objective view of that same world, the person and his viewpoint included" is profound. Combining the two perspectives is "a problem that faces every creature with the impulse and the capacity to transcend its particular point of view and to conceive of the world as a whole" (*View from Nowhere*, 3). Only humans, so far as we know, are troubled by this problem. And not many of those, either.
18. Wittgenstein, *Philosophical Investigations*, para. 464, 133e.
19. See Tallis, *Of Time and Lamentation*, especially §3.6 "Mathematics and Reality".
20. As Wittgenstein said, "Mathematics is a MOTLEY" – quoted in Hacking, "What Mathematics Has Done to Some and Only Some Philosophers".
21. Nagel, *View from Nowhere*, 86.
22. *Ibid.*, 87.
23. See Tallis, "Information" in *Why the Mind Is Not a Computer*.
24. Nagel is again relevant: "We remain, in pursuit of knowledge, creatures inside the world who have not created ourselves, and some of whose processes of thought have simply been given to us (*View from Nowhere*, 118). And: "[T]he most objective view we can achieve will have to rest on an unexamined subjective base" (86). And, finally: "The very idea of objective reality guarantees that such a picture will not comprehend everything; we ourselves are the first obstacles to such an ambition" (13).
25. My skull, my inner organs, my bone marrow, and so on are for the most part silent. Even when (as in illness) they become eloquent, they are experienced as impersonal, external. There is something fundamentally impersonal about a headache, however much it invades my person. And this applies a fortiori to the vast accumulation of objective facts about my body, such as biochemical and haematological parameters. "What it is like to be Raymond Tallis" is not what it is like to be successive time slices of the material of his body. Nagel's assertion that "I am whatever persisting individual in the objective order underlies the subjective continuities of that mental life I call mine" (*View from Nowhere*, 40) overlooks the gap between mental life and whatever it is that secures my place in the objective order – most obviously my body. The gap is most dramatically illustrated by the fact that my brain is innocent of me and I am innocent of what is going on in my brain, even or especially of what accompanies my assertion of such innocence.
26. Quoted in Hillar, "Philo of Alexandria".
27. Which – to hark back to Chapter 2 – makes the meeting of God and the Word, of deity and truth, in the living, breathing, weeping, bleeding, body of Christ even more poignant. It is odd that the Platonic fastidiousness, even ontological snobbishness, of the philosophical tradition on which Philo drew, should have been suspended. That Jesus assumed earthly form is a scandal, as well as a miraculous intersection between time and eternity.
28. Nagel, *View from Nowhere*, 104.
29. An especially poignant commentary on the extent to which we are hostage to the bodies in which the possibility of knowledge and sense-making resides is the dementia that darkened Kant's final years. Thomas de Quincey's *The Last Days of Immanuel Kant* is a harrowing, chastening (and largely plagiarized) account of the disintegration of one of Europe's greatest minds and most influential philosophers.
30. Superbly described in Mark O'Connell's witty and perceptive *To Be a Machine*. O'Connell notes the powerful distaste for the body evident in transhumanism, a distant echo of the Gnostic vision of human beings as divine spirits trapped in corruptible flesh that is a barrier to knowledge.

31. Randal A. Koene's website, Carboncopies: Realistic Routes for Substrate-Independent Minds, quoted in O'Connell, *To Be a Machine*, 44.
32. For a critique of these assumptions, see Tallis, *Why the Mind Is Not a Computer* and "Are Conscious Machines Possible?" in *Reflections of a Metaphysical Flâneur*.
33. O'Connell, *To Be a Machine*, 18.
34. *Ibid.*, 197.

CHAPTER 6

1. Arendt, *The Life of the Mind*, 185, quoted in Safranski, *Martin Heidegger*, 427.
2. Kołakowski, *Positivist Philosophy from Hume to the Vienna Circle*, 146–7.
3. Mach, *Knowledge and Error*, 171.
4. See Tallis "Seeing Time", Chapter 1, *Of Time and Lamentation*.
5. See Tallis, *The Knowing Animal*.
6. Quoted in Welbourne, *Knowledge*, 31. Sense-making even at the relatively basic level pre-supposes certain cognitive capacities, in particular a grasp of concepts. The cat does not have the concepts "bird" or "garden".
7. See Hume, *A Treatise on Human Nature*, Vol. 1, 1.4.2,14–43 and 52.
8. See Tallis, *The Knowing Animal* for an attempt to do both of these things.
9. Wittgenstein, *Tractatus Logico-Philosophicus*, 5.4711.
10. *Ibid.*, 7.
11. Chalmers, *The Conscious Mind: In Search of a Fundamental Theory*, 297.
12. *Ibid.*, 298.
13. Armstrong, *A World of States of Affairs*, 1.
14. *Ibid.*, 3.
15. Robinson, "The Concept of Knowledge", 23.
16. Sellars, "Empiricism and the Philosophy of Mind", para. 32.
17. *Ibid.*, para. 36. This is an opportunity to head off a common claim about animals. Because their behaviour is (necessarily) adaptive, it can be thought of as rational. Given this, we may think of them reasoning themselves to their goals. But of course human reasoning links explicit generalized ends with explicit generalized means and there is no evidence of, or need for this, in animals. In the case of bespoke voluntary action, it is not sufficient that my action should be purposive; I have also to have that purpose in mind. Animals do not, therefore, operate in the space of reasons where items are connected at the level of generality. This Sellarsian connectedness is evident in, say, beliefs. (See Tallis, "Does Rover Believe Anything?" in *Epimethean Imaginings*). Of course, when I act, not all the moments of my action are illuminated by my sense of the reason for it. They do not have to be. It is sufficient that I should be set going, or set myself going, free-wheel, stop when I have arrived, and refresh my sense of what I am doing if I drift, or am blown, off course.
Sellars pointed out that "the 'of-ness' of sensation simply isn't the 'of-ness' of even the most rudimentary thought. Sense grasps no facts, not even such simple ones as something's being red and triangular" (quoted in Levine, "Sellars and Non-Conceptual Content", 865). We may think of "the of-ness" of perceptions, with full-blown intentionality, as half way between non-intentional sensations and thoughts with derived intentionality.
18. Quine, "Two Dogmas of Empiricism", 344. Sellars's distinction of spaces is an acceptable form of the dualism that seems irresistible when we consider the evident truth that the suffering you feel is not in the same space as the beam and the head that banged against

it, and a fortiori your intention to seek legal advice against the owner of the beam. This is not, of course, a dualism of stuffs.

19. It is tempting here to quote G. K. Chesterton who said that "The madman is not the man who has lost his reason. The madman is the man who has lost everything but his reason" ("The Maniac", Chapter 2, *Orthodoxy*). I will however resist this temptation.

20. Propositions do not exist unless they are proposed and, in order to be proposed, they have to be entertained, expressed, materialized in utterances or written expressions. Once, however, they have been expressed, it can seem as if they were already implicitly present in general propositional awareness. There is, however, two-way traffic. While propositions may grow out of propositional attitudes – as when I think my fear to myself – they are in turn fed by propositions – as when someone I think of gives me cause to fear.

21. Strawson, *The Bounds of Sense*, 79. Even this is not entirely true. Much knowing-that is, and remains, implicit, lying beyond the reach of articulation, and know-how is even less amenable to being translated into propositions. Strawson's account of the relationship of propositions to "what-is" is of course more subtle, complex, and hesitant than this. Consider, for example this suggestion in his Introduction to his edited volume *Philosophical Logic*: "Between sentence-meaning and utterance-force lies, sometimes, the proposition", 10–11.

22. Searle, *The Construction of Social Reality*, passim.

23. See Tallis, *The Knowing Animal*.

24. It may seem unnecessary to say this until it is recalled how influential logical atomism was in twentieth-century anglophone philosophy. Logical atomism was, of course, developed by Russell for whom all truths are developed from atomic facts. Truths become identified with the world in virtue of conflating facts with actual objects and their qualities standing in certain relations. Thus are "thatter" and "matter" merged. And thus, too, the opening of the *Tractatus* that we discussed earlier.

25. There is a nice (but only apparent) intersection between thatter and matter in the question of what happens when an irresistible force meets an immovable object. If the force is irresistible there can be no immovable object; and if the object is immovable, there can be no irresistible force. The idea that they might meet is self-contradictory and the contradiction is not in any actual world but only in a world of thatter that postulates possible worlds which are mutually exclusive in as straightforward a manner as "p" and "not-p".

A variation of this invites us into more complex intersections between logic and actuality. If A is pushing against B and B is not moving then B must be pushing against A. This looks like a connection between folk physics, Newton's third law of motion ("action and reaction are equal and opposite"), and a self-evident truth. Thus are the by-ways of "therefore".

26. The determination of the naturalizers of epistemology to wire us in to the material world is illustrated by this passage from Quine: "There is a short-sighted but stubborn notion that a mere string of marks on paper cannot be true, false, doubted, or believed. Of course it can, because of conventions relating it to speech habits and because of neural mechanisms linking speech habits causally to mental activity" (*From Stimulus to Science*, 94). Long live such short-sightedness because it may make it possible to see what is in front of our nose! Among those things that Quine overlooks are "conventions" and "mental activity" which are linked by (not identical with) neural mechanisms.

27. Ladyman, "An Apology for Naturalized Metaphysics", 144. Quine is much less apologetic: "To account for knowledge of an external thing or event … the naturalistic epistemologist looks rather to the external thing or event itself and the causal chain of stimulation from it to one's brain" (Quine, "Naturalism; Or Living Within One's Means", 252).

28. Wittgenstein, *Philosophical Investigations*, para. 476.
29. See, for example, Tallis, *Of Time and Lamentation*, Chapter 12 "Time and Human Freedom".
30. Stroud, "The Significance of Naturalized Epistemology", 456.
31. The theory has many other advocates. The classic statement is Goldman, "A Causal Theory of Knowing". Donald Davidson was an eloquent opponent of the theory but (unfortunately *vide infra*) on behalf of a coherence theory of truth. The notion that beliefs and pieces of knowledge are not stand alone, however, holds up and the point he makes about "neural intake" and knowledge most certainly does: "This causal relation [between sensations and belief] cannot be a relation of confirmation or disconfirmation, since the cause is not a proposition or a belief, but just an event in the world or in our sensory apparatus" (Davidson, "Empirical Content" in *Subjective, Intersubjective, Objective*, 173).
32. Jonathan Bennett aptly noted that true propositions are "categorially wrong for the role of a puller and shover and twister and bender" (*Events and their Names*, 22).
33. Ramsey & Moore, "Facts and Propositions", 155.
34. Quine, *Philosophy of Logic*, quoted in Stolnar & Damnjanovic, "The Deflationary Theory of Truth" – to which I am indebted.
35. See Tallis, *Of Time and Lamentation*, § 8.2.2.4 "Events and Truth-makers".
36. Quine, "Epistemology Naturalized" in *Ontological Relativity and Other Essays*, 26.
37. I am tempted to point out that there was a reason why Václav Havel's *Living in Truth* was not called *Living in Disquotation*. But that might be a rather cheap point.

CHAPTER 7

1. Wilbur, *Epistemology*.
2. Nagel, *View from Nowhere*, 127.
3. There is no connection without explicit separation. At the root of this connection-and-separation is intentionality. There is thus a sense in which, certainly at the level of factual knowledge, the objects of consciousness are cognate to the perceiving subject. The contingency of this relationship, however, differentiates it from being internal in the idealist sense.
4. This is captured in Strawson's notion of real objects being "objects in the weighty sense", sensed as having an existence independent of all experiences of them: they exist not merely independently of my awareness of them but in virtue of anyone's awareness of them. They are not Berkeleian. Importantly, such objects form, or are deposited in, a unified spatio-temporal system and as such their identity is not constructed out of the happenstance of someone's experience (*The Bounds of Sense*, 26).
5. Quine, "Whither Physical Objects?", quoted in Martin, "On the Need for Properties", 221.
6. Quoted in Dainton, *Time and Space*, 200.
7. That is why Quine's claim that "We can say of John's body not only that it broke a leg but that it solved Fermat's Last Theorem" (*From Stimulus to Science*, 85) seems profoundly wrong. Indeed, while being incarnate, and having flesh in some kind of working order, is a necessary condition of John's solving the theorem, it is a mistake to think of John's body or part of it (even the organ inside his skull) as doing the solving; even less as doing it in the way that it, for example, heals a broken leg – or more precisely that such healing happens.
8. I have explored this in several books. The reader might like to consult: *The Kingdom of Infinite Space* or *I Am*.

9. This has negative implications for the popular idea among "transhumanists" of Substrate-Independent Minds "uploaded" on to computers, which we discussed in the Addendum to Chapter 5, "Subjects without Bodies".

10. See Tallis, "The Soup and the Scaffolding" in *In Defence of Wonder and Other Philosophical Reflections*.

11. Quoted in Kołakowski, *Positivist Philosophy from Hume to the Vienna Circle*, 146–7.

12. We are located by being dis-located. All persons are displaced persons.

13. Quine, "Naturalism; Or, Living Within One's Means", 252.

14. *Ibid.*, 253.

15. The curious might be interested in one version of this story – a rational reconstruction of the passage from apehood to personhood – set out in a trilogy of books by the present author: *The Hand*; *I Am*; and *The Knowing Animal*.

16. Keskinen, "Quine on Objects", 139.

17. I am not of course concerned here with knowledge claims and the truth value of my thoughts. Self-evidently, whether or not the thought "It is raining" is true will depend on what is happening out there. My concern is with whether I can know what I am thinking about.

18. Lau & Deutsch, "Externalism about Mental Contents" is an ideal introduction to the topic. Nagel has expressed the central idea of externalism very clearly: "The essence of what a term refers to depends on what the world is actually like and not just on what we have to know to use and understand the term" (*View from Nowhere*, 41).

    We can of course generalize this to an acknowledgement of the limits of the privileged access we have to ourselves (lucidly and comprehensively discussed in Cassam, *Self and World*). In order to articulate ourselves, we need an objective knowledge of the correct use of the language in which we say what we are, and a capacity to choose the most illuminating way of gathering ourselves up into a stretch of prose. Moreover, the notion of the self-transparent self overlooks the degree to which "I" is constructed out of an internalized "we". What is certainly true is that the Other – general or located in another individual – provides the necessary background to any act of making sense. The Other may even be in-house, given that an individual fact, for example, makes sense only against experiences, thoughts and memories whose acquisition has for the most part been forgotten.

    Such thoughts would overlap with the fear that the most sophisticated, seemingly objective, and self-critical inquiry is compromised by external circumstances from which it arises and its own internal history. Michel Foucault spoke of "the unconscious of science" (*The Order of Things*, xi). A later passage is particularly relevant: "Order is one and the same time that which is given in things, as their inner law, the hidden network that determines the way they confront one another, and also that which has no existence except in the grid created by a glance, an examination, a language; and it is only in blank spaces of this grid that order manifests itself in depth as though already there, waiting in silence for its moment of expression" (*ibid.*, xx).

19. McDowell, "Sellars and the Space of Reasons" discusses the notion of "epistemological externalism": "[a]ccording to which it can suffice for a belief to count as knowledge if it results from a way of acquiring beliefs that can be relied on, in the circumstances, to issue in true beliefs, even if that fact about the belief's provenance is beyond the believer's ken" [I have this reference off the net and cannot find a formal reference for it]. In other words, I can know something and yet not know how good are the credentials for my counting it as knowledge. This is a reverse of the usual sceptical anxiety according to which we may not be aware of just how corrupt are the sources of our knowledge.

20. There is the dream of a disembodied mind in the fantasies of the transhumanists discussed in Chapter 4. The point for the present is that the idea of a mind as a free-floating utterly transparent collection of information is of something so purified as to be subjectless and consequently – well, mindless.

21. I have argued that pretty well everything else Lacan said was nonsense in "Lacan-can or the Dance of the Signifier" in *Not Saussure*.

22. This would seem to be what remains indubitably true in Kant's postulation of an unknowable realm underpinning the phenomenal world of experience: "[K]nowledge has to do only with appearances, and must leave the thing in itself as indeed real per se, but as not known by us" (*Critique of Pure Reason*, B, xx).

    The noumenal realm must be thinkable, indeed must be postulated as the transcendental ground of the appearances, to avoid "the absurd conclusion that there can be appearance without anything that appears" (*ibid.*, B, xxvi). While the noumenon shares with the residual opacity of the object of knowledge the characteristic of systematically eluding empirical access, its nature of being intelligible (as the intelligible ground of the sensible world), takes it beyond the complete cognitive resistance of the Lacanian Real.

23. And this does not take into account the intrinsic dynamism of tokenized discourse that, as it were, "runs off". Platonic thoughts are too static and the verbal tokens too mobile.

CHAPTER 8

1. Quine, *Word and Object*, 22.

2. For a critical discussion of some of the literature on the idea that physical science is gradually revealing metaphysical reality, see "Mathematics and Reality" in Tallis, *Of Time and Lamentation*.

3. For a rough calculation of just how ill-read the most voracious reader will be at the end of his/her life – think mile-long beaches and individual grains of sand – see Tallis, "Criticism Terminable and Interminable".

4. Alkhateeb, "Science has outgrown the human mind and its limited capacities", 2.

5. See, for example, "'I kid you not': Knowingness and Other Shallows" in Tallis, *In Defence of Wonder*.

6. Not all of us think in words and there are some whose lives are not accompanied by ceaseless inner chatter, as Charles Fernyhough points out in *The Voices Within: The History and Science of How We Talk to Ourselves*. Leading primatologist Frans de Waal goes further and argues that, "though language assists human thinking by providing categories and concepts, it is not the stuff of thought" (De Waal, "The link between language and cognition is a red herring"). Neither of these facts takes away the force of the point I am making: that, even in the case of thinking to one's self (something after all most of us do for much of our waking life), there is darkness at the heart of our thoughts. For me, linguistically articulated thoughts are a surface manifestation of something deeper, central to, and uniquely characteristic of, human consciousness. The unique human capacity for thought is rooted in something more fundamental than language – a relative parvenu in the history of hominins.

7. Few imagine that animals have a semantic memory for facts – for reasons that hardly need spelling out. A recent paper, however, has claimed that dogs have episodic memories of experiences. Fugazza *et al* argue in "Recall of Others' Action After Incidental Encoding Reveals Episodic-like Memory in Dogs" that dogs do have short duration episodic

memory for particular commands. This, however, comes nowhere near the boundless, multi-dimensional network of past events located in their contexts, the seething recollection, that haunts our every moment.

8. For an excellent discussion of "world-driven scepticism" see Sacks, *Objectivity and Insight*.

9. I believe this striking claim is in Foucault, *The Archaeology of Knowledge*, but I have not been able to pin it down.

10. Quite a few philosophers in the analytical tradition – most notably Quine – would take extreme exception to this.

11. The key reference here is to Michel Foucault's *Les Mots et Les Choses* [*The Order of Things*]. The standard definition of science as "a body of knowledge organized in a systematic manner" presupposes that its system to some degree reflects the order and "system" of the world. The position of Foucault, and of the structuralists from whom he distanced himself, is that Nature tends to be carved at joints defined by the curriculum of human thought, itself shaped by many happy and unhappy accidents of intellectual history.

12. The idea of a "language of things" is beautifully mocked by Swift in *Gulliver's Travels* where the ancient professors in the Academy of Lagado used things instead of words in their endeavour to avoid ambiguity. Some of the most learned, Swift pointed out, would be overwhelmed by the sheer weight of objects they had to carry on their backs in anticipation of their learned conversations. The opposite ambition is expressed in Francis Ponge's ambition to speak for things, taking *Le parti pris des choses* – "the voice of things". In fact, he does not succeed in ventriloquizing on behalf of things but instead engages in lovely reveries on the physical appearance and properties of things. *Les choses* are spoken for, not being allowed to speak.

13. I cannot resist the temptation to quote this, although I cannot locate the source.

14. Wheeler, "Sakharov revisited: It from Bit".

15. Wheeler, "Information, Physics, Quantum", 5.

16. See Barbour, "Bit from It", 1.

17. *Ibid.*, 1.

18. Quoted in Smolin, *Time Reborn*, 293.

19. Julian Barbour argues, against Wheeler, that "structured variety" – instantiated in things – is the ground of being and that bits offer neither structure not variety. Barbour also makes another point which hits at the claim of standard quantum theory to be the last word on what is real: "Probabilities without things are pure nothings" ("Bit from It", 6).

20. "*Die Sprache spricht*" (Heidegger, *Poetry, Language, Thought*, xxv).

21. Tactfully and sympathetically described in Isaacson, *Einstein: His Life and Universe*.

22. Quoted in Dainton, *Time and Space*, 200.

23. Anton Zeilinger quoted in Barbour, "Bit from It", 9.

24. Russell, *An Inquiry into Meaning and Truth*, 13.

25. I owe this point to William Simpson (MPhil dissertation, University of Oxford, 2016).

26. "Of the Outer Life" is available in translation in *The Poem Itself*.

27. Hofmannsthal, *The Lord Chandos Letter*, 133–4.

28. Nagel, *View from Nowhere*, 74.

29. See, for example, Tallis, *Of Time and Lamentation* §11.3 "The Onlooker".

30. Even so, it is very much alive among the transhumanists in California and elsewhere. Their pursuit of transcendence takes them beyond tinkering with the biological body. Zoltan Istvan, a leading transhumanist mused as follows: "What would be a nice scenario ... is that we first get smart drugs and wearable technologies. And then life extension technologies. And then, finally, we get uploaded and colonize space and so on". Humanity would

be "the nucleus ... of some greatly more vast and brilliant phenomenon that would spread across the universe" and "convert a lot of matter and energy into organized form of life in a generalized sense". Ultimately, "Life will eventually control all matter, all energy, and calculate an infinite amount of information" (quoted in O'Connell, *To Be a Machine*, 18–9). It would encompass the Alpha and the Omega; or at least the 0 and the 1 and the nothing in between.

CODA

1. Nagel, *View from Nowhere*, 9.
2. I have not been able to track down the origin of this quote but I am entirely confident it is Valéry's.
3. Sir Thomas Browne, *The Garden of Cyrus*, chapter 4.
4. St John's Gospel 8:11.
5. "Nature and Nature's laws lay hid in the night / God said 'Let Newton be!' and all was light" (Alexander Pope, "An Epitaph Intended for Sir Isaac Newton" in Westminster Abbey).
6. Given that vision is scarcely limited to the human species, and that man is by no means the most visually gifted animal, ascribing uniquely human sense-making to this sense may seem odd. However, human sight is not merely a property of an organism but of an embodied subject facing a world of objects. Behind this observation is a long story, set out in a trilogy of books I published a decade ago. The most relevant volume is *The Knowing Animal*. (Incidentally, as I have had occasion to point out previously, blindness is not a barrier to knowledge. Those who are congenitally blind acquire their knowledge, and the concepts that structure it, by testimony – as, for the most part, do the rest of us.)
7. Of course what is visible in the written word is not what the written word is about: knowledge is colourless. The light that falls on the word is not sufficient to reveal its meaning. This may be one reason behind the rivalry between light and words for priority in establishing to the sense of the world, as discussed in Chapter 2. In the beginning was the Light, says the Old Testament. In the beginning was the Word, says the New. The Old Testament light, however, was brought into being by the word, commanding it (along with the rest of creation) into existence. If we wished to be fanciful, we may think of words as sustaining holographic images of objects of the senses created by their folded light. But we may resist the temptation.
8. A thesis that is argued with great care by Steven Pinker in *The Better Angels of Our Nature: Why Violence Has Declined*. Those for whom pessimism is a mark of depth and optimism correspondingly a measure of shallowness have loathed this book.
9. T. S. Eliot, "Ulysses, Order, and Myth" in Kermode (ed.), *Selected Prose of T. S. Eliot*, 177.
10. For a sceptical view on this, see Tallis, "'I kid you not': Knowingness and Other Shallows" in *In Defence of Wonder*.
11. Parfit, *On What Matters*, 1.
12. It is no longer believed that St John of Patmos was the same St John who wrote the Gospel that begins with "In the beginning was the Logos." It would have made an even better story if this had been true; but the metaphysical point still holds.
13. I can imagine the world without me – that I am not. Or at least I imagine I can, as an extrapolation of my awareness of my absence in every part in the world I am currently not. I am absent from the next room, the next street, the adjacent county, from 99.999 per cent of

England, a greater percentage of the world and of the universe. Thus, the idea of the world without me is simply a matter of closing the last small hole in my universe-wide absence. This, however, is an illusion because the absence my pin-prick of presence punctures is sustained by my awareness of it. After my death, my absence will leave the world as well as my presence (leaving aside the proxy presence I have in others who are aware of my absence, who may miss me, or at least are aware that I am missing).

References

Alkhateeb, A. "Science has outgrown the human mind and its limited capacities". Aeon. 24 April 2017. Available at: https://aeon.co/ideas/science-has-outgrown-the-human-mind-and-its-limited-capacities (accessed 18 January 2018).

Allais, L. "Transcendental Idealism". In A. Morgan (ed.), *The Kantian Catastrophe? Conversations on Finitude and the Limits of Philosophy*, 33–48. Newcastle: Bigg Books, 2017.

Arendt, H. *The Life of the Mind*. New York: Harcourt, 1981.

Armstrong, D. M. *A World of States of Affairs*. Cambridge: Cambridge University Press, 1997.

Augustine. *City of God*. Trans. M. Dods. New York: The Modern Library, 1950.

Austin, J. L. *Sense and Sensibilia*. Oxford: OUP Paperbacks, 1962.

Azeri, S. "Transcendental Self and Empirical Self: Kant's Account of Subjectivity". *Filosofia* 65 (2010): 269–83.

Barbour, J. "Bit from It". www.platonia.com/bit from it.pdf (accessed 17 January 2018).

Barfield, O. *Saving the Appearances: A Study in Idolatry*. Middletown, CT: Wesleyan University Press, 1988.

Barnes, J. (ed.). *Early Greek Philosophy*, second edition. London: Penguin Classics, 2001.

Beckett, S. *Worstward Ho*. New York: Grove Press, 1983.

Bennett, J. *Events and their Names*. Cambridge: Cambridge University Press, 1988.

Bjorge, N. "The Self as Noumenon". Available at: http://thelemistas.org/en/MSS/Bjorge/Nondualism/SelfAsNeumenon (accessed 18 January 2018).

Blackmore, J. T. *Ernst Mach: His Work, Life and Influence*. Berkeley, CA: University of California Press, 1972.

Bodanis, D. *Einstein's Greatest Mistake: The Life of a Flawed Genius*. New York: Little, Brown, 2016.

Bradley, F. H. *Appearance and Reality: A Metaphysical Essay*, second edition. London: Allen & Unwin, 1897.

Browne, T. *The Garden of Cyrus* [1658]. Available at https://en.wikisource.org/wiki/The_Garden_of_Cyrus (accessed 17 January 2018).

Burnet, J. *Early Greek Philosophy*, second edition. London: A & C Black, 1908.

Burtt, E. A. (ed.). *The Metaphysical Foundations of Modern Science*. Garden City, NY: Doubleday Anchor, 1954.

Carter, B. "Large Number Coincidences and the Anthropic Principle in Cosmology". In M. S. Longair (ed.) *Confrontation of Cosmological Theories with Observational Data*, 291–8. Dordrecht: Reidel, 1974.

Cassam, Q. *Self and World*. Oxford: Clarendon Press, 1997.

Chalmers, D. *The Conscious Mind: In Search of a Fundamental Theory*. Oxford: Oxford University Press, 1996.

Chesterton, G. K. *Orthodoxy* [1908]. Available at http://www.gutenberg.org/ebooks/130 (accessed 17 January 2018).

Cornford, F. M. *From Religion to Philosophy: A Study in the Origins of Western Speculation*. London: Arnold, 1912.

Craig, E. (ed.). *The Routledge Encyclopaedia of Philosophy*, 10 volumes. London: Routledge, 1988.

Cross, F. L. & E. A. Livingstone (eds). *The Oxford Dictionary of Christian Thought*. Oxford: Oxford University Press, 1997.

Dainton, B. *Time and Space*, second edition. Durham: Acumen, 2010.

Davidson, D. "Empirical Content" [1982]. In D. Davidson, *Subjective, Intersubjective, Objective: Philosophical Essays Volume 3*, 159–76. Oxford: Oxford University Press, 2001.

Dawkins, R. *The Extended Phenotype: The Long Reach of the Gene*. Oxford: Oxford University Press, 1990.

De Quincey, T. "The Last Days of Immanuel Kant" [1827]. *Blackwood's Magazine*. Available at: https://ebooks.adelaide.edu.au/d/de_quincey/thomas/last-days-of-immanuel-kant/ (accessed 18 January 2018).

Dennett, D. *The Intentional Stance*. Cambridge, MA: MIT Press, 1987.

Dennett, D. *From Bacteria to Bach and Back: The Evolution of Minds*. London: Allen Lane, 2017.

Einstein, A. "Physics and Reality". Trans. Jean Piccard, *Journal of the Franklin Institute* 221 (March 1936), 349–82.

Eliot, T. S. *Selected Prose of T. S. Eliot*. Edited with an Introduction by Frank Kermode. London: Faber & Faber, 1975.

Fernyhough, C. *The Voices Within: The History and Science of How We Talk to Ourselves*. New York: Basic Books, 2016.

The Festal Menaion: The Service Books of the Orthodox Church. Trans. Mother Mary & Kallistos Ware. Waymart, PA: STM Press, 1998.

Fodor, J. "Semantics, Wisconsin Style". *Synthese* 59 (1984), 231–50.

Foucault, M. *The Order of Things: An Archaeology of the Human Science*. London: Tavistock, 1970.

Foucault, M. *The Archaeology of Knowledge*. London: Tavistock, 1972.

Frank, A. "Minding Matter". *Aeon*, 13 March 2017. Available at https://aeon.co/essays/materialism-alone-cannot-explain-the-riddle-of-consciousness (accessed 17 January 2018).

Friston, K. "The Mathematics of Mind-Time". *Aeon*, 18 May 2017. Available at https://aeon.co/essays/consciousness-is-not-a-thing-but-a-process-of-inference (accessed 17 January 2018).

Fugazza, C. *et al.* "Recall of Others' Action After Incidental Encoding Reveals Episodic-like Memory in Dogs". *Current Biology* 26:23 (2016), 3209–13.

Gardner, S. *Kant and the Critique of Pure Reason*. London: Routledge, 1999.

Gibson, J. J. *The Ecological Approach to Visual Perception*. Boston, MA: Houghton, Mifflin, Harcourt, 1979.

Goff, P. "Bertrand Russell and the Problem of Consciousness". In S. Leach & J. Tartaglia (eds), *Consciousness and the Great Philosophers*, 185–91. London: Routledge, 2016.

Goff, P. "Panpsychism is crazy, but it's also most probably true". *Aeon*, 1 March 2017. Available at: https://aeon.co/ideas/panpsychism-is-crazy-but-its-also-most-probably-true (accessed 17 January 2018).

Goff, P. "Panpsychism". In S. Schneider & M. Velmans (eds), *The Blackwell Companion to Consciousness*, second edition, 106–24. Chichester: Wiley-Blackwell, 2017.

Goldman, A. "A Causal Theory of Knowing". *Journal of Philosophy* 64:12 (1967), 357–72.

Gomes, A. "Kant, the Philosophy of Mind, and Twentieth-Century Analytic Philosophy". In A. Gomes & A. Stephenson (eds), *Kant and the Philosophy of Mind: Perception, Reason and the Self*, 5–24. Oxford: Oxford University Press, 2017.

Gray, J. *Straw Dogs: Thoughts on Humans and Other Animals*. London: Granta, 2002.

Grosseteste, R. *De Luce* [On Light]. Trans. Clare Riedl. Milwaukee, WI: Marquette University Press, 1942.

Guttenplan. S. (ed.). *Mind and Language*, Wolfson College Lectures 1974. Oxford: Oxford Clarendon Press, 1975.

Hacking, I. "What Mathematics Has Done to Some and Only Some Philosophers". In T. Smiley (ed.), *Mathematics and Necessity*, 83–138. London: British Academy, 2000. Available at: http://www.cs.bham.ac.uk/research/projects/cogaff/misc/hacking-mathematics-1998.pdf (accessed 17 January 2018).

Hahn, L. E. & P. A. Schilpp (eds). *The Philosophy of W. V. Quine*, second edition. Chicago, IL: Open Court, 1998.

Harvey, A. E. *A Companion to the New Testament*, second edition. Cambridge: Cambridge University Press, 2004.

Hastings, A. & A. Mason (eds). *The Oxford Companion to Christian Thought*. Oxford: Oxford University Press, 2000.

Hastings, J., J. A. Seible & L. A. Gray (eds). *Encyclopaedia of Religion and Ethics*, 13 volumes. London: T & T Clark, 1908–26.

Heidegger, M. *Being and Time*. Trans. J. Macquarrie & E. Robinson. San Francisco, CA: Harper & Row, 1962.

Heidegger, M, "Die Sprache" [1950]. In *Poetry, Language, Thought*. Trans. Albert Hofstadter. New York: Harper Perennial, 1975.

Heidegger, M. *Early Greek Thinking: The Dawn of Western Philosophy*. Trans. D. Farrell Krell & F. Capuzzi. New York: Harper & Row, 1975.

Hillar, M. "Philo of Alexandria". *Internet Encyclopaedia of Philosophy* (2001). Available at: http://www.iep.utm.edu/philo/ (accessed 18 January 2018).

Hofmannsthal, H. von. "The Lord Chandos Letter". In Hofmannsthal, *Selected Prose*. Trans. M. Hottinger. New York: Pantheon, 1952.

Hope-Moncrieff, A. R. *Classic Myths and Legends*. London: Gresham Publishing, 1950.

Hume, D. *An Enquiry Concerning Human Understanding*. Edited by Peter Millican. Oxford: Oxford World's Classics, 2008.

Hume, D. *A Treatise of Human Nature*. Edited by D. F. Norton & M. J. Norton. Oxford: Oxford University Press, 2000.

Isaacson, W. *Einstein: His Life and Universe*. New York: Simon & Schuster, 2007.

Kant, I. *Critique of Pure Reason*. Trans. N. Kemp Smith. London: Macmillan, 1967.

Kant, I. *Prolegomena to Any Future Metaphysic*. Edited by G. Hatfield. Cambridge: Cambridge University Press, 2004.

Keskinen, A. "Quine on Objects: Realism or Anti-Realism?". *Theoria* 78:2 (2012), 128–45.

Kołakowski, L. *Positivist Philosophy from Hume to the Vienna Circle*. Trans. N. Guterman. London: Penguin, 1972.

Lacan, J. *The Seminar of Jacques Lacan Book 1: Freud's Papers on Technique 1953–1954*. Trans. J. Forrester. New York: Norton, 2013.

Lack, D. "The Behaviour of the Robin". *Proceedings of the Zoological Society of London* A109, 2–3 (1939), 169–219.

Ladyman, J. & D. Ross, with D. Spurrett & J. Collier, *Everything Must Go: Metaphysics Naturalized*. Oxford: Oxford University Press, 2007.

Ladyman, J. "An Apology for Naturalized Metaphysics". In M. H. Slater & Z. Yudell (eds), *Metaphysics and the Philosophy of Science*, 141–62. Oxford: Oxford University Press, 2017.

Lau, J. & M. Deutsch. "Externalism about Mental Content". *The Stanford Encyclopedia of Philosophy* (Winter 2016 Edition), Edward N. Zalta (ed.). Available at: https://plato.stanford.edu/archives/win2016/entries/content-externalism/ (accessed 17 January 2018).

Leach, S. & J. Tartaglia (eds). *Consciousness and the Great Philosophers*. London: Routledge, 2016.

Levine, S. "Sellars and Non-Conceptual Content". *European Journal of Philosophy* 24:4 (2016), 855–78.

Locke, J. *An Essay Concerning Human Understanding*. Edited by P. Phemister. Oxford: Oxford World's Classics, 2008.

Longair, M. S. (ed.) *Confrontation of Cosmological Theories with Observational Data*. Dordrecht: Reidel, 1974.

Macdonald, G. & D. Papineau, "Introduction: Prospects and Problems for Teleosemantics". In G. Macdonald & D. Papineau (eds), *Teleosemantics*, 1–23. Oxford: Clarendon Press, 2006.

Mach, E. *Knowledge and Error: Sketches on the Psychology of Enquiry*. Translated by T. J. McCormack & P. Fouldes. Dordrecht: Reidel, 1976.

Mach, E. *The Analysis of Sensations and the Relation of the Physical to the Psychical*. Trans. C. M. Williams. La Salle, IL: Open Court, 1984.

Marsh, H. *Admissions: A Life in Brain Surgery*. London: Weidenfeld & Nicolson, 2017.

Martin, C. "On the Need for Properties: The Road to Pythagoreanism and Back". *Synthese* 112:2 (1997), 193–231.

MacCulloch, D. *A History of Christianity: The First Three Thousand Years*. London: Penguin, 2010.

McDowell, J. "Sellars and the Space of Reasons". Available at: http://www.scribd.com/doc/137428240/John-McDowell-Sellars-and-the-Space-of-Reasons#scribd (accessed 17 January 2018).

McKirahan, R. D. *Philosophy Before Socrates*. Indianapolis, IN: Hackett, 1994.

McLeese, A. "The Soul Archaeology of Darwin". *Harvard Crimson*, 24 February 2009.

Meillassoux, Q. *After Finitude: An Essay on the Necessity of Contingency*. Trans. R. Brassier. London: Continuum, 2007.

Merquior, J. G. *Foucault*. London: Fontana, 1985.

Millikan, R. "Useless Content". In G. Macdonald & D. Papineau (eds), *Teleosemantics*, 100–14. Oxford: Clarendon Press, 2006.

Morgan. A. (ed.). *The Kantian Catastrophe? Conversations on Finitude and the Limits of Philosophy*. Newcastle: Bigg Books, 2017.

Nesic, J. "Panpsychism and the Deflation of the Subject", *Filozofija I Drusto* XXVIII (4) (2017), 1102–21.

Nietzsche, F. *Philosophy in the Tragic Age of the Greeks*. Trans. M. Cowan. Chicago, IL: Henry Regnery, 1962.

O'Connell, M. *To Be a Machine*. London: Granta, 2017.

O'Connor, J. & E. Robertson. "William Van Orman Quine". MacTutor History of Mathematics archive, University of St Andrews. October 2003. Available at: http://www-history.mcs.st-and.ac.uk/Biographies/Quine.html (accessed 21 February 2018).

Parfit, D. *On What Matters*. Oxford: Oxford University Press, 2011.

Patočka, J. *Body, Community, Language, World*. Trans. E. Kohák. La Salle, IL: Open Court, 1998.

Petkov, V. (ed.). *Space, Time and Space-Time: Physical and Philosophical Implications of Minkowski's Unification of Space and Time*. Berlin: Springer, 2010.

Pinker, S. *The Better Angels of Our Nature: Why Violence Has Declined*. New York: Viking, 2011.

Plato, *Complete Works*. Edited by J. M. Cooper. Indianapolis, IN: Hackett, 1997.

Plotinus, *The Enneads*. Edited by J. Dillon and translated by S. MacKenna. London: Penguin Classics, 1991.

Pojman, P. "Ernst Mach". *The Stanford Encyclopedia of Philosophy* (Winter 2011 Edition), Edward N. Zalta (ed.). Available at: https://plato.stanford.edu/archives/win2011/entries/ernst-mach/ (accessed 17 January 2018).

Pollok, K. "The Understanding Prescribes Laws of Nature: Spontaneity, Legislation, and Kant's Transcendental Hylomorphism". *Kant-Studien* 105:14 (2004), 509–13.

Popper, K. *Objective Knowledge: An Evolutionary Approach*. Oxford: Clarendon Press, 1972.

Quine, W. V. O. "Two Dogmas of Empiricism. *Philosophical Review* 60 (1951), 20–43.

Quine, W. V. O. "Mr. Strawson on Logical Theory". *Mind* LXII (1953), 248–53.

Quine, W. V. O. *Word and Object*. Cambridge, MA: MIT Press, 1960.

Quine, W. V. O. *Philosophy of Logic*. Englewood Cliffs, NJ: Prentice-Hall, 1970.

Quine, W. V. O. "The Nature of Natural Knowledge". In S. Guttenplan (ed.), *Mind and Language*. Oxford: Clarendon Press, 1975.

Quine, W. V. O. "Whither Physical Objects?" In R. Cohen, P. Feyerabend & M. Wartofsky (eds), *Essays in Memory of Imre Lakatos*. Boston Studies in the Philosophy and History of Science Volume XXXIX, 497–504. Dordrecht: D. Reidel, 1976.

Quine, W. V. O. "Epistemology Naturalized". In *Ontological Relativity and Other Essays*. New York: Columbia University Press, 1986.

Quine, W. V. O. "Naturalism; Or Living Within One's Means". *Dialectica* 49:2–4 (1995), 251–61.

Quine, W. V. O. *From Stimulus to Science*. Cambridge, MA: MIT Press, 1995.

Quine, W. V. O. "Reply to Hilary Putnam". In L. E. Hahn & P. A. Schilpp (eds), *The Philosophy of W. V. Quine*, second edition, 427–31. Chicago, IL: Open Court, 1998.

Radford, T. "Gravity's Engines: The Something Side of Black Holes", *The Guardian*, 12 December 2012.

Ramsey, F. P. & G. E. Moore "Facts and Propositions". *Proceedings of the Aristotelian Society* 7, supplementary (1927), 153–70.

Redding, P. "Georg Wilhelm Friedrich Hegel". *The Stanford Encyclopedia of Philosophy* (Winter 2017 Edition), Edward N. Zalta (ed.). Available at: https://plato.stanford.edu/archives/win2017/entries/hegel/ (accessed 18 January 2018).

Rees, M. "Curtains For Us All? A Conversation with Martin Rees". *Edge*, 31 May 2017. Available at: https://www.edge.org/conversation/martin_rees-curtains-for-us-all (accessed 18 January 2018).

Robinson, R. "The Concept of Knowledge". *Mind* LXXX (1971), 17–28.

Rosenberg, A. "Eliminativism Without Tears: A Nihilistic Stance on the Theory of Mind". Unpublished manuscript. Available at: http://docplayer.net/410618-Eliminativism-without-tears-1.html (accessed 20 January 2018).

Russell, B. *The Analysis of Matter*. London: Kegan Paul, 1927.

Russell, B. *An Inquiry into Meaning and Truth*. London: Allen & Unwin, 1940.

Russell, B. "Knowledge by Acquaintance and Knowledge by Description". In *Mysticism and Logic and Other Essays*, 197–218. London: Pelican, 1953.

Sacks, M. *Objectivity and Insight*. Oxford: Clarendon Press, 2000.

Sagan, C. *Cosmos*. New York: Random House, 1980.

Safranski, R. *Martin Heidegger: Between Good and Evil*. Trans. Ewald Osers. Cambridge, MA: Harvard University Press, 1998.

Santayana, G. "Introduction". In Everyman Selection of *The Works of Spinoza: Ethics and "De Intellectus Emendatione"*. London: Dent, 1910.

Schneider, S, & M. Velmans (eds). *The Blackwell Companion to Consciousness*, second edition. Chichester: Wiley-Blackwell, 2017.

Schrödinger, E. "Mind and Matter". In *What is Life and Other Essays*, 93–164. Cambridge: Cambridge University Press, 1967.

Searle, J. *Intentionality: An Essay in the Philosophy of Mind*. Cambridge: Cambridge University Press, 1983.

Searle, J. *The Construction of Social Reality*. London: Allen Lane, 1995.

Sellars, W. "Empiricism and the Philosophy of Mind". In H. Feigl & M. Scriven (eds), *Minnesota Studies in the Philosophy of Science* vol. 1, 253–329. Minneapolis, MN: University of Minnesota Press, 1956.

Simpson, W. "Causal Powers of the Scientific Image". MPhil dissertation, University of Oxford, 2016.

Sinclair, R. "Quine's Naturalized Epistemology and the Third Dogma of Empiricism". *Southern Journal of Philosophy* XLV (2007), 455–72.

Slater, M. & Z. Yudell (eds). *Metaphysics and the Philosophy of Science: New Essays*. Oxford: Oxford University Press, 2017.

Slowik, E. "The Fate of Mathematical Place: Objectivity and the Theory of Lived Place from Husserl to Casey". In V. Petkov (ed.), *Space, Time and Space-Time: Physical and Philosophical Implications of Minkowski's Unification of Space and Time*, 291–311. Berlin: Springer, 2010.

Smolin, L. *Time Reborn: From the Crisis of Physics to the Future of the Universe*. London: Allen Lane, 2013.

Stace, W. "Man Against Darkness". *Atlantic Monthly* (September 1948), 53–9.

Stoljar, D. & N. Damnjanovic, "The Deflationary Theory of Truth". *The Stanford Encyclopedia of Philosophy* (Fall 2014 Edition), Edward N. Zalta (ed.). Available at https://plato.stanford.edu/archives/fall2014/entries/truth-deflationary/ (accessed 18 January 2018).

Strauss, M. "Our Universe is too vast for even the most imaginative sci-fi". *Aeon*, 22 February 2017. Available at: https://aeon.co/ideas/our-universe-is-too-vast-for-even-the-most-imaginative-sci-fi (accessed 18 January 2018).

Strawson, G. "Real Naturalism", *Proceedings and Addresses of the American Philosophical Association* 86:2 (2012), 124—55.

Strawson, P. F. *The Bounds of Sense*. London: Methuen, 1966.

Strawson, P. F. (ed.). *Philosophical Logic*. Oxford: Oxford University Press, 1967.

Stroud, B. "The Significance of Naturalized Epistemology". *Midwest Studies in Philosophy* 6:1 (1981), 455–71.

Suddendorf, T. *The Gap: The Science of What Separates us from Other Animals*. New York: Basic Books, 2013.

Tallis, R. *Not Saussure*. Basingstoke: Macmillan, 1988, 1995.

Tallis, R. *The Explicit Animal: A Defence of Human Consciousness*. Basingstoke: Macmillan, 1991.

Tallis, R. "Criticism Terminable and Interminable: the Place of Literary Criticism in a Life of Finite Duration", *PN Review* 18:2 (1992), 47–51.

Tallis, R. *A Conversation with Martin Heidegger*. Basingstoke: Palgrave Macmillan, 2002.

Tallis, R. *The Hand: A Philosophical Inquiry into Human Being.* Edinburgh: Edinburgh University Press, 2003.

Tallis, R. *I Am: A Philosophical Inquiry into First-Person Being.* Edinburgh: Edinburgh University Press, 2004.

Tallis, R. *Why the Mind Is Not a Computer.* Exeter: Imprint Academic, 2004.

Tallis, R. *The Knowing Animal: A Philosophical Inquiry into Knowledge and Truth.* Edinburgh: Edinburgh University Press, 2005.

Tallis, R. *Michelangelo's Finger: An Exploration of Everyday Transcendence.* London: Atlantic, 2010.

Tallis, R. *In Defence of Wonder and Other Philosophical Reflections.* Durham: Acumen, 2012.

Tallis, R. *Reflections of a Metaphysical Flâneur and Other Essays.* Durham: Acumen, 2013.

Tallis, R. *Epimethean Imaginings: Philosophical and Other Meditations on Everyday Light.* Durham: Acumen, 2014.

Tallis, R. *Of Time and Lamentation: Reflections on Transience.* Newcastle: Agenda, 2017.

Tallis, R. "Time, Reciprocal Containment, and the Ouroboros". *Philosophy Now*, Oct/Nov 2017

Uexkull, J. von. *Theoretical Biology.* Trans. D. L. MacKinnon. New York: Harcourt, Brace, 1926.

Valéry, P. "On Poe's 'Eureka'". In *Leonardo, Poe, Mallarmé* volume 8 of *The Collected Works of Paul Valéry.* Trans. M. Cowley & J. R. Lawler. London: Routledge & Kegan Paul, 1972.

Waal, F. de. "The link between language and cognition is a red herring". *Aeon*, 30 June 2016. Available at: https://aeon.co/ideas/the-link-between-language-and-cognition-is-a-red-herring (accessed 18 January 2018).

Waal, F. de. *Are We Smart Enough to Know How Smart Animals Are?* New York: Norton, 2016.

Welbourne, M. *Knowledge.* Chesham: Acumen, 2002.

Wheeler, J. A. "Sakharov revisited: 'It from Bit'". In M. Mank'ko (ed.) *Proceedings of the First International A. D. Sakhorov Memorial Conference on Physics, Moscow, 1991.* Commack, NY: Nova Science Publishers, 1991.

Wheeler, J. A. "Information, Physics, Quantum: The Search for Links". In W. H. Zurek (ed.) *Complexity, Entropy and the Physics of Information.* Redwood City, CA: Addison-Wesley, 1990.

Whitehead, A. N. *The Concept of Nature.* Cambridge: Cambridge University Press, 1920.

Wilbur, R. "Epistemology". In *Collected Poems, 1943–2004.* New York: Harcourt Books, 2004.

Wittgenstein, L. *Tractatus Logico-Philosophicus.* Trans. D. F. Pears & B. F. McGuinness. London: Routledge & Kegan Paul, 1961.

Wittgenstein, L. *Philosophical Investigations.* Trans. G. E. M. Anscombe. Oxford: Basil Blackwell, 1963.

Yeats, W. B. "The Circus Animals' Desertion". In *The Collected Poems of W. B. Yeats: A New Edition,* edited by R. J. Finneran. London: Macmillan, 1991.

Index

249